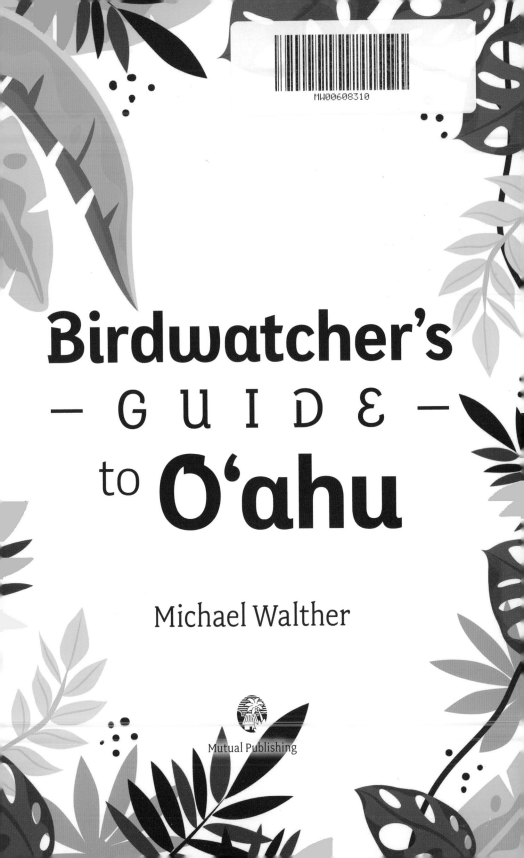

Birdwatcher's
— G U I D E —
to Oʻahu

Michael Walther

Mutual Publishing

Copyright ©2023 by Mutual Publishing, LLC

All rights reserved. No part of this book
    may be reproduced in any form or by
    any electronic or mechanical means,
    including information storage and
    retrieval devices or systems, without
    prior written permission from the
    publisher, except that brief passages
    may be quoted for reviews.

Library of Congress Control Number:
    2023936077

ISBN: 978-1-949307-43-6

All photos © Michael Walther, unless
        otherwise noted
Design by Courtney Tomasu

First Printing, August 2023

Mutual Publishing, LLC
1215 Center Street, Suite 210
Honolulu, Hawaiʻi 96816
Ph: 808-732-1709
Fax: 808-734-4094
info@mutualpublishing.com
www.mutualpublishing.com

Printed in South Korea

CONTENTS

PREFACE

I have lived on the beautiful island of O'ahu since 1995 and guided hundreds of birding tours while visiting the best places to observe and photograph birds on this tropical isle. I wrote this book to help both non-residents and local birders find and identify the birds on the island nicknamed "The Gathering Place."

This volume provides you with the necessary information to plan a visit to twenty-four of the best locations on O'ahu to see our fascinating avifauna. This guide is unique in Hawai'i because it contains every species recorded on O'ahu including all of the "official Hawai'i" list species plus every introduced and extinct species. *Birdwatcher's Guide to O'ahu* is divided into seven geographic regions and includes birding hotspots in the island's coastal, rainforest, urban, and offshore environments.

My goal, twenty-eight years ago, was to photograph all of the bird species in the Southeastern Hawaiian Islands. As of 2023, I have photographed 198 of the 261 extant species on the official list. Many of these are very rare vagrants and obtaining photos of those not found on O'ahu involved flying to one of the outer islands, renting a car, and reserving overnight accommodations. Thankfully, most of these exciting chases resulted in seeing and photographing the rare vagrant I was seeking. My photographs of Hawai'i's rare birds and other resident, migrant, and winter visiting species are included in this guide. Photographs of bird species occurring in the Hawaiian Islands that I photographed in the mainland United States or in another country have the location in bold green in the photo caption.

It is hoped that the reader, after seeing our island's endangered bird species, will be inspired to help conserve them by donating to the non-profits mentioned in this book. Hawai'i is the bird extinction capital of the world and together, all of us who appreciate and have a passion for birds, need to prevent any more species loss so that the birds will survive and future generations will be able to enjoy them as we have.

ACKNOWLEDGMENTS

Thanks to Bennett Hymer and Jane Gillespie at Mutual Publishing Company for the opportunity to write this book. Special thanks to Courtney Tomasu for her excellent graphic design work, great comments and editing, and for helping to create *Birdwatcher's Guide to Oʻahu*.

Thanks to all scientists, field biologists, and managers working to save Oʻahu's forest birds. I especially thank Robert L. Pyle, Peter Pyle, Eric Vanderwerf, and H. Douglas Pratt.

Most of the data for each species status and distribution on Oʻahu and all of the seabird charts are from the comprehensive and very thorough on-line database by Robert L. Pyle and Peter Pyle. Pyle, R.L., and P. Pyle. *The Birds of the Hawaiian Islands: Occurrence, History, Distribution, and Status.* B.P. Bishop Museum, Honolulu, HI, U.S.A. Version 2 (1 January 2017) http://hbs.bishopmuseum.org/birds/rlp-monograph. Thanks to Peter for allowing me to use his data.

The following excellent sources were consulted to write the species descriptions and measurements:

Birds of Western North America by David Sibley
Birds of Hawaii by the Hawaii Audubon Society
Photographic Guide to the Birds of Hawaiʻi by Jim Denny
Birds of Hawaiʻi and the Tropical Pacific by H.D. Pratt
"Birds of the World" online by the Cornell Lab of Ornithology
All About Birds by the Cornell Lab of Ornithology
Wikipedia accounts
New Zealand Birds online
Field Guide to the Birds of Australia by Graham Pizzey and Frank Knight
www.whatbird.com
United States Fish and Wildlife Service bird accounts
"The Birds of France" https://www.oiseaux.net/birds/france.html

Thanks to the authors who created these great books and websites and to all the photographers whose excellent images of bird species appear in this book.

I thank my parents, Harold and Marie, for choosing to live near the Everglades in Florida and in a semi-rural suburb of Los Angeles. It was at these special places I developed a love and appreciation for nature. To my brother, Mark, for his generosity and his help in founding Oʻahu Nature Tours and for keeping it going during the difficult early years.

Thanks to all the birders that I was able to share the great birds of Oʻahu with and for all of their excellent stories about birding in Hawaiʻi and around the world.

Special thanks to my wife, Cecilia, for her love, friendship, great advice, support, and for building Oʻahu Nature Tours together into a successful company. Her tireless efforts organizing, managing, and staffing our eco-tour business has enabled me to pursue photographing Oʻahu's birds and writing books about nature in Hawaiʻi.

INTRODUCTION

The island of Oʻahu is the third largest island in the state of Hawaiʻi at 597 square miles. It is composed of three highly eroded, ancient shield volcanoes: Kaʻena, Waiʻanae, and Koʻolau. The five-million-year-old Kaʻena volcano is completely submerged off the northwest point of the island. The 3.9 million year old Waiʻanae volcano is twenty-two miles long and its tallest peak, Mount Kaʻala, is the highest point on Oʻahu at 4,025 feet. The Koʻolau volcano is 2.5 million years old and thirty-four miles long.[1] The highest peak in the Koʻolau range is Mount Konahuanui at 3,149 feet. Between the two volcanoes is a flat area known as the Schofield Plateau that was created by lava flows from both volcanoes. The lochs at Pearl Harbor, south of the plateau, were formed by the submergence of stream valleys.

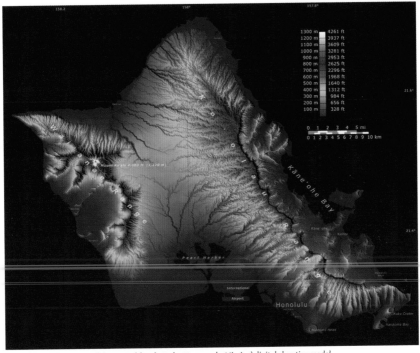

Oʻahu SRTM (Shuttle Radar Topography Mission) digital elevation model.

Ever since the trio of volcanoes that formed Oʻahu emerged from the sea, powerful, erosional forces worked against them. The effects of constant pounding surf, strong winds, and abundant rainfall combined to weather the enormous mountains. Huge amphitheater valleys, separated by steep-sided ridges, were carved into their pristine flanks. Mānoa, Pālolo, Nuʻuanu, Makua, Laulaulei, Kaʻaʻawa, and Kahana were partially created by fresh-water streams cutting through the ancient basalt since the first rains fell on their exposed slopes. The time worn, remnant volcanoes have been greatly dissected and because of the severe deformation they are called ranges today.

When you travel up Oʻahu's scenic windward or eastern coast you see many offshore islands and islets beginning with Kāohikaipu, a cinder cone located close to the southern end of the Koʻolau volcano at Makapuʻu Point. Nearby is Mānana Islet, a former tuff cone. Both of these and many of the other offshore islands are bird sanctuaries that are closed to the public. As you precede up the coast to the north shore, another fourteen islands can be seen. Perhaps the most famous is Mokoliʻi, also known as Chinaman's Hat, which is an eroded remnant of part of a former balsaltic ridge of the Koʻolau volcano. Oʻahu's coastline is 227 miles long. Wetlands on Oʻahu are limited, and unfortunately very few are open to the public at this time.

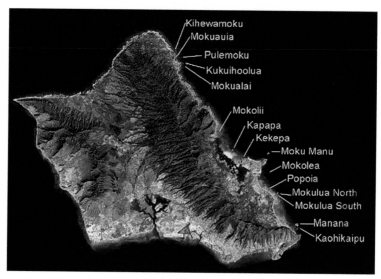

Oʻahu offshore islets.

The most recognizable features caused by past events and processes that shaped Oʻahu are those included in the Honolulu Volcanic Series. Famous landmarks including Lēʻahi or Diamond Head Crater, Puowaina or Punchbowl Crater, Hanauma Bay, Kohelepelepe or Koko Crater, Kuamoʻokāne or Koko Head, Salt Lake, and the miniature Kaimukī shield volcano plus thirty-three other tuff cones, cinder cones and lava flows were created between 30,000 to 800,000 years ago when the Koʻolau volcano came back to life after being dormant for almost a million years.[2]

The northern most place on Oʻahu is Kahuku Point at 21° 42'42.86" N. Diamond Head Crater is the southernmost point at 21° 15'16.26"N. Located south of the Tropic of Cancer, the island has a mild climate that is relatively uniform throughout the year. Average annual high temperature in Honolulu is 84.5°F and the average low 70.7°F.

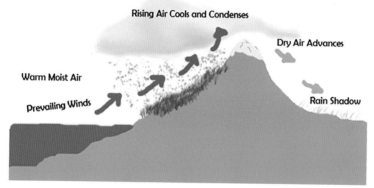

Orographic effect.

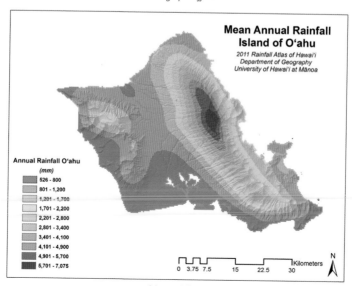

Oʻahu rainfall map.

The refreshing east to west trade winds, Oʻahu's primary source for rain, are the most prominent weather characteristic of the island and occur as much as eighty percent of the days in some years. There are two major seasons; the wet season, hoʻoilo, from November to April and the dry season, kau, from May to October.

The two parallel mountain ranges have a significant impact on rainfall patterns because of the orographic effect. When moisture bearing air masses move from lower elevations on the windward side up and over the Koʻolau and Waiʻanae volcano, clouds are formed and the majority of rain falls near the summits of the mountains. On the leeward side of the two ranges dry conditions exist due to the rain shadow effect. Windward Oʻahu areas have an average of eighty inches of annual rainfall while drier areas on the leeward side including, Honolulu and Mākaha, less than twenty inches of rain per year. The wettest part of the Koʻolau volcano averages over 240 inches of rain each year!

Oʻahu is an excellent place for birding. Below are twelve reasons why every birder should include a visit to Oʻahu while staying in the Hawaiian Islands.

1)   Oʻahu has 218 species on the official bird list compiled by Robert L. Pyle and Peter Pyle (http://hbs.bishopmuseum.org/birds/rlp-monograph/SEHIlist.htm). This is twenty more species than the next best island for birding, Hawaiʻi. I have followed this checklist for the order of species in this guide.

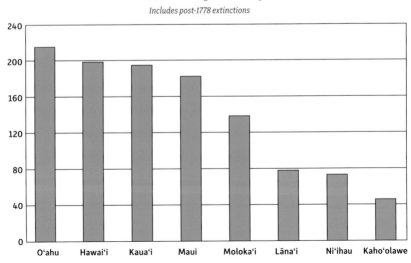

Number of Bird Species by Island

Includes post-1778 extinctions

2) O'ahu has more breeding seabirds on the island (145,465) than any other in the Southeastern Hawaiian Islands. Kaua'i is second with 30,425.

In the following tables, B represents a species known to breed on the island in historic times (since 1778) but not known to be breeding during the 2000 to mid-2010s, and M indicates that the species has been recorded on the island or island group but is not known to breed there.

Southeastern Hawaiian Islands

COMMON NAME	SEHI	KA'ULA	LEHUA	NI'IHAU	KAUA'I	O'AHU	MOLOKA'I	LĀNA'I	KAHO'OLAWE	MAUI	HAWAI'I
Laysan Albatross	610	65	90	25?	295	135	M	M		M	M
Black-footed Albatross	45	5	40		M	M					
Hawaiian Petrel	5,955			M	1,500	M	50	2,500	5	1,600	300
Bulwer Petrel	1,100	50	50	M	30	425	50	45	50	300	100
Wedge-tailed Shearwater	87,825	2,000	23,000	?	15,000	40,000	1,900	300	200	5,025	400
Christmas Shearwater	155	100		M		55	M			M	
Newell Shearwater	10,300			M	10,000	M	50	M		50	200
Band-rumped Storm-Petrel	330		M		250	M				30	50
White-tailed Tropicbird	1,550	B	M	M	750	75	250	75	M	150	250
Red-tailed Tropicbird	1,035	325	150	B	400	80	10	35	30	M	5
Masked Booby	350	300	B	M	M	50	M			M	M
Brown Booby	1,000	400	500	M	B	100	M	M	B	M	M
Red-footed Booby	4,500	300	1,400	B	1,800	1,000					
Great Frigatebird	B	M	M	M	M	B	M			M	
Brown Noddy	26,010	4,000	B			22,010					
Black Noddy	2,035	100	200	M	400	160	350	75	250	200	300
White Tern	815	15				800					
Sooty Tern	132,500	42,500	M			90,000					
Gray-backed Tern	525	500	M			25					
Least Tern	B					B				M	B
TOTALS	276,810	50,120	25,430	?	30,425	145,465	2,660	3,030	535	7,355	1,605

Oʻahu Islets, Hawaiian Islands, Breeding Seabird Populations (Pairs)

COMMON NAME	MOKUʻAUIA	MOKOLIʻI	KAPAPA	KEKEPA	MOKUMANU	MŌKŌLEA	POPOIʻA	MOKULUA ISLETS	MĀNANA	KĀOHIKAIPU
Bulwer Petrel			10	10	100	10	125	150	10	10
Wedge-tailed Shearwater	2,500	200	300		2,000		1,500	10,000	12,000	400
Christmas Shearwater					50		5			
White-tailed Tropicbird			2							
Red-tailed Tropicbird									15	
Masked Booby					50					
Brown Booby					100					
Red-footed Booby					200					
Great Frigatebird					B					
Brown Noddy					2,000	10			20,000	
Black Noddy					75	20			10	5
Sooty Tern					15,000				75,000	
Gray-backed Tern					25					
TOTALS	2,500	202	310	10	19,590	40	1,625	10,155	107,025	415

Breeding Seabird Populations (Pairs)

3) Oʻahu is the best island to see the rare **Bristle-thighed Curlew** with 126 individuals present in 2014.[3] The wintering population is centered around the restricted access James Campbell National Wildlife Refuge, but birds can be usually found in the adjacent Kahuku Golf Course area. The next best island to look for Bristle-thighed Curlews is Hawaiʻi which had a high count of twenty to thirty in 1965 at South Point.

Kahuku, Oʻahu.

4) O'ahu is the only island with breeding **White Terns** and has over 1,000 pairs that can be found mostly in urban areas between the Honolulu airport and Hawai'i Kai on the southeast coast. There are excellent opportunities to locate this very photogenic species in Waikīkī and nearby parks. They are extremely rare on all of the other southeastern Hawaiian Islands.

Kapi'olani Park, O'ahu.

5) O'ahu is the only accessible island in the southeastern Hawaiian Islands with breeding **Christmas Shearwaters**. Fifty pairs breed on Mokumanu Islet off Kāne'ohe. They are most easily seen during pelagics around Mokumanu and rarely from land.

6) O'ahu is the only accessible island in the southeastern Hawaiian Islands with breeding **Masked Boobies**. A minimum of fifty pairs nest on Mokumanu Islet. Individuals are occasionally seen from shore at Makapu'u Point, Makapu'u Beach Park, and Lā'ie Point. If you are able to arrange a pelagic to the waters offshore of Makapu'u Point your chances of seeing this species will be increased.

Christmas Shearwater.

Adult Masked Booby, Kaiwi Channel.

7) O'ahu is the only accessible island in the southeastern Hawaiian Islands with breeding **Gray-backed Terns**. A minimum of twenty-five pairs nest on Mokumanu Islet. Individuals are occasionally seen from shore at Makapu'u Beach Park. If you are able to arrange a pelagic to the waters offshore of windward O'ahu your chances of seeing this species will be increased.

Juvenile Gray-backed Tern, Mokumanu, O'ahu.

8) Oʻahu is the only accessible island in the southeastern Hawaiian Islands with breeding **Sooty Terns**. A minimum of 75,000 pairs nest on Mānana Islet and another 15,000 nest on Mokumanu Islet. One of the most spectacular birding experiences on Oʻahu is going to Makapuʻu Beach Park to see tens of thousands of Sooty Terns swarming around, above and on Mānana Islet. Huge groups of these black and white terns spiral thousands of feet above Mānana in invisible thermals. Occasionally, if wind conditions are suitable, some Sooty Terns will fly over Sandy Beach Park on

Sooty Tern, Offshore Honolulu, Oʻahu.

their way to the breeding colony at Mānana Islet. The birds begin to arrive in December, in some years, but January is more reliable. They breed on the islands, and most of them depart towards the equator by the end of July.

9) Oʻahu has the highest number of breeding **Bulwer's Petrels** with 425 pairs. Several small islands close to Kailua Beach, Popoia, and the twin Mokulua islets have 100 breeding pairs each. Bulwer's Petrel is occasionally seen during Oʻahu pelagic trips.

Bulwer's Petrel, Offshore Honokōhau, Hawaiʻi Island

10) Oʻahu is the only island with **Mariana Swiftlets**. They are found most often on the ʻAiea Ridge Trail and the ʻAiea Loop Trail. The best strategy to see these rare birds is to walk up the ʻAiea Ridge trail and find a clear view on the side of the ridge above the H-3 freeway. Wait and watch for the Swiftlets to arrive. They usually hunt insects together in small groups and fly just above the treetops. I have observed them going back and forth continuously over this area on several occasions. You might also encounter them lower on the ʻAiea Loop Trail but tall trees and the rapid flight of the Swiftlets provide only very brief views.

Mariana Swiftlet, ʻAiea Ridge Trail, Oʻahu.

11) O'ahu is the only island to see the rarest **'Elepaio** species which has a population of only 1,200 birds. Tragically, these island-endemic birds are being devastated by Avian Malaria and Avian Pox which are transmitted by introduced mosquitoes. Their numbers are also reduced by introduced predators especially the tree-climbing Black Rat. The number of males exceed the number of females because only the females incubate at night and many of them are eaten by Black Rats. Competition with non-native birds and loss of habitat are additional factors causing population declines.

'Elepaio, 'Aiea Loop Trail.

12) Pacific Rim Conservation (PRC) and the United States Fish and Wildlife Service have begun a project at James Cambell National Wildlife Refuge (JCNWR) on O'ahu's North shore to establish new breeding colonies of **Bonin Petrels**, **Tristram's Storm-Petrels**, and **Black-footed Albatross**. In an effort to mitigate seabird loss due to rising ocean levels from global warming, a sixteen-acre fenced enclosure was created at the refuge.

In 2017 to 2018, they moved forty Black-footed Albatross chicks from Midway and Tern Island to JCNWR, of which thirty-six fledged. In 2018, PRC moved fifty-three Bonin Petrel chicks and twenty-eight Tristram's Storm-Petrel chicks from Midway and Tern Island, with 100% survival in both species. In 2018 to 2019, they moved sixty-five Black-footed Albatross chicks from Midway and Tern Island to JCNWR, of which sixty-one fledged.

In 2018 to 2019, they moved 129 Bonin Petrel chicks and seventy-one Tristram's Storm-Petrel chicks from Midway and Tern Island, of which 129 and sixty-seven fledged, respectively. In 2019, the first individual Bonin Petrel and Tristram's Storm-Petrel returned after just one year. In 2020, eight Bonin petrels returned, including male-female pairs in burrows. In 2020, they moved some of the Tristram's Storm-Petrels and Bonin Petrels to predator-free offshore islets (Kekepa and Mokumanu) a few days before fledging in hopes that they will imprint on those sites and return to them as adults.[4]

By 2023, the returning birds will be successfully reproducing at the new colony which will continue to grow as more birds return. All three of these species previously nested on O'ahu, but their populations were eliminated due to predation and habitat loss. It is hoped all three species will thrive at their new home, and eventually birders will be able to observe these once rare species again from the north shore coastline and during offshore pelagics.

O'ahu's 212 extant bird species are composed of the following groups:

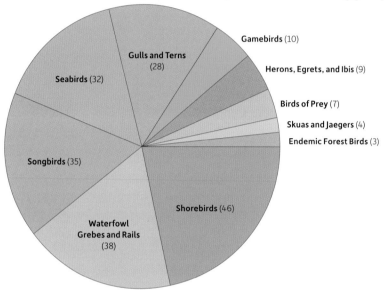

The following chart depicts the status of O'ahu's bird species. The residents, breeding visitors, and winter visitors contain all of the endemic and indigenous species found on O'ahu and are the most likely targets for birders. Many of the migrants and all of the vagrants are rare, and most of these will not be seen during brief birding visits. While the naturalized species are interesting, they are not an original part of O'ahu's avifauna and some of them are considered pests. One of the great aspects of observing many of O'ahu's introduced species is that you can see birds from around the world without having to travel to far-off countries.

I have followed the status codes from the excellent online database cited below.

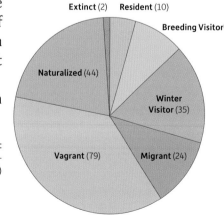

Pyle, R.L., and P. Pyle. "The Birds of the Hawaiian Islands: Occurrence, History, Distribution, and Status." B.P. Bishop Museum, Honolulu, HI, U.S.A. Version 2 (1 January 2017) http://hbs.bishopmuseum.org/birds/rlp-monograph

A minimum of 341 bird species have been recorded on O'ahu and are included in this guide. This total includes the following:

- 212 species on the official bird list that is created by the Hawai'i Bird Records Committee (HBRC).
- Nineteen endemic species that are extinct before 1778 and are based on subfossil remains.
- Seven endemic species that are extinct after 1778.
- Two introduced and established species that are now extinct.
- Sixteen introduced species that are non-established and are present on O'ahu. These species are included in ebird but not included in O'ahu's official list.
- Eighty-two species that were introduced to O'ahu but are extirpated on the island.
- Three species on the hypothetical list.

Composition of O'ahu's Total Bird Species

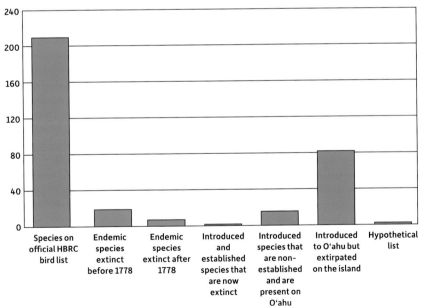

The information above was derived from:

Pyle, R.L., and P. Pyle. "The Birds of the Hawaiian Islands: Occurrence, History, Distribution, and Status." B.P. Bishop Museum, Honolulu, HI, U.S.A. Version 2 (1 January 2017) http://hbs.bishopmuseum.org/birds/rlp-monograph

The "Places to See Birds on Oʻahu" chapter in this book is divided into seven geographical areas. The areas are:

1. Honolulu Area
2. Southeast
3. East
4. North Shore
5. Central
6. Koʻolau Range
7. Pelagics

Most of the locations can be reached in a vehicle and are mainly located on or near the coast. Several require walking on trails in the mountain forests. The pelagics require chartering a boat from either Kewalo Basin in Honolulu, Hāleʻiwa Boat Harbor, Hawaiʻi Kai Marina, or Heʻeia Boat Harbor depending on where you would like to go in Oʻahu's offshore waters.

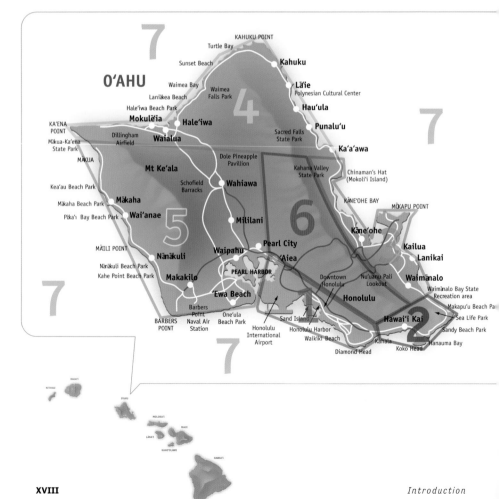

Due to space limitations, many female and juvenile duck photographs were not included in the species accounts. I also did not include photographs for some of the female and juvenile naturalized species. To help with bird identifications further please consult with several excellent field guides including H.D. Pratt's *Birds of Hawai'i and the Tropical Pacific* and David Sibley's *Field Guide to the Birds of Western North America.*

When birding on O'ahu please consider doing the following so you have a safe and enjoyable experience.

1) Never leave any valuables or what might appear as valuables (bags, cases, etc.) in your vehicle. Unfortunately, vehicle break-ins are very common on the island especially at trail parking areas.

2) Wear sunscreen, hat, and closed-toed shoes. Use mosquito protection and take lots of water on trails.

3) Let someone know the name of the trail and your expected return if you are hiking on mountain trails.

4) Please do not play tape recordings to endangered forest birds since this results in them wasting energy.

5) Consider reporting your bird sightings on ebird so other interested birders might be able to see the birds you observed.

While exploring O'ahu looking for many of its birds it is important to contemplate how many species have been lost since the arrival of the first humans only 1,000 years ago. The present-day avifauna of O'ahu is only a meager remnant of the many species that were once found in this former bird paradise. Only four of the original thirty-one native land bird species survive. One of the four, the O'ahu 'Elepaio is extremely endangered. This is an 87% loss of endemic forest bird diversity on the island. Sadly, just the O'ahu 'Amakihi and 'Apapane, two of the original eighteen Hawaiian Honeycreepers, still contribute to a very, very muted dawn chorus.

The once mega-seabird colonies which had hundreds of thousands of individuals per species have been decimated and only relic populations exist today. Hawai'i is the extinction capital of the world. Please consider helping the dedicated scientists who are trying to save the last remaining O'ahu 'Elepaios by donating to Pacific Rim Conservation at their website (https://pacificrimconservation.org/donations/form/).

Hopefully Wolbachia-infected mosquitoes will be released into Oʻahu's forest soon in an effort to eliminate disease carrying mosquitoes. You can support this very important effort by donating to the American Bird Conservancy's "Birds not Mosquitoes" program at their website (https://abcbirds.org/program/hawaii/mosquitoes/). These unique birds need all of our help to survive in a once pristine environment that humans have mostly destroyed.

Thank you for helping our birds, and best of luck in finding many species on Oʻahu.

Aloha,
Michael Walther
Honolulu, Hawaiʻi
2023

O‘AHU
BIRD
SPECIES
ACCOUNTS

Waiakea Pond, Hilo, Hawai'i Island.

Kodiak National Wildlife Refuge, Alaska.
LISA HUPP, USFWS

Greater White-fronted Goose
(Speckle-belly, White-fronted Goose)
Anser albifrons

RARE VAGRANT
LENGTH 64–81 cm. (25–32 in.)
WINGSPAN 130–165 cm. (51–65 in.)
WEIGHT 1,995–3,400 g. (4.4–7.5 lb.)

A large gray-brown goose with a barred and speckled light gray breast. Has distinctive patch of white feathers bordering the base of pink bill. The rump and undertail are white. Tail feathers have a white tip. Sexes similar. Juvenile has no white at base of duller colored bill. Might be confused with feral Graylag geese which are occasionally seen on O'ahu. Graylag geese are larger, have a heavier bill with very little or no white at base, and a striped neck. A minimum of thirty-six adult and juvenile Greater White-fronted Geese have been recorded on O'ahu. The best locations to look for these rare Arctic visitors are James Campbell National Wildlife Refuge (NWR) and Pearl Harbor NWR.

Emperor Goose
(Beach Goose, Painted Goose)
Chen canagica

VERY RARE VAGRANT
LENGTH 66–76 cm. (26–30 in.)
WINGSPAN 122–142 cm. (48–56 in.)
WEIGHT 2,766–3,129 g. (6.1–6.9 lb.)

A thick-bodied bluish-gray goose with white head and hindneck, black throat, and pink bill. Tail is white. Legs and feet orange. Sexes similar. Juveniles are mostly gray. Breeds in Arctic and sub-arctic Alaska and Russia. Estimated world population is 100,000 and they are considered near-threatened.

A minimum of twenty-six have been recorded in the Hawaiian Islands with three records for O'ahu; one in 1956 and two in 1960.

Graylag Goose
Blondous River, Iceland.

Kawaiele Waterbird Sanctuary, Kaua'i.

Kahuku Aqua Ponds, O'ahu.

Snow Goose

Chen careulescens

RARE VAGRANT
LENGTH 64–79 cm. (25–31 in.)
WINGSPAN 135–165 cm. (53–65 in.)
WEIGHT 1,995–2,676 g. (4.4–5.9 lb.)

A mostly white goose with dark primaries, pink bill, legs, and feet. Two color morphs; white and dark. Sexes are similar but female often smaller. Immature has gray upperparts and a dull brownish bill and legs.

A minimum of fifteen individual snow geese have been recorded on O'ahu including five juveniles. O'ahu's premier wetland preserves; James Campbell NWR, Pearl Harbor NWR, and Nu'upia Ponds Wildlife Management Area (WMA) are the best locations to find this Arctic species. Surprisingly, three adults overwintered at Kaena Point, one of the hottest and driest locations on the island, from November 2019 to March 2020.

Immature Snow Goose,
Fir Island, Washington.

Brant
(Brent Goose, Black Brant)

Branta bernicla

VAGRANT
LENGTH 55–66 cm. (22–26 in.)
WINGSPAN 106–121 cm. (42–48 in.)
WEIGHT 861–2,222 g. (1.9–4.9 lb.)

A small Arctic goose with black head, neck, wings, breast and tail. Conspicuous white patch on side of neck. White flanks and rump. Bill, legs and feet are black. Both sexes identical in plumage. Immatures have gray flanks and belly and no white neck band.

Thirty-eight Brant have been recorded on O'ahu. Most have been found at James Campbell NWR and Nu'upia Ponds WMA. In May 2016, a single individual was photographed at Kaena Point.

Waiakea Pond, Hawai'i Island (this is an introduced bird).

James Campbell NWR, O'ahu.

Cackling Goose
Branta hutchinsii minima

WINTER VISITOR

LENGTH 61–66 cm. (25–26 in.)
WINGSPAN 108–111 cm. (42.5–43.7 in.)
WEIGHT 1,270–2,404 g. (2.8–5.3 lb.)

A dark brown goose with a black head and neck with a white throat patch. The bill is short and black. Legs and feet black. Very similar to the larger Canada Goose but can be half the size depending on subspecies.

Two subspecies have occurred in the Hawaiian Islands: *Leucopareia* and *Taverneri*. There are fifty-four records for O'ahu as fall and winter visitors. The best locations on O'ahu to look for Cackling Goose are James Campbell NWR, Pearl Harbor NWR (Honouliuli), and less frequently, Nu'upia Ponds WMA.

Canada Goose
Branta canadaensis

RARE VAGRANT

LENGTH 75–106 cm. (30–42 in.)
WINGSPAN 127–185 cm. (50–73 in.)
WEIGHT 2,404–6,486 g. (5.3–14.3 lb.)

Large, brown goose with black head, bill and neck. Chin and cheeks are white. The neck is long and black. The breast is pale. White upper tail coverts. Sexes similar. Primary differences from Cackling Goose are the longer bill and neck and larger size in most of the seven subspecies of Canada Goose.

Canada Geese are rare visitors to the Hawaiian Islands. Only three Canada Geese have been recorded on O'ahu; one each at Mokapu Peninsula, James Campbell NWR, and Pearl Harbor NWR.

Mana Road, Hawaiʻi Island.

Waiakea Pond, Hilo, Hawaiʻi Island.

Hawaiian Goose
Nēnē

Branta sandvicensis

RESIDENT ENDEMIC THREATENED

LENGTH 55–66 cm. (22–26 in.)
WINGSPAN 109–119 cm. (43–47 in.)
WEIGHT 1,496–3,039 g. (3.3–6.7 lb.)

A medium sized, gray-brown goose with a black head and hindneck. The cheeks are buff colored and the neck is heavily furrowed. The bill, legs, and feet are black. Has two calls; a soft "nay-nay" and a loud "haw." Sexes similar but females slightly smaller. Nēnē are close relatives of Canada and Cackling Geese but have no white throat patch. They spend most of the time on the ground.

Nēnē are the world's rarest geese and have the smallest range of any goose species. It is the official state bird of Hawaiʻi. Reduced by hunting and habitat loss to fewer than thirty in the wild in 1950s; the population has now grown to over 3,000. In 2019 they were reclassified from endangered to threatened.

Significant populations exist today on Hawaiʻi Island, Maui, and Kauaʻi but they are extremely rare on Oʻahu. One was observed at Kaʻena Point in 2008. In

Gadwall

Mareca strepera

WINTER VISITOR

LENGTH 46–56 cm. (18–22 in.)
WINGSPAN 78–90 cm. (31–35 in.)
WEIGHT 498–1,043 g. (1.1–2.3 lb.)

A medium sized duck. Male is mostly gray with a pale gray-brown head, light chestnut wings, white speculum and a black rump. Bill is short and black. Legs are orange. Female resemble a female Mallard but is smaller, has a dark orange-edged bill, and a white speculum.

A minimum of twenty-eight individuals have been reported between 1967 to 2023 on Oʻahu. Most of these were at the island's premier wetland birding locations; James Campbell NWR and Pearl Harbor NWR.

2014, a pair that had been translocated from Kauaʻi to Hawaiʻi Island decided to fly back to Kauaʻi but stopped at James Campbell NWR and nested; producing three goslings. A few Nēnē were reported occasionally at various wetlands on Oʻahu until early 2019.

Sakai, Osaka, Japan. LAITCHE

Female, Anchorage, Alaska.

Eurasian Wigeon

Mareca penelope

WINTER VISITOR

LENGTH 42–52 cm. (17–20 in.)
WINGSPAN 71–81 cm. (28–32 in.)
WEIGHT 498–907 g. (1.1–2.0 lb.)

A medium sized duck. Male has a dark rufous head with a buffy forehead and crown. A gray body with pinkish breast, white patch on upper wings, dark green speculum, white hip patch and black rump. Female is very similar to female American Wigeon but has browner head, and a slightly grayer body. Both sexes have a short blue-gray bill with a black tip.

In Hawaii, Eurasian Wigeon occur every year between October and March often together with American Wigeon. A minimum of eighty birds have been recorded on Oʻahu since 1944 with high counts of nine together in 1988, 2002, and 2012.

American Wigeon (Baldplate)

Mareca americana

WINTER VISITOR

LENGTH 42–52 cm. (17–20 in.)
WINGSPAN 71–81 cm. (28–32 in.)
WEIGHT 499–907 g. (1.1–2.0 lb.)

A medium sized brown and gray duck. Male has a finely streaked grayish-brown head with a white forehead and green stripe that extends from the eye to the back. Small blue-gray bill with black tip. The body, back and sides are light brown and the forewing has a large white patch. Rump is black with a contrasting white hip patch. Female has a plain gray head with dark area around the eye.

American Wigeon are recorded every year on Oʻahu arriving in October and usually leaving in March but can stay until May. Best locations to find this species are James Campbell NWR, Pearl Harbor NWR, and Nuʻupia Ponds WMA. They are found less often at Kaelepulu Pond, Pouhala Marsh, and Paiko Lagoon Wildlife Sanctuary.

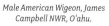

Male American Wigeon, James Campbell NWR, Oʻahu.

Male (top) and female (bottom), Waiākea Pond, Hilo, Hawai'i Island.

Mallard

Anas platyrhynchos

WINTER VISITOR
LENGTH 50–65 cm. (20–26 in.)
WINGSPAN 81–98 cm. (32–39 in.)
WEIGHT 680–1,360 g. (1.5–3.5 lb.)

A common large duck in North America but rare in the Hawaiian Islands. Male has a glossy green head, white neck ring, chestnut breast, and grayish body. Speculum bluish-purple bordered with white. Tail is white and tail coverts black. Bill yellow and legs orange. Female is plain mottled brown and has an orange and brown bill.

Beginning in the 1800s Mallards were imported to the Southeastern Hawaiian Islands as stock mostly for food. Feral populations are established on O'ahu. Occasionally wild Mallards arrive in the fall but they cannot be distinguished from those in the naturalized population.

Male (both photos), Hanalei NWR, Kaua'i.

Hawaiian Duck
Koloa

Anas wyvilliana

RESIDENT ENDEMIC ENDANGERED
LENGTH 40.6–50.8 cm. (16–20 in.)
WINGSPAN 81–98 cm. (32–39 in.)
WEIGHT 453–589 g. (1–1.3 lb.)

Hawaiian ducks evolved from ancient hybridization between Mallards and Laysan Ducks and closely resemble female Mallards but are smaller.[1] Both sexes are mottled brown and have a green or blue speculum bordered by white. The tail is dark, unlike the black and white tail of Mallards. Legs and feet are orange. Males are slightly larger, more reddish-brown than females, and have olive-green bills. Females have a dull orange and black bill.

A recent genetic study determined there are no pure Hawaiian Ducks on O'ahu but some Koloa sampled at James Campbell NWR are 80 percent Koloa and 20 percent Mallard.[2] The best location to see pure Koloa is at Hanalei NWR on Kaua'i. Recent population estimate for Kaua'i was 2,000. Hawaiian Ducks are threatened with extinction due to hybridization with feral Mallards, predation, and disease.

Seedskadee National Wildlife Refuge, Wyoming.
TOM KOERNER, USFW

Blue-winged Teal

Spatula discors

WINTER VISITOR

LENGTH 35.5–40.6 cm. (14–16 in.)
WINGSPAN 55.8–61 cm. (22–24 in.)
WEIGHT 281–499 g. (9.9–17.6 oz.)

A small duck that has a comparatively long bill. Adult male has a white facial crescent between the bill and eye, black spotted brown breast, white hip patch, and black tail. Female is mottled brown and has a small white area at the base of bill. Both sexes have blue wing coverts, green speculum, bluish-black bill and yellow-orange legs and feet.

There are seventy-four records of Blue-winged Teal on Oʻahu from 1946 to 2023. Most of these observations were at James Campbell NWR. and Pearl Harbor NWR. Additional locations where this Teal has been found include Kaʻelepulu wetland and Nuʻupia Ponds WMA. Twelve were together at Honouliuli, Pearl Harbor NWR on March 20, 1978.

Henderson Bird Preserve, Nevada (top).
Blue-winged Teal × Cinnamon Teal hybrid (bottom),
Kahuku, Oʻahu.

Cinnamon Teal

Spatula cyanoptera

VAGRANT

LENGTH 38.1–43.1 cm. (15–17 in.)
WINGSPAN 53.3–58.4 cm. (21–23 in.)
WEIGHT 335–400 g. (11.8–14.1 oz.)

A small duck similar in size to Blue-winged Teal. Breeding plumage male has deep reddish-brown head and body. The speculum is green. The bill is black and the eyes are red. Female has a pale brown head, mottled brown body, brown eyes and a gray bill. Both sexes have a blue forewing; the male's being brighter. Legs and feet are orange. Female is very similar to female Blue-winged Teal but is a little larger and has a slightly longer bill and a warmer brown color.

There are only nine records for this species on Oʻahu. Most of these were at James Campbell NWR with five birds recorded there in late December 1993.

Oʻahu Bird Species Accounts

Male (top) and female (bottom), Kahuku, Oʻahu.

Northern Shoveler
(Spoonbill)
Koloa Mohā
Spatula clypeata

WINTER VISITOR
LENGTH 43–56 cm. (17.7–22 in.)
WINGSPAN 69–84 cm. (27.1–33 in.)
WEIGHT 470–1,000 g. (1–2.2 lb.)

Medium sized duck with a large spatulate (shovel-like) bill, pale blue forewing, green speculum and orange legs. Breeding male has an iridescent green head, yellow eyes, black bill, white breast, chestnut sides and belly, blue forewing, green speculum and black rump. Female is similar to female Mallard and is mottled brown, forewing is gray and the bill is orange.

Northern Shoveler are one of the most common migratory ducks on Oʻahu and arrive every Autumn. High counts in 2021 were fifteen at Pearl Harbor NWR and ten at James Cambell NWR.

Male, Kapolei, Oʻahu.

Northern Pintail
Koloa Mapu
Anas acuta

WINTER VISITOR
LENGTH 51–66 cm. (20–26 in.)
WINGSPAN 80–95 cm. (31–37 in.)
WEIGHT 454–1,135 g. (0.99–3 lb.)

A medium sized duck with a slender neck and long pointed tail. Male has a narrow vertical white stripe that extends from the back of its dark brown head down to its neck. The breast is white, flanks are gray, hip patches are white and the rump and tail are black. Female is smaller, mottled brown and has a shorter tail. Both sexes have blue-gray bills and gray legs and feet.

Northern Pintails are the most common wintering duck in the Hawaiian Islands. Besides the Northern Shoveler, it is the only other migratory duck to be named by pre-contact Hawaiians. During the 1950s, 7,000 to 8,000 individuals were counted in Hawaiʻi but these numbers have declined precipitously due to draining of many important wetlands. Recent counts on Oʻahu average between 100 and 150 annually. Best locations to look for this migratory duck on Oʻahu include James Campbell NWR, Pearl Harbor NWR, Nuʻupia Ponds WMA, Pouhala Marsh and Salt Lake.

Female Northern Pintail, Kapolei, Oʻahu.

Male, Estanque de San Lázaro, Trujillo, Spain.
CHARLES J. SHARP

Garganey
Spatula querquedula

RARE VAGRANT

LENGTH 37–41 cm. (14.5–16.1 in.)
WINGSPAN 58–69 cm. (22.8–27.1 in.)
WEIGHT 300–440 g. (10.5–15.5 oz.)

A small dabbling duck. Breeding male has a brown head and broad white crescent above the eye that extends to the nape. The breast is brown and flanks are pale gray. Female has a distinctive white spot at base of upper mandible and a dark line from bill through eye that divides whitish facial stripes. Both sexes have gray bill, blue-gray forewing, white bordered blue-green speculum, and gray legs.

Garganeys breed across the Palearctic and are rare migrants to the Hawaiian Islands. Twenty-five individuals have been reported on Oʻahu from 1967 to 2023. A pair was observed from October 2017 through March 2018 at Pearl Harbor NWR.

Male (top), Henderson Bird Preserve, Nevada.
Female (bottom), Kahuku, Oʻahu.

Green-winged Teal
Anas crecca

WINTER VISITOR

LENGTH 31–39 cm. (12.2–15.3 in.)
WINGSPAN 52–59 cm. (20.5–23.2 in.)
WEIGHT 311–397 g. (11–14 oz.)

Smallest of the dabbling ducks. Breeding male has chestnut head, green eye patch, vertical white bar on side of chest, gray flanks, and a buff patch at side of tail that is bordered in black. Male Eurasian Green-winged teal are similar but have a white horizontal stripe above the wing. Female is speckled brown with a faint stripe above the eye and a pale buffy streak on tail coverts. Both sexes have a green speculum.

Green-winged Teal are regular visitors at Oʻahu's wetland refuges every year from October to April.

Kahuku, O'ahu.

Male, Henderson Bird Preserve, Nevada.

Canvasback

Aythya valisineria

RARE VAGRANT

LENGTH 48–56 cm. (19–22 in.)
WINGSPAN 79–89 cm. (31–35 in.)
WEIGHT 862–1,600 g. (1.9–3.52 lb.)

A medium size duck with a distinctive sloped forehead, long black bill and long neck. Male has a chestnut red head and neck, red eyes, white back and sides and a black rump. Female has a light brown head and neck, dark brown chest and grayish-brown sides. Both sexes have a black bill and bluish-gray legs and feet.

Eighteen Canvasbacks have been recorded on O'ahu between 1953 and 2023.

Redhead

Aythya americana

VERY RARE VAGRANT

LENGTH 42–54 cm. (16.5–22 in.)
WINGSPAN 75–79 cm. (29.5–31 in.)
WEIGHT 630–1,500 g. (1.3–3.3 lb.)

A medium sized diving duck. Breeding male has a round rufous head and neck, yellow eye, and black breast. Back and sides are gray and the tail is light black. Female is warm brown with a white belly. Both sexes have a bluish gray bill with a black tip separated by a narrow white ring.

Redheads are very rare vagrants to the Hawaiian Islands. Only six individuals have been reported on O'ahu from 1977 to 2023.

Female Redhead,
Kahuku, O'ahu.

Pahranagat NWR, Nevada.

P. DAVIS, USFWS

James Campbell NWR, Oʻahu.

Tufted Duck

Aythya fukigula

RARE VAGRANT

LENGTH 40–47 cm. (15.7–18.5 in.)
WINGSPAN 65–72 cm. (25.5–28.3 in.)
WEIGHT 600–1,000 g. (1.3–2.2 lb.)

A small diving duck that breeds across the northern Palearctic. The breeding adult male is all black except for white flanks and black-tipped blue-gray bill. The head has a purplish gloss and a conspicuous long, black tuft. Eyes are yellow. Female is dark brown with paler flanks and has a shorter crest that might not always be visible.

Forty-six Tufted Ducks have been recorded in the Southeastern Hawaiian Islands since 1975. Twenty-six of these were found on Oʻahu, mostly at James Campbell NWR. Three Tufted Ducks overwintered at Kaʻelepulu Pond in 2014 and 2015.

Ring-necked Duck
(Ringbill)

Aythya collaris

WINTER VISITOR

LENGTH 38–45.7 cm. (15–18 in.)
WINGSPAN 62–63 cm. (24.4–24.8 in.)
WEIGHT 490–910 g. (1.08–2.0 lb.)

A medium-sized diving duck. Breeding male has a black head, neck, and back, gray sides, and a white spur on the side. The bill is dark blue-gray with two white bands, narrow at the base and wider near the tip. Female has a grayish brown head and body, pale face and throat, and white eye rings.

Ring-necked Ducks migrate to the Hawaiian Islands during most years and are usually found in small numbers on Oʻahu at James Campbell NWR and Pearl Harbor NWR They also might be located at Loko Ea Fishpond in Haleʻiwa and Nuʻupia Ponds WMA.

Male (left) and female (right), Pearl Harbor, Oʻahu.

Westchester Lagoon, Alaska.

Greater Scaup

Aythya marila

WINTER VISITOR

LENGTH 38–53 cm. (15–22 in.)
WINGSPAN 71–84 cm. (28–33 in.)
WEIGHT 720–1,360 g. (1.6–3.0 lb.)

Greater Scaup are very similar to Lesser Scaup but have more rounded heads that are less peaked. Breeding male's head is a glossy green. The eyes are yellow. The bill is bright blue and has a large, dark nail at tip. The breast is black while the flanks are white. Female is mostly brown and has white around the base of a dull, blue bill.

Between 1946 and 2023 a minimum of thirty-one individuals have been recorded on Oʻahu.

Lesser Scaup

Aythya affinis

WINTER VISITOR

LENGTH 38–48 cm. (15–19 in.)
WINGSPAN 68–78 cm. (27–31 in.)
WEIGHT 454–1,089 g. (1–2.4 lb.)

A medium size duck that is very similar to Greater Scaup. Breeding male has a narrow black head with a purple gloss and a high crown. The eyes are bright yellow. The bill is blue with a narrow black tip. Back is whitish-gray and flanks are pale gray. Female is dark brown with a white patch at base of bill. Eyes are brownish-yellow.

Lesser Scaup are regular winter visitors to the Hawaiian Islands and are far more common than Greater Scaup in Hawaiʻi. The highest count recorded on Oʻahu was on December 4, 2004, when fifty-five Lesser Scaup were at James Campbell NWR.

Female (left) and male (right), Kachemack Bay, Alaska.

Barrow, Alaska.

Surf Scoter

Melanitta perspicillata

EXTREMELY RARE VAGRANT

LENGTH 48–61 cm. (19–24 in.)
WINGSPAN 76–84 cm. (30–33 in.)
WEIGHT 900-1,295 g. (1.9–2.8 lb.)

Breeding male is mostly black except for white patches on the forehead and nape. The colorful, triangular-shaped bill is a combination of yellow, white, red, orange, and black. The iris is white. Female is slightly smaller than the male, browner and has a dark bluish-black bill with a vertical white spot at the base of the bill.

This large North American sea duck is an extremely rare vagrant to the Hawaiian Islands with only two individuals recorded. On December 24, 1959, an emaciated juvenile female was found in the surf at Waikīkī Beach, Oʻahu. Almost half a century later, a juvenile was found on November 22, 2003 at the Kawaiʻele Waterbird Sanctuary on Kauaʻi.

Long-tailed Duck (Oldsquaw)

Clangula hyemalis

EXTREMELY RARE VAGRANT

LENGTH 38–47 cm. (15–18.5 in.)
WINGSPAN 73–79 cm. (28–31 in.)
WEIGHT 650–1,100 g. (1.4–2.4 lb.)

A brightly plumaged sea duck that breeds in the arctic and subarctic regions of Eurasia and North America. In the winter, male has a white crown, neck, and upper breast and a dark, gray cheek patch. The body is white and black. The bill is short and has a pink band. During the breeding season, the crown and neck are black and the cheek is grayish-white. The tail is 10 to 15 cm long. Female has a brown head and body and a short-pointed tail. In the winter, the head and neck are white with a dark crown and dark patch on the cheek. In the summer, the head is dark.

Long-tailed Ducks are extremely rare in the Hawaiian Islands with four records for the state and only one on Oʻahu. A juvenile male was observed at Haleʻiwa from December 4, 1993 to February 9, 1994.

Male (top), Henderson Bird Preserve, Nevada.
Male immature (bottom), Kaunakakai, Moloka'i.

Bufflehead

Bucephala lbeola

WINTER VISITOR
LENGTH 32–40 cm. (13–16 in.)
WINGSPAN 50.8–60.9 cm. (20–24 in.)
WEIGHT 270–550 g. (9.5–19.4 oz.)

A small diving sea duck with short bill. Breeding male strikingly white with black back. The head is iridescent green and purple with a large white patch behind the eye. Female and first winter male are gray-brown overall and have an oval white patch on cheek.

Most of the eighty-eight records of Buffleheads in the Hawaiian Islands from 1903 to 2023 are first-year individuals in female-like plumage. Only ten adult male Buffleheads have been recorded.

Male (left) and female (right), Denali NP, Alaska.

Common Goldeneye

Bucephala clangula

VERY RARE VAGRANT
LENGTH 40–51 cm. (15–20 in.)
WINGSPAN 77–83 cm. (30–32 in.)
WEIGHT 770–1,000 g. (1.7–2.2 lb.)

A medium-sized sea duck. Breeding male is mostly white with a greenish-glossed, dark head and a white, round patch below a golden eye. Bill is gray-black and short. Female has a chocolate-brown head, gray back, wings, and tail. Bill is mostly black with a yellow-orange tip.

Common Goldeneyes are extremely rare vagrants to the Hawaiian Islands with four records for the state and one for O'ahu. A female was observed at a wetland on the north shore on January 21, 2012. The next day it was recorded at Waiawa, Pearl Harbor NWR.

Female, Waiākea Ponds, Hilo, Hawaiʻi.

Hooded Merganser
Lophodytes cucullatus

RARE VAGRANT

LENGTH 40–50 cm. (16–19 in.)
WINGSPAN 56–70 cm. (22–28 in.)
WEIGHT 450–880 g. (1–1.9 lb.)

A small diving sea duck with a long, thin, serrated bill. Breeding male has a black head with a white patch, black neck and breast, two black spurs on chest and rusty flanks. Female's head has a rusty brown crest and a pale white spot behind eye. The body is grayish-brown. Both sexes have retractable crests.

Hooded Mergansers are rare vagrants to Hawaiʻi, with a total of twenty-four individuals since 1966. Most of these were female with only two males in breeding plumage. Fourteen have been recorded on Oʻahu including an adult male at Salt Lake on March 7, 2003.

Male (top) and female (bottom), Virgin River, Zion NP, Utah.

Common Merganser
Mergus merganser

EXTREMELY RARE VAGRANT

LENGTH 58–72 cm. (22.8–19 in.)
WINGSPAN 78–96 cm. (22–28 in.)
WEIGHT 907–2,086 g. (2–4.6 lb.)

A large sea duck that inhabits rivers and lakes in Europe, Asia, and North America. Breeding male is mostly white with a dark green head and a bright red bill. The back is black, and the rump and tail are gray. Female is mostly gray with a reddish-brown head, white chin and white secondary feathers on the wing.

A female Common Merganser reached the Southeastern Hawaiian Islands and was recorded on three islands between 1986 and 1998. It was present on Oʻahu at Waimea Valley on February 21, 1991.

Henderson Bird Preserve, Nevada.

Ruddy Duck

Oxyura jamaicensis

VERY RARE VAGRANT
LENGTH 35–43 cm. (14–17 in.)
WINGSPAN 53–61 cm. (21–24 in.)
WEIGHT 300–850 g. (0.66–1.8 lb.)

Male (top), **Kenai River, Alaska.**
Female (bottom), Ka Iwi Scenic Shoreline, O'ahu.

Red-breasted Merganser

Mergus serrator

VERY RARE VAGRANT
LENGTH 51–62 cm. (20–24 in.)
WINGSPAN 70–86 cm. (28–34 in.)
WEIGHT 800–1,350 g. (1.7–3 lb.)

Breeding male has a dark green head, white neck, and rusty breast. The eyes and narrow bill is red. The back is black, and the rump gray brown. Female has a rusty head and mottled gray back and sides.

Twelve Red-breasted Mergansers have reached the Southeastern Hawaiian Islands. The first record for O'ahu is 1901. A second Merganser was observed at Nu'upia Ponds in December, 1976. The last record for O'ahu (pictured above, bottom photo) is from Sandy Beach, November 8 to 29, 2011.

A small, compact, thick-necked duck with a broad bill and long, stiff tail. Breeding male has a black head, white cheek patches, and a scoop-shaped, bright blue bill. The body is reddish-brown, and the tail is black. Female has a dark brown crown and whitish cheek patch divided by a pale, dark line. The body is grayish-brown.

Eleven Ruddy Ducks have been record-. ed in the Hawaiian Islands. Six on O'ahu. December 23, 1945, a pair was at Ka'elepu-lu Wetland. Two males at He'eia Wetland December 16, 1984 moved to Waipio and were joined by a third male on January 22, 1985. The last record for O'ahu was at the West Loch of Pearl Harbor January 8, 2005.

Haleakalā NP, Maui.

Chukar

Alectoris chukar

POSSIBLY NATURALIZED
LENGTH 30–38 cm. (12–15 in.)
WINGSPAN 48–53 cm. (19–21 in.)
WEIGHT 530–765 g. (1.1–1.6 lb.)

A large, pale partridge native to Europe and Asia. Sexes are similar. Adults are pale gray above with lighter underparts. A black band runs through the eye and extends onto the cream-colored throat. The eyes are black with a red ring. The flanks are boldly marked with black bars. Bill and feet are red. Call is a repeated loud chuck.[3]

From 1931 to 1941, Chukars were raised at the Mokapu Game Farm on Mokapu Peninsula, Oʻahu. When World War II started, the military used the birds to help feed the troops. Chukars were first introduced to Oʻahu in 1923, but this introduction failed by 1933.[4] Additional introductions to Oʻahu of 30 birds in 1954 and 48 birds in August 1961[5] resulted in a few sightings from Pearl Harbor to Kaʻena Point through the 1950s and 1960s, but Chukars had become extirpated on Oʻahu by the 1970s.

On March 30, 2018, Chukars were ob-

Pālehua Road, Oʻahu.

Gray Francolin
(Gray Partridge)

Ortygornis pondicerianus

NATURALIZED RESIDENT
LENGTH 26–34 cm. (10.2–13.4 in.)
WINGSPAN 36–41 cm. (14–16 in.)
WEIGHT 200–340 g. (0.44–0.74 lb.)

A plump gray and brown game bird with chestnut upperparts, heavily barred, dark brown on back and finely barred on chest and flanks. The cheeks and forehead are rufous buff. The tail is short, rounded, and chestnut colored. Legs are reddish-brown. The male has small spurs on the legs. Call is a repeated *Ka-tee-tar-tee-tar*.[6]

Gray Francolins are native to India and the Middle East. They were introduced to Oʻahu in the 1980s and were first observed in the Diamond Head area, where they can still be found today. Two of the best locations to look for this species are Honouliuli and Kaʻena Point.

served and photographed in the Waiʻanae Mountains at the top of Palehua Road. It is possible a small population is now naturalized on Oʻahu or these might be recent game bird releases.

Pu'u Anahulu, Hawai'i Island.

Pu'u Anahulu, Hawai'i.

Black Francolin

Francolinus francolinus

NATURALIZED RESIDENT
LENGTH 33–36 cm. (12.9–14.2 in.)
WINGSPAN 45–50 cm. (17–19 in.)
WEIGHT 400–490 g. (0.88–1 lb.)

Male has a black head with a prominent white patch below the eye and a chestnut collar. The flanks have white spots and the back and wings are scalloped with gold, buff, and tawny brown. Female is paler and has mottled brown back and wings and a light chestnut nape. Face and broad eyebrow are buffy-white with a narrow black malar stripe. Both sexes have reddish-brown legs. Call is a loud *cheek-cheek-cheerakik*.[7]

Black Francolins occur in Central Asia and were successfully introduced to west O'ahu in 1994. They are found at Ka'ena Point and in the Wai'anae mountains.

Erckel's Francolin
(Erkel's Spurfowl)

Pternistis erkelli

NATURALIZED RESIDENT
LENGTH 38–43 cm. (15–17 in.)
WINGSPAN 36–41 cm. (14–16 in.)
WEIGHT 900–1,587 g. (2–3.5 lb.)

Sexes are similar. Adults have a chestnut crown, black supercilium and small white spot behind the eyes. Throat is white, and the bill is black. The breast is gray with elongated white and chestnut stripes. Legs and feet are yellow. Male produces a series of cackles that increase in speed and descend in pitch.[8]

Erckel's Francolins are native to North Africa. On O'ahu, they are released at the Kuaokalā Game Management Area in the northern Wai'anae range where they are hunted. They can be found most accessibly at Ka'ena Point.

Erckel's Francolin was described in 1835 by the German naturalist Eduard Rüppell from specimens collected in the mountains of Ethiopia. The specific epithet was chosen by Rüppell to honor his assistant, Theodor Erckel (1811–1897), who had helped with the collection of specimens.[9]

Japanese Quail

INGRID TAYLAR

Coturnix japonica

NATURALIZED RESIDENT
POSSIBLY EXTINCT ON OʻAHU?
LENGTH 11–20 cm. (4.5–8 in.)
WINGSPAN 32–35 cm. (12.5–14 in.)
WEIGHT 90–100 g. (3.1–3.5 oz.)

A small brown quail that is very secretive and seldom seen. Male is reddish-brown and has a white eyebrow and rufous throat. Female is pale brown and has a white throat. The bill is gray. Call is a wheezy *chik whir*.[10]

Forty Japanese Quail were released on Oʻahu in 1930.[11] Munro indicated that Japanese Quail were increasing rapidly after release on Oʻahu in 1930[12]; however, there are very few documented reports since. Schwartz and Schwartz record two observations on the southwest slopes of the Koʻolau mountains above Pearl City and above Helemanu.[13] They were reportedly present near Palikea Peak in the Waianae mountains in June, 1966 (E 28:18). Subsequently, individuals were flushed on Waipiʻo Peninsula January 9, 1977, found dead on the highway near Waileʻe, along the North Shore October 27, 1985 and heard near Kaiwailoa along the North Shore July 16, 1986. Small populations of this cryptic species possibly persist in the remote West Waiʻanae range, North Koʻolau mountains, and/or elsewhere in rural sections of Oʻahu.[14] There are no reports of Japanese Quail on Oʻahu in eBird.

Gallus gallus, *Kaeng Krachan National Park, Thailand.*
FRANCESCO VERONESI

Gallus gallus domesticus, *Lyon Arboretum, Oʻahu.*

Red Junglefowl
Moa
Gallus gallus

EXTINCT ON OʻAHU
LENGTH 42–75 cm. (16–29.5 in.)
WINGSPAN 38–51 cm. (15–20 in.)
WEIGHT 900–1,450 g. (2–3.2 lb.)

Red Junglefowl, the ancestral species to modern day poultry, are smaller than domesticated chickens. They are native to the Himalayan region, Southeast Asia, and Indonesia.[15] The male is brightly colored with yellow-orange feathers on the back and neck. The face and comb are red, and the long sickle-shaped tail feathers are iridescent, bluish-green. Females are smaller and mostly brown with a pale red face and a very small comb.

In the Southeastern Hawaiian Islands, wild populations of Red Junglefowl were formerly present on most or all islands, but they have become extirpated or integrated into populations of domestic chickens (other variants of *Gallus gallus*) on all islands except Kauaʻi.

Original Red Junglefowl persist in relatively unaltered form only in upland Kauaʻi, where there was an estimated population of 1,390 individuals in 1946–1947.[16] The wild population or original stock is centered at Kōkeʻe SP and on the Alakaʻi Plateau, but they interbreed regularly with domestic chickens on the periphery of this range,[17] and genetic studies show infusion from European strains throughout the population.[18 19]

Male, Puʻu Anahulu, Hawaiʻi Island.

Kalij Pheasant

Lophura leucomelanos

NATURALIZED RESIDENT
LENGTH 50−74 cm. (20−29 in.)
WINGSPAN 50−74 cm. (35−40 in.)
WEIGHT 564−1,025 g. (1.2−2.2 lb.)

Male is iridescent blue-black with a purple-green wash. The head and crown are black with a bright red patch surrounding the eye and a backward pointing crest. The bill is pale gray. The breast is grayish-white. The tail is mostly black. Legs and feet are brown. Female is dark brown with white edged feathers and a brown tail. The red patch on the face is smaller than the males and the crest is shorter and browner.

The Kalij Pheasant is a game bird native to Central Asia. Occasionally sightings occur in the Waiʻanae mountains. They were first introduced to the area in 2003 as an unauthorized introduction and are now established with a growing population.[20]

Palawai Basin, Lānaʻi.

Common Pheasant
(Ring-necked Pheasant)

Phasianus colchicus

NATURALIZED RESIDENT
LENGTH 50−89 cm. (20−35 in.)
WINGSPAN 56−86 cm. (22−34 in.)
WEIGHT 500−2,990 g. (1.1−6.6 lb.)

Male is brightly colored and has a green head, red facial skin, pale yellow beak, and a prominent white neck ring. The breast is copper colored and wings are white with black spots. The rump is gray, and the brown tail is long and barred. Female is mottled brown with a pale breast and shorter tail. Call is a loud, harsh *uurk-iik*.[21]

Ring-necked Pheasants are native to Asia. Mongolian Pheasants (P.c. mongolius) were brought to Honolulu by the botanist W. Hillebrand in June through July 1866 at the request of King Kamehameha V, who encouraged the importation of a variety of pheasants for aesthetics and hunting.[22] The best locations to see this colorful species are Kaʻena Point and James Campbell NWR.

Female, Puʻu Anahulu, Hawaiʻi Island.

Waimea Valley, Oʻahu.

Puʻu Anahulu, Hawaiʻi Island.

Indian Peafowl

Pavo cristatus

NATURALIZED RESIDENT
LENGTH 100–225 cm. (39–89 in.)
WINGSPAN 56–86 cm. (22–34 in.)
WEIGHT 2,700–6,350 g. (6–14 lb.)

Male has an iridescent blue and green crown with a fan-shaped crest and bare white skin above and below the eye. The neck and breast are bluish-green. The back has scaly bronze-green feathers with copper and black markings. The primaries are chestnut, and the secondaries black. The tail is dark brown. The spectacular multicolored train has many eyespots. Female has a rufous-brown head with a chestnut-green crest. The upper body is mostly brown and underparts whitish.

The Indian Peafowl is native to India, Nepal, Pakistan, and Sri Lanka. Introductions to Oʻahu occurred in the 1860s. They are occasionally seen at Kaʻena Point, Mākaha Valley, Haleʻiwa, Waimea Valley, Byodo-In Temple in Kahaluʻu, and the grounds of Honolulu Zoo.

Wild Turkey

Meleagris gallopavo

NATURALIZED RESIDENT
LENGTH 76–124 cm. (30–49 in.)
WINGSPAN 124–162 cm. (49–64 in.)
WEIGHT 2,494–10,886 g. (5.5–24 lb.)

An unmistakable large gamebird. Male is mostly black with a mix of iridescent red, green, purple, copper, and bronze feathers. The head is featherless with red wattles on the throat and neck. The wings are glossy bronze-gold. The fan-shaped tail is long and dark. Female is smaller and mostly brown and gray.

First introduced to Hawaiʻi in 1778. Wild Turkeys can be observed in the Waiʻanae Mountains especially in the areas above Kaʻena Point.

(top) KAREN LEBBING, USFWS

Alaska Maritime National Wildlife Refuge (bottom). USFWS

Pacific Loon

Gavia pacifica

EXTREMELY RARE VAGRANT
LENGTH 58–74 cm. (23–29 in.)
WINGSPAN 110–128 cm. (43–50 in.)
WEIGHT 997–2,404 g. (2.2–5.3 lb.)

Adult in breeding plumage has a pale gray nape, thin white lines on the neck, and a black throat. The body is black with small white patches on the back. Non-breeding adults and immature birds are drabber and have white chins and forenecks. The back is duller black.

In January 1982 a first-cycle Pacific Loon was reported by marine biologists near Coconut Island in Kāneʻohe Bay, Oʻahu. The exceptionally rare bird stayed until early March. This is the only accepted record for the Hawaiian Islands.

Wakodahatchee Wetlands, Delray Beach, Florida. DORI

Pied-billed Grebe

Podilymbus podiceps

RARE VAGRANT
LENGTH 31–38 cm. (12–15 in.)
WINGSPAN 45–62 cm. (18–24 in.)
WEIGHT 253–568 g. (0.55–1.2 lb.)

A small, stocky, mostly grayish-brown grebe with a short, white bill that has a black circle in the summer. The crown and back are darker. Throat is black in the spring and summer. The underparts are lighter brown.

Pied-billed Grebes are rare vagrants to the Hawaiian Islands with all records being from the Southeastern Hawaiian Islands. From 1985 to 1993 a small breeding colony became temporarily established on Hawaiʻi Island.

There are five records for Oʻahu; one or two birds were at James Campbell National Wildlife Refuge December 19, 1978 to March 20, 1979, singles were observed at Kailua January 1–19, 1996, at Pearl Harbor NWR November 6, 2011 to March 14, 2012, at Lāʻie February 13–29, 2016, and James Campbell NWR on February 14, 2017.

Adult breeding. Henderson Bird Preserve, Nevada.

Eared Grebe
Podiceps nigricollis

VERY RARE VAGRANT
LENGTH 28–34 cm. (11–13 in.)
WINGSPAN 51–56 cm. (20–22 in.)
WEIGHT 275–450 g. (9.7–15.8 oz.)

Adult in breeding plumage has a blackish-brown head, neck, breast, and upperparts. A tuft of yellow feathers extends behind the bright red eye. The flanks are rufous. Sexes are similar. Non-breeding adult has a black head and a white area below the eye and grayish-black upperparts. The neck is brownish-gray.

There are four substantiated records for the Hawaiian Islands. The only record for the Northwestern Hawaiian Islands is of a well-described bird in basic plumage on the saline lake on Laysan November 11–26, 1998. In the Southeastern Hawaiian Islands, an Eared Grebe in formative or basic plumage appeared at the Lowe Aquafarm near Kahuku, O'ahu February 19, 1983 and had molted into alternate plumage when last seen on April 1. This is the only record for O'ahu.

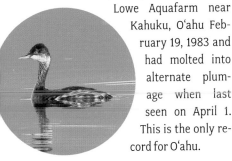

Adult nonbreeding Eared Grebe, Kealia Pond NWR, Maui.

Ka'ena Point, O'ahu (both photos).

Laysan Albatross
Moli
Phoebastria immutabilis

BREEDING VISITOR
LENGTH 76–81 cm. (30–32 in.)
WINGSPAN 195–203 cm. (77–80 in.)
WEIGHT 1,905–4,082 g. (4.2–9 lb.)

Adult has a white head, pink bill with a dark tip, and a black patch around the eye. The upper wings, rump, and tail are brownish-black. Underwings are white with black margins. The legs and feet are pink. Immature has a gray bill.

Ninety-nine percent of the world's Laysan Albatross breed in large colonies in the Northwestern Hawaiian Islands. Fortunately, at least 800 pairs nest in the accessible Southeastern Hawaiian Islands. One of the most important birds to see while visiting O'ahu is this magnificent species. Every birder should consider walking to Ka'ena Point between November and July to view the Laysan Albatross colony and amazing scenery.

Black-footed Albatross with chick.
WIETEKE HOLTHUIJZEN, USGS VOLUNTEER

Black-footed Albatross
Ka'upu

Phoebastria nigripes

BREEDING VISITOR
LENGTH 68–74 cm. (27–29 in.)
WINGSPAN 195–203 cm. (77–80 in.)
WEIGHT 2,585–4,309 g. (5.7–9.5 lb.)

A large gray-brown albatross with long, slender wings. Pale face has white at the base of the bill and behind the eye. There is a white band at the base of the tail above. Bill and legs are grayish.

Black-footed Albatross breed primarily in the Northwestern Hawaiian Islands between October and June. They are rarely seen during O'ahu pelagics. The best place to look for this majestic species is Ka'ena Point. James Campbell NWR and Pacific Rim Conservation have begun efforts to establish a Black-footed Albatross colony on the refuge. Hopefully as the colony increases, birders will have more opportunities to observe this species on O'ahu.

Light Morph, Gardur, Iceland.

Northern Fulmar

Fulmarus glacialis

RARE WINTER VISITOR
LENGTH 38–74 cm. (15–23 in.)
WINGSPAN 102–112 cm. (40–44 in.)
WEIGHT 450–1,000 g. (1–2.2 lb.)

A medium-sized petrel that has two morphs, light and dark. The light morph has a white head and body with gray wings and tail. The bill is pale yellow. The dark morph is uniformly gray with a yellow bill.

Northern Fulmars rarely reach the Hawaiian Islands between November and March, with most records being of birds found weak or dead onshore. There are seven records for O'ahu and no pelagic observations. All of the Northern Fulmars reaching Hawai'i were dark morph individuals except one light morph.

Light morph, Kīlauea Point NWR, Kauaʻi.

Kermadec Petrel

Pterodroma neglecta

RARE MIGRANT
LENGTH 36–40 cm. (14–16 in.)
WINGSPAN 90–94 cm. (35–37 in.)
WEIGHT 370–590 g. (13–20.8 oz.)

Kermadec Petrels are medium-sized gad-fly petrels that are polymorphic with light, dark, and intermediate morphs. All types have white feather shafts on the upper-wing that enhance their resemblance to skuas and jaegers. They use this resemblance to parasitize other seabirds for their food. The underwing is dark with white bases to the primaries. Light morph birds have a mostly white head, dark eye patch, white underparts, and a gray band on the breast. Dark morphs are mostly sooty brown with white feathers on the forehead and throat. Leg color varies from pink to back.

Kermadec Petrels breed in the Ker-madec and other island groups across the South Pacific and disperse into the North Pacific. They occur uncommonly in Hawaiian waters, mostly beyond 90 kilometers offshore, with greater abundance reported in fall and winter.

The only record for Oʻahu was a dark morph observed seven kilometers west of Oʻahu on April 11, 1997.

ROBBIE KOHLEY, USFWS

Murphy's Petrel

Pterodroma ultima

RARE MIGRANT
LENGTH 36–40 cm. (14–16 in.)
WINGSPAN 89–97 cm. (35–38 in.)
WEIGHT 335–435 g. (11.8–15.3 oz.)

Grayish-brown petrel with a short, dark bill, white patches on the face and throat, and a pale 'M' pattern across the wings and back. Legs are pink.

Murphy's Petrels were described by Robert Cushman Murphy an American ornithologist in 1949. They breed in the Austral, Tuamotu, and Pitcairn Islands in the central South Pacific and are uncommon but regular transients through Hawaiian waters. There are three records for Oʻahu; an adult male was collected seven miles southwest of Barbers Point October 29, 1966, one found stranded at an unknown locality on Oʻahu January 17, 1995, and one that flew aboard a ship off Honolulu on January 18, 2005. It died the next day.

Mottled Petrel

Pterodroma inexpectata

MIGRANT

LENGTH 33–35 cm. (12.9–14 in.)
WINGSPAN 74–82 cm. (29–32 in.)
WEIGHT 247–441 g. (8.7–15.5 oz.)

A medium-sized petrel with a distinctive gray patch across the lower breast and belly. The face is mottled gray and white, with dark areas around the eyes. The bill is short and black. The upperparts are gray and have a distinct 'M' pattern. The white underwings have bold, black bars. Legs and feet are pink.

Mottled Petrels breed on islands south of New Zealand from December to May and disperse widely during the non-breeding season, with part of the population traveling to the North Pacific. They migrate through Hawaiian waters regularly, with most records during brief periods in spring and autumn. There are at least fifteen records of Mottled Petrels in O'ahu's offshore waters. Most of these were in the first two weeks of April.

Juan Fernandez Petrel

Pterodroma externa

RARE MIGRANT

LENGTH 42–45 cm. (16.5–17.7 in.)
WINGSPAN 95–97 cm. (37–38 in.)
WEIGHT 310–555 g. (10.9–19.5 oz.)

A large petrel with dark brownish-gray upperparts that have an 'M' pattern across the wings. The face is white with a grayish-black cap that extends below the eyes. The bill is black and has a hook at the tip. The underparts are mostly white with a small but variable black carpal bar extending diagonally in from the elbow joint.

Juan Fernandez Petrels breed in the Juan Fernandez Islands west of Chile December to May and disperse northward into the subtropical North Pacific and westward as far as the Hawaiian Islands. There are a minimum of eleven records for O'ahu, with most sightings from late August to October.

Offshore Honokōhau, Hawai'i Island.

Near Eaglehawk Neck, Tasmania, Australia. JJ HARRISON

Hawaiian Petrel
'Ua'u

Pterodroma sandwichensis

BREEDING VISITOR ENDEMIC
ENDANGERED
LENGTH 38–40 cm. (15–16 in.)
WINGSPAN 94–99 cm. (37–39 in.)
WEIGHT 362–453 g. (12.7–15.9 oz.)

A large, long-winged, slender petrel that is dark above and white below. The head is white with a sooty, black hood. The underwing is white with black margins and bold, dark diagonal bars on the leading edge of the wings. Legs and feet are pink and black.

There are about 6,000 breeding pairs of endangered Hawaiian Petrels, most of which nest on Lāna'i, Maui, and Kaua'i. Birds arrive at the colonies in February, and the young fledge October through November. They formerly occurred on O'ahu in great numbers, but these colonies were destroyed after the arrival of humans about 1,000 years ago. Recent acoustical searches of O'ahu's mountainous areas detected Hawaiian Petrels at one location, which could indicate they are once again breeding on the island or possibly looking for potential nesting sites.[23] There are a minimum of twenty-five records of Hawaiian Petrels foraging in O'ahu's offshore waters.

White-necked Petrel

Pterodroma cervicalis

RARE MIGRANT
LENGTH 41–45 cm. (16–18 in.)
WINGSPAN 95–105 cm. (37–41 in.)
WEIGHT 380–545 g. (13.4–19.2 oz.)

White-necked Petrels have a black cap, white collar, and dark gray back. The underwing is white with a thin, dark leading edge and a short, narrow diagonal bar.

They breed in the Kermadec Islands north of New Zealand. A minimum of seventy have been recorded on pelagic trips from Kaua'i and Hawai'i Island but only a few from O'ahu. Most of these observations are from October to December with twelve March to May.

USFWS

Bonin Petrel

Pterodroma hypoleuca

BREEDING VISITOR
LENGTH 30–33 cm. (12–13 in.)
WINGSPAN 63–71 cm. (25–28 in.)
WEIGHT 218–226 g. (7.6–7.9 oz.)

A small petrel with a gray-black head and back. Forehead, chin and throat are white. Upperparts are white with a prominent 'M' pattern across the wings and rump. The underwing is white with dark margins, a black diagonal bar, and a distinctive oval patch at the carpal joint. Legs and feet are pink and the toes black.

Bonin Petrels breed on low, vegetated, sandy islands throughout the Northwestern Hawaiian Islands. They also breed in the Bonin Islands and on Volcano Island south of Japan, and disperse northward after breeding. Adults arrive on the breeding grounds in late July to August, and the young fledge in May to June. They once lived on O'ahu but became extinct after the arrival of Polynesians about 1,000 years ago. Only four Bonin Petrels have been recorded on O'ahu.

Pacific Rim Conservation and the United States Fish and Wildlife Service began a restoration program on O'ahu in 2018 when fifty-three Bonin Petrels were translocated from Tern and Midway Islands to a

Offshore Kāne'ohe, O'ahu (both photos).

Black-winged Petrel

Pterodroma nigripennis

MIGRANT
LENGTH 28–30 cm. (11–11.8 in.)
WINGSPAN 63–71 cm. (25–28 in.)
WEIGHT 131–228 g. (4.6–8 oz.)

Black-winged Petrels are small seabirds with long, narrow wings. They have pale, gray heads with a white forehead, black patch around the eyes, and a short black beak. A gray collar extends onto the white underparts. The underwing is white with a distinctive, bold, black diagonal bar. The pointed tail is gray with a dark tip.

Black-winged Petrels breed on the Kermadec Islands and other islands around New Zealand in December to April, many dispersing to the subtropical and temperate North Pacific. They are one of the more common visiting Pterodroma in the Hawaiian Islands, with records year-round but with a peak in May to December. There are a minimum of eighteen records for O'ahu's offshore waters with fifteen individuals observed on September 22, 2010.

sixteen-acre fenced area at James Campbell NWR.[24] The first Bonin Petrel chicks fledged from the refuge in August 2021.[25] Hopefully the population will continue to expand and flourish while providing new opportunities for birders on O'ahu.

JJ HARRISON

Offshore Kāneʻohe, Oʻahu.

Cook's Petrel

Pterodroma cookii

MIGRANT
LENGTH 25–30 cm. (9.8–11.8 in.)
WINGSPAN 65–66 cm. (25.5–26 in.)
WEIGHT 112–300 g. (3.9–10.5 oz.)

Named after the famous explorer Captain James Cook, this small gray and white petrel has long, narrow wings. The upperwings have a dark 'M' pattern. It has a gray cap and white forehead. The bill is black. The tail has a black tip. Underparts are mostly white except for narrow black margins on the wings.

Cook's Petrels breed on islands off New Zealand from October to April and disperse northeastward to the central and East Pacific. They occur in Hawaiian waters rarely in April and are fairly common June to November. There are a minimum of eight records of Cook's Petrel in the offshore waters of Oʻahu mostly in mid to late September. High count was from a pelagic trip off Kāneʻohe, with twenty on September 20, 2005.

Stejneger's Petrel

Pterodroma longirostris

RARE MIGRANT
LENGTH 26–31 cm. (10–12 in.)
WINGSPAN 53–66 cm. (21–26 in.)
WEIGHT 160–200 g. (5.6–7 oz.)

Stejneger's Petrel was named after Leonhard Stejneger, a Norwegian-born American ornithologist.[26] A small petrel with a distinctive dark gray cap that contrasts with its lighter gray back. The forehead is white and the slender, hooked bill is black. A triangle of white extending toward the ear from the neck separates the dark gray cap from the lighter, partial breast band. The upperwing surface has a bold 'M' pattern. The tip of tail is black. Underwings are mostly white with small black bars at the wrists.

Stejneger's Petrels breed in the Juan Fernandez Islands off Chile from November to May and disperse to the eastern North Pacific. They have occurred in Hawaiian waters primarily from September to November, with four additional records from May to June. There are only four records of Stejneger's Petrels for Oʻahu's offshore waters.

Offshore Honokōhau, Hawai'i Island.

Offshore Kāne'ohe, O'ahu.

Bulwer's Petrel
'Ou

Bulweria bulwerii

BREEDING VISITOR

LENGTH 25–29 cm. (9.8–11.4 in.)
WINGSPAN 78–90 cm. (31–35 in.)
WEIGHT 100–110 g. (3.5–3.8 oz.)

A small sooty-brown petrel with a long, pointed tail. It has distinctive, diagonal light brown bars on the upperwings. The bill is black.

Named after the English naturalist James Bulwer after he collected a specimen of an unknown petrel in the Madeira Islands in 1825.[27] Most breed in the Northwest Hawaiian Islands from Pearl and Hermes east to Nihoa and Ka'ula Rock, and very few on small coastal islets around the Southeastern Hawaiian Islands. They arrive in the Hawaiian Islands April and May, and the last fledglings leave in September to October. They are absent from Hawaiian waters from November to March, dispersing southeastward into the tropical Pacific. Offshore of O'ahu an estimated 425 pairs nest on several islets along the Northeast coast.

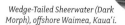

Wedge-Tailed Sheerwater (Dark Morph), offshore Waimea, Kaua'i.

Wedge-tailed Shearwater
'Ua'u Kani

Ardena pacifica

BREEDING VISITOR

LENGTH 43–48 cm. (17–19 in.)
WINGSPAN 97–104 cm. (38–41 in.)
WEIGHT 320–490 g. (11.2–17.2 oz.)

Pale morph Wedge-tailed Shearwaters are grayish brown above. The underparts are mostly white with dark wing margins and undertail-coverts. The tail is distinctly wedge-shaped when fanned. They have slender, gray, hooked bills. The legs and feet are pale pink. Dark morphs are uniformly dark brown above and dark gray below.

Wedge-tailed Shearwaters are found throughout the tropical Pacific and Indian oceans and are very common in the Hawaiian Islands. They breed on almost every island in the archipelago and on many small offshore islets. Adults arrive at the colonies in March and depart September–November and remain away from colonies for a short time in January–February. Most are light morphs. Approximately five percent are dark morphs. Large breeding colonies are located at Mānana, Mokulua, Mokumanu, and Moku'auia islets off the eastern coast of O'ahu and at Ka'ena Point NAR. O'ahu has a minimum of 25,000 breeding pairs of Wedge-tailed Shearwaters.

GREGORY "SLOBIRDR" SMITH

Kaiwi Channel between O'ahu and Moloka'i.

Buller's Shearwater

Puffinus bulleri

MIGRANT
LENGTH 46–47 cm. (18–19 in.)
WINGSPAN 97–99 cm. (38–39 in.)
WEIGHT 342–425 g. (12–15 oz.)

Buller's Shearwaters were named after Sir Walter Lawry Buller, a New Zealand ornithologist.[28] It is a large, long-tailed shearwater with a distinctive dark 'M' pattern on its bluish-gray upperwings. Black cap contrasts with white on the cheeks. Bill is grayish-black. Underside is bright white.

Buller's Shearwaters breed on Poor Knights Islands off northern New Zealand from October to April and disperse widely across the north and south Pacific Oceans. They occur regularly in small numbers in Hawaiian waters, primarily as northbound transients, from April–August and southbound transients during October and November. There is a minimum of nineteen records for O'ahu. Most of these were sighted during single-day trips offshore with a few observed from shore.

Sooty Shearwater

Puffinus griseus

MIGRANT
LENGTH 40–51 cm. (16–20 in.)
WINGSPAN 94–110 cm. (37–43 in.)
WEIGHT 650–950 g. (1.4–2.1 lb.)

A medium sized, dark brown shearwater with long, narrow wings that have silver-gray areas underneath. The bill is long and dark. The tail is short and narrow.

Sooty Shearwaters breed on islands off Southeast Australia, New Zealand, and the southern tip of South America from October to May. After breeding, they disperse throughout the world's oceans including the entire Pacific. They have been observed migrating commonly through Hawaiian Island waters, northward during March and April and southward between September and November. There are many records of Sooty Shearwaters from O'ahu's offshore waters.

Sooty Shearwater, Kaiwi Channel between O'ahu and Moloka'i.

Christmas Shearwater

Puffinus nativitatis

DUNCAN WRIGHT, USFWS

BREEDING VISITOR

LENGTH 35.5–38 cm. (14–15 in.)
WINGSPAN 71–81 cm. (28–32 in.)
WEIGHT 320–360 g. (11.2–12.6 oz.)

Christmas Shearwaters are medium sized, chocolate-brown shearwaters with a short, rounded tail. The bill is shiny black. The underparts are paler than the upperparts. Underside of primaries are dull white.

Christmas Shearwaters are named after Christmas Island (now Kritimati), which was discovered by Captain Cook the day before Christmas 1777. They breed throughout the Tropical Pacific and reach their northernmost nesting area in the Northwestern Hawaiian Islands. Adults return to breeding grounds in the Hawaiian Islands in February, eggs are laid in late spring, chicks fledge in early fall, and most or all individuals depart Hawaiian waters by early November to winter south and east of Hawai'i.

There are about 165 pairs of Christmas Shearwaters breeding in the Southeastern Hawaiian Islands. Fifty of these are on Mokumanu off the coast of Kāne'ohe, O'ahu. The best opportunity for birders to see this species is to charter a boat from Kāne'ohe and look for the birds as they fly to and from the small island. It is very important to check with the Coast Guard and Marine Corps Base Hawai'i at Kāne'ohe, while planning any pelagic trip to determine if the waters around Mokumanu might be closed due to live fire practice. There are a minimum of thirty records for O'ahu with the majority being from the Mokumanu area and Makapu'u Point.

Offshore Waimea, Kaua'i. (both photos)

Newell's Shearwater
'A'o

Puffinus newelli

MIGRANT ENDEMIC
CRITICALLY ENDANGERED
LENGTH 30−35 cm. (12−14 in.)
WINGSPAN 76−89 cm. (30−35 in.)
WEIGHT 340−426 g. (12−15 oz.)

A small shearwater that is brownish-black above and white below. The bill is black and has a sharp hook at the tip. Black cap contrasts with white cheeks. The underwing is white with dark borders. There is a distinctive white patch on the flanks that extends onto the sides of the rump. The legs are pink with dark toes.

Newell's Shearwater was named by H. W. Henshaw after Brother Matthias Newell who had received specimens from local residents on Maui. They had captured several birds in Waihe'e Valley in 1894.[29] They only breed in the Southeastern Hawaiian Islands, primarily in burrows on steep forested mountain slopes at medium elevation. Adults return to the breeding grounds during the first week of April and most depart in early fall, primarily toward the south and east.

Prior to the arrival of Polynesians there were large colonies of Newell's Shearwaters on O'ahu, but there are currently no known breeding locations on the island. A minimum of forty-five grounded birds have been found on O'ahu since 1954. They encounter bright lights and are hit by cars. There are a minimum of twenty records of Newell's Shearwaters in O'ahu's offshore waters found during pelagic trips and sea watches from land.

Offshore Honokōhau, Hawai'i Island.

Leach's Storm-Petrel

Hydrobates leucorhous

WINTER VISITOR
LENGTH 18–21 cm. (7–8.2 in.)
WINGSPAN 43–48 cm. (17–19 in.)
WEIGHT 38–46 g. (1.3–1.6 oz.)

In 1820, Coenraad Jacob Temminck named the Leach's Storm-Petrel after William Elford Leach, an English Zoologist and Marine Biologist. Leach had purchased a specimen for the British Museum from William Bullock in 1819.[30]

Storm Petrels with white rumps observed in Hawaiian waters need careful analysis to determine species. Leach's Storm-Petrels are very difficult to differentiate from Band-rumped Storm-Petrels. One of the more reliable characteristics is the shape of the tail. Please refer to this excellent article for further information.[31]

Leach's Storm-Petrels are medium-sized dark blackish-brown storm-petrels with deeply notched tails and a white rump patch that is usually but not always divided by a dark line. Upperwings have a broad, pale diagonal bar.

Leach's Storm-Petrels breed in the North Atlantic and Pacific and migrate to temperate and tropical waters in winter. They are found commonly in Hawaiian waters, with most records from October to April.

Offshore Port Allen, Kaua'i.

Band-rumped Storm-Petrel
'Ake'ake

Hydrobates castro

MIGRANT ENDANGERED
LENGTH 19–21 cm. (7.4–8.2 in.)
WINGSPAN 43–46 cm. (17–18 in.)
WEIGHT 44–49 g. (1.5–1.7 oz.)

A fairly large, dark brown storm-petrel with a narrow, white rump band that wraps around the sides. There is a pale band on the upperwing. The tail is slightly notched.

Band-rumped Storm-Petrels breed in localized populations and disperse widely throughout the world's tropical and subtropical oceans. In the Pacific, breeding has been documented at the Galapagos, Hawaiian Islands, and Japan. Small colonies exist in the Southeastern Hawaiian Islands. Estimated pairs are 350 on Kaua'i, 30 on Maui, and 50 on Hawai'i Island. They are very rare in O'ahu's offshore waters, with only six records. The best opportunity to see this rare species is a pelagic from Hale'iwa on O'ahu's North Shore into the Ka'ie'ie Waho Channel which separates O'ahu and Kaua'i.

Nihoa Island. USFWS

Tristram's Storm-Petrel

Hydrobates tristrami

BREEDING VISITOR

LENGTH 24–27 cm. (9.6–10.6 in.)
WINGSPAN 54–57 cm. (21–22 in.)
WEIGHT 71–120 g. (2.5–4.2 oz.)

The species is named after Reverend Henry Baker Tristram, an English clergyman, bible scholar, traveler, and ornithologist. Tristram was a founding member of the British Ornithologists' Union and was appointed a fellow of the Royal Society in 1868.[32] It is the largest storm-petrel species. Dark brown overall with a pale gray bar on upperwings. The wings are long and pointed. The tail is forked.

Tristram's Storm-Petrels breed on islands off Japan and in the Northwestern Hawaiian Islands. Most birds arrive to colonies in late October to November, and chicks fledge primarily in late March to mid-May. The only records of Tristram's Storm-Petrels for Oʻahu are one fledgling found at Kualoa Regional Park[33], and one seen offshore June 28, 2004.

Twenty-eight Tristram's Storm-Petrel chicks were moved from Midway Atoll and Tern Island to a safe enclosure at James Campbell NWR.[34] This was done to establish a population due to sea level rise

Offshore Honolulu, Oʻahu.

White-tailed Tropicbird
Koaʻe ʻula

Phaethon lepturus

BREEDING VISITOR

LENGTH 71–81 cm. (28–32 in.) including tail streamers
WINGSPAN 89–96 cm. (35–37 in.)
WEIGHT 220–410 g. (7.7–14.4 oz.)

Offshore Molokaʻi.

White-tailed Tropicbirds are the smallest tropicbird species. They are mostly white with distinctive diagonal black bars on the upperwings and black outer primaries. They have black eye stripes. The bill color is usually yellow but can be yellow-orange or orange-red. The tail streamers are long and white, but in the golden morph (above photo) the tail is yellow. Immature tropicbirds lacks tail streamers and have a yellow-green bill.

White-tailed Tropicbirds are nearly pantropical, being scarce only in the Eastern Tropical Pacific. Locations to look for White-tailed Tropicbirds on Oʻahu include Halona Point, Makapuʻu Lookout, Kualoa Regional Park, and the cliffs above Kaʻena Point.

caused by global warming. Breeding on Oʻahu is expected soon which should eventually create opportunities for Oʻahu birders to see this rare storm-petrel in Oʻahu's offshore waters, particularly offshore of Kahuku, Oʻahu.

Hālona, southeast coast, Oʻahu (both photos).

Red-billed Tropicbird

Phaethon aethereus

RARE VAGRANT
LENGTH 90–107 cm. (35–42 in.) including tail streamers
WINGSPAN 90–106 cm. (35–41.7 in.)
WEIGHT 600–900 g. (1.3–1.9 lb.)

Red-billed Tropicbirds are the largest of the three tropicbird species. They are mostly white and have a finely barred back and black outer primaries. The bill is red and a black patch extends behind the eyes. The tail has long, white streamers. Immature tropicbirds have a yellow bill and no tail streamers.

Unlike White-tailed and Red-tailed Tropicbirds, the Red-billed Tropicbird is not regularly found in the Hawaiian Islands, occurring primarily in the subtropical and tropical Eastern Pacific, Atlantic, and Indian oceans. Approximately fifteen individuals have been recorded as vagrants to the Hawaiian Islands.

On Oʻahu, an adult was observed interacting with Red-tailed Tropicbirds along the rocky southeast coast near Hālona Point on March 3, 2006. Two Red-billed Tropicbirds were observed together in the same area in 2007 and were banded. The following year, a new unbanded individual was observed from February 26 to July 26 and it was incubating an abandoned Red-tailed Tropicbird egg on the last date. After a pause in observations, a Red-billed Tropicbird returned to the area in 2018. Two were seen together in 2020 and continued into 2021. On January 31, 2023, two were also seen together suggesting potential nesting might occur in this area soon.

The best place for visiting birders to look for this species is along the southeast coast of Oʻahu between Lānaʻi Lookout and Hālona Point from January to May. This is the most accessible and probably best place on earth to possibly see all three tropicbird species together.

Southeast coast of O'ahu (all photos).

Red-tailed Tropicbird
Koa'e 'Ula
Phaethon rubicauda

BREEDING VISITOR
LENGTH 95–104 cm. (37–41 in.) including tail streamers
WINGSPAN 111–119 cm. (44–47in.)
WEIGHT 600–830 g. (1.3–1.8 lb.)

The adult Red-tailed Tropicbird is mostly white and has a bright red bill, a black eye patch, a white tail, and two elongated, red tail feathers. The legs and feet are blue-black. Immature Tropicbirds are white with prominent black barring on the upperparts and have no tail streamers.

Red-tailed Tropicbirds breed throughout the tropical and subtropical Pacific and Indian Oceans. In Hawai'i, they are present at colony sites from February to October but virtually absent November to January. Birders can enjoy spectacular views of Red-tailed Tropicbirds along O'ahu's southeast coast, where at least ninety pairs are located.[35]

Adult female, Kīlauea Point NWR, Kaua'i.

Great Frigatebird
'Iwa

Fregata minor

BREEDING VISITOR
LENGTH 85–105 cm. (33–41 in.)
WINGSPAN 205–230 cm. (81–91 in.)
WEIGHT 1,000–1,590 g. (2.2–3.5 lb.)

Immature, Kaiwi Channel.

Adult male, Kīlauea Point NWR, Kaua'i.

The Great Frigatebird is large seabird that is lightly built, enabling it to soar effortlessly without flapping its long, angular wings. Many people see a resemblance to a Pterodactyl when they observe it flying high above. It is mostly black and has a forked tail. Adult male has an inflatable red throat patch and purple-green sheen on the scapular feathers. Adult female is larger than the male and has a white throat and breast. Immature has variable white and rust coloring on the head, throat, and breast.

Great Frigatebird is nearly a pantropical species, being absent only from the Atlantic Ocean north of the equator. There are an estimated 10,000 breeding pairs in the Northwestern Hawaiian Islands with seventy-five percent of these at Laysan and Nihoa Islands. They roost in large numbers on several islets off O'ahu's eastern shore but only two nests have been documented in the Southeastern Hawaiian Islands. Some of the best places to look for this species on O'ahu are Mōkapu Peninsula, Makapu'u Point, and along the North Shore.

Java, Indonesia. RON KNIGHT

Lesser Frigatebird
Fregata ariel

VERY RARE VAGRANT
LENGTH 68–81 cm. (26–32 in.)
WINGSPAN 155–193 cm. (61–76 in.)
WEIGHT 625–955 g. (1.3–2.1 lb.)

Lesser Frigatebirds are the smallest frigatebird species. Adult male is black with a white patch on the flank that extends onto the underwing and a red gular sac. Female is larger than male and duller in color and has a white breast and white collar. Immature has a tawny brown head and neck.

Lesser Frigatebirds breed in the tropical and subtropical west and central Pacific east to the Phoenix, Line, Tuamotu, and Marquesas Islands, and in the Indian and South Atlantic oceans. There are six records of this very rare species in the Southeastern Hawaiian Islands, and only one for Oʻahu.

Adult, Kaiwi Channel.

Masked Booby
ʻĀ

Sula dactylatra

BREEDING VISITOR
LENGTH 75–85 cm. (30–33 in.)
WINGSPAN 160–170 cm. (63–67 in.)
WEIGHT 1,179–2,222 g. (2.6–4.9 lb.)

The Masked Booby is the largest booby species. Adult is white with black on the trailing edge of wings. The tail is black. Bill is yellow and the bare skin on the face is black giving it a masked appearance. Iris is yellow. Immature has a white neck and underside. The head is mottled gray-brown and the bill is dull yellow.

Masked Boobies breed worldwide on tropical and subtropical islands; in the Pacific they are found from Australia and Japan to Chile and Mexico. They remain at the breeding islands year-round and range at sea generally in the vicinity of breeding grounds, but can also disperse far to sea when not breeding. A minimum of fifty pairs breed on Mokumanu Islet off the coast of Kāneʻohe, Oʻahu. Best areas on Oʻahu to see this very uncommon species are Makapuʻu Point, Lāʻie Point, Kaʻena NAP, or a pelagic offshore of east Oʻahu.

Immature Masked Booby.
Mokumanu, Oʻahu.

Galapagos Islands. FLOODMFX

Nazca Booby

Sula granti

VERY RARE VAGRANT

LENGTH 75–85 cm. (30–33 in.)
WINGSPAN 160–170 cm. (63–67 in.)
WEIGHT 1,179–2,222 g. (2.6–4.9 lb.)

Nazca Booby is very similar to Masked Booby but has an orange bill. Adult is white with black on the trailing edge of wings. Bare black skin on face and a black tail.

Nazca Boobies breed in the tropical east Pacific, primarily on the Galapagos Islands, with smaller numbers on several other islands off Ecuador, Columbia, and Mexico. There are nine records for the Hawaiian Islands. There are only two records for Oʻahu, both from Mokumanu Islet, a single bird associating with Masked Boobies on February 28, 2006 and a distant view of a single bird on September 25, 2017.

Offshore Honolulu, Oʻahu.

Brown Booby

ʻĀ

Phaethon rubicauda

BREEDING VISITOR

LENGTH 64–85 cm. (25–33.5 in.)
WINGSPAN 132–155 cm. (52–61 in.)
WEIGHT 950–1,700 g. (2–3.7 lb.)

Brown Boobies are relatively large seabirds with long wings and tail and a yellow pointed bill (bill color can vary). Adults are chocolate-brown above with a sharply contrasting white chest. The short legs and feet are bright yellow. Male face color is blue, yellow in females. Immature is light brown overall. Male of the subspecies brewsteri has a pale-gray head and neck. This subspecies has been observed in Oʻahu's offshore waters.

Brown Boobies breed widely across the tropical Pacific on islands and off the west coast of Central America. Breeding occurs from January to September. They are fairly common offshore of Oʻahu, with many being observed resting on buoys.

*Immature Brown Booby,
Mokumanu Islet, Oʻahu.*

Adult, Makapuʻu, Oʻahu.

Red-footed Booby
ʻĀ

Sula sula

BREEDING VISITOR
LENGTH 69–79 cm. (27–31 in.)
WINGSPAN 134–150 cm. (53–59 in.)
WEIGHT 850–1,100 g. (1.8–2.4 lb.)

This is the smallest booby species. There are three morphs in Hawaiʻi. In the most common morph, the adult is mostly white with black wing tips and secondaries, pale blue or greenish bill, brightly colored pink, red, and blue facial skin, white tail, and bright red legs. Immature is gray-brown above and grayish-white below with an indistinct border on breast. The bill is dark and the legs are pale pink.

Red-footed Boobies inhabit tropical oceans around the world. In the Southeastern Hawaiian Islands, they breed year-round. Approximately 1,000 pairs nest on the Mokapu Peninsula and Mokumanu Islet. The best place to see and photograph this colorful species is at Makapuʻu Beach Park. Hundreds of Red-footed Boobies pass low over the coastline early in the morning as they fly to their offshore fishing areas.

SANDRA UECKER, USFWS

American Bittern

Botaurus lentiginosus

EXTREMELY RARE VAGRANT
LENGTH 58–85 cm. (25–33 in.)
WINGSPAN 92–115 cm. (36–45 in.)
WEIGHT 370–1,072 g. (0.8–2.3 lb.)

A medium-sized brown and white heron with a long neck and pointed bill. A black streak extends from the eye down the side of neck. The eyes are surrounded by yellow skin and the irises are pale yellow. Immature is similar to adult but lacks a black neck streak.

American Bitterns breed across southern Canada and the northern United States and winter in southern parts of the breeding range, south through Mexico, and the Caribbean. They are extremely rare in the Hawaiian Islands with only two records. The first was at a watercress farm near the north end of the Middle Loch of Pearl Harbor, Oʻahu from January 20, 2013 to March 29, 2013. The second was at James Campbell NWR November 3, 2018 to February 12, 2019.

Immature Red-footed Booby, Makapuʻu, Oʻahu.

James Campbell NWR

Great Blue Heron

Ardea herodias

RARE VAGRANT
LENGTH 91–137 cm. (36–54 in.)
WINGSPAN 167–201 cm. (66–79 in.)
WEIGHT 1,814–3,583 g. (4–7.9 lb.)

Adult Great Blue Heron has a white face and a pair of black plumes that extend from above the eye to the back of the head. The bill is dull yellow becoming orange during the breeding season. Neck is brownish buff with black and white steaking down the front. The wings, belly, and back are blue-gray. Thighs are red-brown. Immature has a black cap, no plumes, and is brownish-gray.

Great Blue Herons breed throughout North America and migrate as far as northern South America for the winter. There are a minimum of ten records for Oʻahu. Locations where this species has been found include Pearl Harbor NWR, James Campbell NWR, and Nuʻupia Ponds WMA.

Hawaiʻi Kai, Oʻahu.

Great Egret

Ardea alba

VERY RARE VAGRANT
LENGTH 80–104 cm. (31–41 in.)
WINGSPAN 131–170 cm. (52–67 in.)
WEIGHT 700–1,500 g. (1.5–3.3 lb.)

The Great Egret is large, long-necked, long-legged, and all white except for the yellow bill and black legs and feet. In non-breeding plumage, the facial skin is yellow. During breeding season, the facial skin turns green and both sexes grow long, flowing plumes on the back. There are six records for Great Egrets in the Hawaiian Islands; three of these are from Oʻahu.

Great Blue Heron.
Merritt Island NWR, Florida.

Santa Barbara, California.

Snowy Egret

Egretta thula

EXTREMELY RARE VAGRANT

LENGTH 56–66 cm. (21–26 in.)
WINGSPAN 90–105 cm. (35–41 in.)
WEIGHT 350–400 g. (12–14 oz.)

A medium-sized, slender, white heron with a black bill, yellow lores, black legs, and distinctive, bright yellow feet. During breeding season, the lores are reddish and the nape, neck, and back have long plumes. Sexes are similar in appearance. Immature has duller yellow lores.

Snowy Egrets breed in most of the contiguous United States and throughout Central and South America. There are five confirmed records of Snowy Egrets in the Hawaiian Islands. Two of these were on Oʻahu. The first was at Nuʻupia Ponds WMA from March 6 to 31, 1980 and the second Snowy Egret was at James Campbell NWR from November 15, 1997 to March 10, 1998.

Merritt Island NWR, Florida.

Little Blue Heron

Egretta caerulea

EXTREMELY RARE VAGRANT

LENGTH 64–76 cm. (25–30 in.)
WINGSPAN 99–104 cm. (39–41 in.)
WEIGHT 283–397 g. (10–14 oz.)

A small, mostly grayish-blue heron with a purplish head and neck. The bill is gray with a black tip. The legs are dull green. Sexes are similar in appearance. Juvenile is all white and has a pale gray bill with dark tip.

Little Blue Herons breed and winter from the southern United States to northern South America. There is only one amazing record for the Hawaiian Islands. A single adult Little Blue Heron was observed in the restricted wetlands around Pearl Harbor one or two times each year from 1966 until 1993.

Kualoa Regional Park, Oʻahu (top).
Juvenile, Waipiʻo, Oʻahu (bottom).

Cattle Egret

Bubulcus ibis

NATURALIZED RESIDENT
LENGTH 46–56 cm. (18–22 in.)
WINGSPAN 88–96 cm. (35–38 in.)
WEIGHT 270–512 g. (9.5–18 oz.)

Adult breeding Cattle Egret is all white except for orange-buff plumes on the crown, breast, and back. The short bill and legs are yellow. Juvenile has a black bill and black legs.

In 1959, the Hawaiʻi Board of Agriculture and Forestry imported young Cattle Egrets from southern Florida and released them on several cattle ranches on Oʻahu and Kauaʻi. They eventually spread to all the major islands. The estimated population in 1980 was 30,000 birds. Today they are very common at Oʻahu's parks and golf courses.

Merritt Island NWR, Florida.

Green Heron

Butorides virescens

VERY RARE VAGRANT
LENGTH 41–46 cm. (16–18 in.)
WINGSPAN 64–68 cm. (25–27 in.)
WEIGHT 170–226 g. (6–8 oz.)

Adult Green Heron has a glossy, black-ish-green cap and a dark, rufous neck with a white line. The wings and back are greenish. The bill is dark with a sharp point. Legs and feet are yellow.

Green Herons live in North and Central America south to Panama. There are eight records for the Hawaiian Islands. The only record of Green Heron on Oʻahu was a bird at Waimanalo on October 2, 1987.

James Campbell NWR, Oʻahu.

Immature, Koʻolina, Oʻahu (fishing with bread bait).

Black-crowned Night-Heron
Nycticorax nycticorax

RESIDENT

LENGTH 58–66 cm. (23–26 in.)
WINGSPAN 115–118 cm. (45–46.5 in.)
WEIGHT 727–1,014 g. (1.6–2.2 lb.)

A stocky, pale gray heron with a black crown and back. The bill is black and the eyes orange-red. The wings are pale gray and the underparts white. Legs and feet are yellow. Sexes similar in appearance, but males are larger. Breeding adults have white plumes on the back of the head. Immature is gray-brown on the back and wings with many pale spots. The underparts are streaked with brown. The eyes are yellow-orange, and the legs are dull greenish-yellow.

A cosmopolitan species, Black-crowned Night-Herons live in the Americas from southern Canada to southern Chile and in Eurasia and Africa east to the Philippines, East Indies, and the Hawaiian Islands. They are very common on Oʻahu and can be found at most wetlands, golf course ponds, and at Ala Moana Park. Some Black-crown Night-Herons have learned to fish with bread that is thrown into the water by people. The herons push the bread underwater and catch the fish that are attracted to the bait.

Pearl Harbor NWR, Honouliuli, O'ahu.

White-faced Ibis

Plegadis chihi

VAGRANT
LENGTH 46–56 cm. (18–22 in.)
WINGSPAN 90–93 cm. (35–37 in.)
WEIGHT 450–590 g. (1–1.3 lb.)

A medium-sized, long-legged wader with a long, curved, gray bill. The eyes are red and the bare facial skin is pink. Breeding adult has narrow, white borders on the face. Body is iridescent purple-red with green and bronze in the wings. The legs are pinkish-red. Immature has dull blue-gray facial skin, a dull gray-brown head, neck, back, and belly. The legs are gray-green.

White-faced Ibis breed in western North America from Oregon and California Southeast to Louisiana. There are a minimum of twenty-two records for O'ahu. Since 2018, they have been present every year at Pearl Harbor and James Campbell NWRs. There is a possibility this species breeds in Hawai'i, but so far this is unproven.

Pearl Harbor NWR, Honouliuli, O'ahu.

Osprey
(Fish Hawk)

Pandion haliaetus

WINTER VISITOR
LENGTH 56–63 cm. (22–25 in.)
WINGSPAN 127–180 cm. (50–71 in.)
WEIGHT 1,400–2,000 g. (3–4.4 lb.)

Ospreys are dark brown above and white below. The head is white with a prominent black eye stripe that extends onto the sides of the neck. The irises are yellow. The bill is black with a blue cere. Feet are white with black talons. Females are larger, and the brown speckling on the breast is more pronounced.

Ospreys are found worldwide. They are annual winter visitors to the Hawaiian Islands with one to four birds present in the islands every year. The best places to look for Osprey on O'ahu are Pearl Harbor NWR, James Campbell NWR, Nu'upia Ponds WMA, and Pouhala Marsh Wildlife Sanctuary.

Female, James Campbell NWR, Oʻahu.

Birding Center, Port Aransas, Texas.
ELAINE R. WILSON

Northern Harrier
(Marsh Hawk)

Circus cyaneus

RARE VAGRANT
LENGTH 41–52 cm. (16–20 in.)
WINGSPAN 97–122 cm. (38–48 in.)
WEIGHT 290–750 g. (0.6–1.6 lb.)

Northern Harrier is a slender, medium-sized raptor with broad wings and a long, rounded tail. They have a distinctive white rump patch. The facial disk gives them an owl-like appearance. Adult female is dark brown above and buff below with brown streaks on the chest. Adult male is gray above and light below. The wing tips are black, and there are reddish spots on the chest. Immature is similar to female but has an un-streaked cinnamon-colored breast, and the back and wings are darker.

Northern Harriers occur throughout Eurasia and North America. A minimum of forty individuals have been recorded in the Southeastern Hawaiian Islands from 1976 to 2023. Sixteen are from Oʻahu. Most records are of first-fall birds.

Sora

Porzana carolina

EXTREMELY RARE VAGRANT
LENGTH 19–30 cm. (7.5–11.7 in.)
WINGSPAN 35–40 cm. (13.7–15.7 in.)
WEIGHT 49–112 g. (1.7–4.0 oz.)

The Sora is a marsh dwelling bird with short, rounded wings. The face is blue-gray with black at the base of the short, yellow bill and on the throat. The back is reddish brown and streaked with white. The flanks have black and white barring. The breast is gray. Sexes are similar in appearance. Immatures lack the black facial markings and are browner.

The Sora breeds from southeast Alaska across North America. There are four records for the Hawaiian Islands with two of these from Oʻahu.

Male Northern Harrier.
Old Denali Highway, Alaska.

James Campbell NWR, Oʻahu.

Common Gallinule
ʻAlae ʻUla
Gallinula galeata sandvicensis

RESIDENT ENDANGERED
LENGTH 32−35 cm. (12.6−13.8 in.)
WINGSPAN 54−62 cm. (21.3−24.4 in.)
WEIGHT 310−456 g. (10.9−16.1 oz.)

The adult Hawaiian Common Gallinule has a black head and neck with a large, red frontal shield over a red bill that has a yellow tip. It is dark brown above and slate-blue below. The undertail coverts are mostly white and the flanks have white stripes. Legs and feet are yellow-greenish. Sexes are similar in appearance. Immature is grayish-brown with a pale yellow or brown bill.

The Hawaiian Gallinule is considered a subspecies of Common Gallinule. It has a more extensive frontal shield then a Common Gallinule and a reddish blush on the front of its legs.[36] It was formerly found on all of the main Hawaiian Islands, but because of hunting, loss of habitat, and predation by non-native mammals it now only occurs on Kauaʻi and Oʻahu. The population on Oʻahu fluctuates annually. A high of 230 in August 2006 and a low of 55 in 1996 were recorded during surveys. Great places to see this secretive bird are James Campbell NWR, Hāmākua Marsh Wildlife

Red Shield morph (bottom), Kaʻelepulu Wetland, Oʻahu.

Hawaiian Coot
ʻAlae Kea
Fulica alai

RESIDENT ENDANGERED
LENGTH 33−40.6 cm. (13−16 in.)
WINGSPAN 58−71 cm. (22.8−28 in.)
WEIGHT 600−700 g. (1.3−1.5 lb)

The adult Hawaiian Coot has a black head, red eyes, and a white frontal shield and bill. The body is slate gray with white undertail feathers. The

Juvenile (left)

feet are lobed and greenish-gray. It is smaller than the American Coot and has a larger frontal shield above the bill. Most Hawaiian Coots have white shields, but a small percentage have a red or brown shield. Immature is light gray and has a dull white bill.

Hawaiian Coots occur on all of the main Hawaiian Islands except Kahoʻolawe. The population on Oʻahu varies annually from 500 to 1,000 birds.

Sanctuary, and Kaʻelepulu Wetland Bird Preserve.

Creamers Field, Fairbanks, Alaska.

Adult (left) and immature (right),
James Campbell NWR, O'ahu.

Black-necked Stilt
Ae'o

Himantopus mexicanus knudseni

RESIDENT ENDANGERED
LENGTH 35–39 cm. (13.8–15.3 in.)
WINGSPAN 71.5–75.5 cm. (28–29.7 in.)
WEIGHT 150–176 g. (5.3–6.2 oz.)

A very slender shorebird with a long, thin, black beak and long, pink legs. It is black on the back and has a white eyebrow, forehead, throat, and underside. Sexes are similar, but female has a tinge of brown on its back while the male's back is glossy. Immature has a brownish back and more extensive white on the cheeks and forehead. Compared to the North American subspecies, the Hawaiian Stilt is blacker on the neck, and the black is lower on its face. They can be seen at Pearl Harbor and James Campbell NWRs, Paiko Lagoon Wildlife Sanctuary, Ka'elepula Bird Preserve, Hāmākua Marsh Wildlife Sanctuary, and Nu'upia Ponds WMA.

The Hawaiian Stilt is considered an endemic subspecies of the Black-necked Stilt of North and South America to which it is very similar. The population in the Hawaiian Islands varies annually from 1,500 to 2,000 individuals. The United States Fish and Wildlife Service is currently considering down listing this species to threatened status.

Sandhill Crane

Grus canadensis

EXTREMELY RARE VAGRANT
LENGTH 112–122 cm. (44–48 in.)
WINGSPAN 165–200 cm. (65–79 in.)
WEIGHT 2,721–6,714 g. (6–14.8 lb.)

Adult Sandhill Crane has a red crown, white cheeks, and a long, pointed bill. It is gray overall and has long legs. Sometimes the feathers are reddish-brown due to preening with iron rich mud. Immature has a rusty brown crown and neck.

Sandhill Cranes breed from northeast Siberia to Baffin Island and south to northeast California and Ohio. In the Southeastern Hawaiian Islands, there is a single record. On October 23, 1933, a farmer captured a first-fall Sandhill Crane in a field near Kahuku, O'ahu. Despite attempts to keep it alive, it perished, and the specimen was sold to the Bishop Museum for $5.00.[37]

Black-bellied Plover
(Gray Plover)

Pluvialis squatarola

WINTER VISITOR
LENGTH 27–30 cm. (11–12 in.)
WINGSPAN 71–83 cm. (28–33 in.)
WEIGHT 190–280 g. (6.7–9.9 oz.)

Pearl Harbor, Oʻahu.

A medium-sized shorebird with short legs and a thick, black bill. In breeding plumage, the face, throat, breast, and belly are black with white stripes extending from the forehead down the sides of the neck. The rump is white. The tail is white with black barring. In non-breeding plumage it is brown and gray above with a gray speckled breast and white rump and belly. In all plumages the inner flanks and base of the underwing are black. Sexes look similar, but the male is more brightly colored. Juvenile has more streaking on the breast and sides.

Black-bellied Plovers breed throughout Holarctic regions. They are regular migrants in small numbers to the Hawaiian Islands. In the Southeastern Hawaiian Islands, they have been recorded annually since the mid-1950s. There are a minimum of fifty records for Oʻahu since 1939. They can be occasionally be found at Oʻahu's refuges and wetland preserves.

Pacific Golden-Plover, Kualoa Regional Park, Oʻahu.

He'eia Pier, O'ahu (Leucistic).

Pacific Golden-Plover
Kōlea
Pluvialis fulva

Ala Moana Beach Park, O'ahu.

WINTER VISITOR
LENGTH 23–30 cm. (9.1–11.8 in.)
WINGSPAN 60–72 cm. (23.6–28.5 in.)
WEIGHT 128–134 g. (4.5–4.7 oz.)

A medium-sized shorebird with long wings and an upright posture. In breeding plumage, it is spotted gold, black, and white on the crown, wings, nape, and back and has a black face, throat, belly, and flanks bordered by white. In non-breeding plumage the forehead and face are pale buff with a distinct whitish eyebrow and blackish ear patch. Upperparts are brownish-white with yellow-buff speckling on the crown, back, wings, and tail. Belly and undertail coverts are white. Immature is like non-breeding adult but has more streaking on the breast and flanks and a yellowish eyebrow. Bill is black and the rump is dark. Legs are black to gray.

Pacific Golden-Plovers breed in Siberia and western Alaska and migrate to wintering grounds from Africa to Australia to California and islands throughout the Pacific. They are the most common migratory shorebird in the Hawaiian Islands and can be found at most of O'ahu's parks, wetlands, golf courses, and athletic fields. They are very adapted to urban areas. The fossil record indicates their presence in the Hawaiian Islands for at least 120,000 years.[38] Some young birds and unhealthy adults over-summer in Hawai'i.

Fairbanks, Alaska (top).
James Campbell NWR, Oʻahu (bottom).

Semipalmated Plover

Charadrius semipalmatus

WINTER VISITOR

LENGTH 14–20 cm. (5.5–7.9 in.)
WINGSPAN 35–56 cm. (14–22 in.)
WEIGHT 22–63 g. (0.78–2.2 oz.)

A small shorebird with a stubby bill, short neck, gray-brown back, and white underparts. In breeding plumage, it has brown cap, white forehead with black above, orange bill with black tip and a narrow, black band at base of upper mandible. Throat and back of neck are white and the neckband is black. The legs and feet are orange. Non-breeding plumage is paler overall. The bill is mostly dark with minimum orange. Neckband is pale brown and the legs are dull yellow.

Semipalmated Plovers breed throughout arctic North America. Every year, a few individuals arrive in the Hawaiian Islands during fall migration. They are most likely to be found at Pearl Harbor and James Campbell NWRs.

Kealia Pond NWR, Maui.

Killdeer

Charadrius vociferus

RARE VAGRANT

LENGTH 20–28 cm. (7.9–11 in.)
WINGSPAN 59–63 cm. (23–25 in.)
WEIGHT 72–121 g. (2.5–4.3 oz.)

A large plover with a short, dark bill, white forehead with a black bar above, brown crown, and a white "eyebrow" above red, bare skin around eyes. It has a white collar, two black breast bands, and mostly brown upperparts with rufous fringes. The rump is red and the tail is brown. The legs are flesh colored. It is the only plover in North America with two breast bands. Sexes are alike and the plumages are essentially identical throughout the year. Immature is very similar to adult. Downy juvenile has a single breast band.

The Killdeer is a New World species, breeding in southeast Alaska and across North America. There are a minimum of forty-two individuals recorded in the Southeastern Hawaiian Islands; nine of these are from Oʻahu. Places where this rare migratory shorebird has been observed on the island include James Campbell NWR and Nuʻupia Ponds WMA.

VEDANT RAJU KASAMBE

Blue Mesa Reservoir, Colorado (left).
James Campbell NWR, Oʻahu, September 19, 2006 (right).

Terek Sandpiper

Xenus cinereus

EXTREMELY RARE VAGRANT
LENGTH 22–25 cm. (8.7–9.8 in.)
WINGSPAN 36–45 cm. (14.2–17.7 in.)
WEIGHT 50–126 g. (1.8–4.4 oz.)

A unique medium-sized shorebird with a distinctive upturned bill. Plumage is gray overall with white underparts and white trailing edge on the wings. The bill is long and black with orange at the base. The eyes are dark brown and surrounded by a white eye ring. The legs are bright orange. In breeding plumage dark streaks appear on the head and neck and black lines are on the scapulars.

Terek Sandpipers breed across central Russia and winter in the southern hemisphere from South Africa to Australia. They are named after the Terek River, which flows into the Caspian Sea, as they were first observed in this area.[39] On January 9, 2014, a Terek Sandpiper was found at James Campbell NWR. This is the only record for the Hawaiian Islands.

Spotted Sandpiper

Actitis macularius

RARE VAGRANT
LENGTH 18–20 cm. (7.1–7.9 in.)
WINGSPAN 37–40 cm. (14.6–15.8 in.)
WEIGHT 34–50 g. (1.2–1.8 oz.)

A medium-sized shorebird with a short neck and short legs. In breeding plumage, the Spotted Sandpiper is brown above and has dark brown spots on its bright, white chest. The bill is orange with a black tip. The supercilium is white. Legs are light yellow to pinkish. In non-breeding plumage the back is grayish-brown and the chest has brown on the sides but no spots. The bill is pale yellow with a black tip. Male and female look similar but the female is slightly larger. Juvenile plumage is similar to non-breeding adult plumage.

Spotted Sandpipers breed across North America and winter as far south as central South America. A minimum of twenty-three individuals have been recorded on Oʻahu from 1976 to 2023. Interesting locations on the island where this rare species has been observed recently include Heʻeia State Park and the Kaiwi State Scenic Shoreline Park. Most sightings have been at Oʻahu's two NWRs.

Glenn Highway, Alaska.

Solitary Sandpiper
Tringa solitaria

EXTREMELY RARE VAGRANT
LENGTH 18–23 cm. (7.1–9.1 in.)
WINGSPAN 55–57 cm. (21.6–22.4 in.)
WEIGHT 31–65 g. (1.1–2.3 oz.)

James Campbell NWR, Oʻahu.

A medium-sized shorebird with dark olive-brown upperparts, mostly white underparts and a black and white tail. It has a distinctive white eye ring and an olive-green bill. The legs are dark olive. In breeding plumage, the upperparts are finely spotted with white dots. In non-breeding plumage, the back is mostly unspotted and the breast is washed with brown.

Solitary Sandpipers breed from Alaska across Canada and winter in Mexico through south central South America. There are five records for the Hawaiian Islands, with three of these from Oʻahu.

Ka'ena Point State Park.

Gray-tailed Tattler
Tringa brevipes

VERY RARE VAGRANT
LENGTH 23–27 cm. (9–11 in.)
WINGSPAN 60–65 cm. (23–26 in.)
WEIGHT 80–162 g. (2.8–5.7 oz.)

A medium-sized shorebird with gray up-perparts and a white eyebrow. The black bill is long, straight, and has a pale base. Legs are yellow. In breeding plumage, the underparts are barred dark brown. In non-breeding plumage the underparts are almost completely white.

Gray-tailed Tattlers and Wandering Tattlers are very similar in appearance. Several characteristics of Gray-tailed Tattlers that help separate them from Wandering Tattlers include: the eyebrow meets on the forehead and extends behind the eye, and they have a shorter nasal groove. The best characteristic to separate these two species is the call. The most common call is a two-note "too-lee." Immature birds are similar to adults in non-breeding plumage.

Gray-tailed Tattlers breed in Siberia and winter in Southeast Asia, Australia, and the western Pacific. There are a minimum of seven records for O'ahu.

James Campbell NWR, O'ahu (both photos).

Wandering Tattler
'Ūlili
Tringa incana

WINTER VISITOR
LENGTH 26–30cm. (10.2–11.8 in.)
WINGSPAN 50–55 cm. (19.7–21.6-26 in.)
WEIGHT 60–169 g. (2.1–6 oz.)

A medium-sized gray shorebird with a long, black bill, white eye ring, a thin white eyebrow that ends at the eye, and dull yellow legs. Adults in breeding plumage are heavily barred underneath. In non-breeding plumage the underparts are gray.

Wandering Tattlers breed along the North Pacific Rim from northeast Siberia to Yukon and northwest British Columbia. They are fairly common on O'ahu and can be found at Ala Moana Beach Park, Paiko Lagoon Wildlife Sanctuary, and all of the major wetland refuges and preserves.

Morro Bay, California State Park Marina. MIKE BAIRD

Greater Yellowlegs

Tringa melanoleuca

RARE VAGRANT

LENGTH 29–40cm. (11–16 in.)
WINGSPAN 66–76 cm. (26–30 in.)
WEIGHT 111–250 g. (4–8.8 oz.)

Westchester Lake, Alaska.

A medium-sized mottled, gray-brown wader with white underparts and long, yellow legs. The distinctive dark bill is much longer than the length of the head and slightly upturned. This characteristic helps to differentiate it from Lesser Yellowlegs. In breeding plumage, it has dark bars on the flanks and is brighter overall.

Greater Yellowlegs breed from southern Alaska to Newfoundland. A minimum of twenty-five have been recorded in the southeastern Hawaiian Islands since 1955; fifteen of these were O'ahu sightings.

Coyote Point Wetlands, California.

Willet

Tringa semipalmata

VERY RARE VAGRANT

LENGTH 33–41 cm. (13–16 in.)
WINGSPAN 66–76 cm. (26–30 in.)
WEIGHT 200–330 g. (7–11.6 oz.)

Willet is a large grayish-brown shorebird with a distinctive, bold black-and-white wing pattern. It has a fairly long and thick bill, a white rump, and gray tail band. The legs are gray. Willets in the eastern population have heavy barring on the breast and heavy mottling on the back. In the western population breeding plumage is lighter.

Two populations of Willet exist in North America: the western subspecies *(Tringa semipalmata inornata)* breeds in the Great Basin and winters along the Pacific Coast, and the nominate eastern subspecies breeds along the Atlantic Coast and winters as far south as South America. There are nine records for the Southeastern Hawaiian Islands; three of these are from O'ahu.

Willet. Coyote Point Wetlands, California.

Fairbanks, Alaska, May 25, 2016.

Lesser Yellowlegs

Tringa flavipes

MIGRANT

LENGTH 23–27 cm. (9–10.6 in.)
WINGSPAN 59–64 cm. (23–25 in.)
WEIGHT 80–91 g. (2.8–3.2 oz.)

Lesser Yellowlegs are a medium-sized, slender, gray-brown shorebird with bright yellow legs. The dark bill is straight and the length is only slightly longer than the length of the head. This is a distinctive characteristic to separate the Lesser from the Greater Yellowlegs. The underparts and rump are white. In breeding plumage, the breast has darker streaks and the flanks are lightly barred. Juvenile is grayer and less distinctly marked.

Lesser Yellowlegs breed from Alaska to western Quebec and winter from the southern U.S. through South America. They are one of the more common migratory shorebird species in the Hawaiian Islands. Every year one or two Lesser Yellowlegs are recorded on Oʻahu.

Borit, Gojal, Gilgit-Baltistan, Pakistan. GILGIT2

Marsh Sandpiper

Tringa stagnatilis

EXTREMELY RARE VAGRANT

LENGTH 22–26 cm. (8.7–10.2 in.)
WINGSPAN 55–59 cm. (22–23 in.)
WEIGHT 45–120 g. (1.6–4.2 oz.)

A slender, pale, medium-sized shorebird with a needle-like bill. The legs are yellow-green. In breeding plumage, the head and neck are heavily streaked dark brown, and the flanks and lower breast have dark bars or chevrons. In non-breeding plumage, it has a gray-brown upper body with a white neck and breast. Immature has more heavily marked upperparts than non-breeding adult.

Marsh Sandpipers breed in northcentral Asia and winter from Africa through Australia. There are only three records for the Hawaiian Islands. One of these was of a Marsh Sandpiper present at Pouhala Marsh Wildlife Sanctuary, Oʻahu from November 18, 2002 to March 3, 2003.

Pouhala Marsh, Oʻahu

Numenius phaeopus hudsonicus, *Waiʻanae, Oʻahu.*   *Iceland.*

Whimbrel

Numenius phaeopus

WINTER VISITOR
LENGTH 37–47 cm. (15–19 in.)
WINGSPAN 75–90 cm. (30–35 in.)
WEIGHT 270–493 g. (0.5–1 lb.)

A large, grayish-brown shorebird with a long, decurved bill that is kinked instead of smoothly curved. The striped head has a brown crown and a distinct buffy white supercilium. The upperparts are dark brown and the neck and belly are pale with dark streaks. The legs are blue-gray. *Numenius phaeopus variegatus* has a barred white rump. *Numenius phaeopus hudsonicus* has a brown rump. Juveniles are similar to adults, but have light spots on their back, a less distinct crown stripe, more buff on the breast, and finer streaking on the neck and chest.

The Whimbrel is a Holarctic breeding species with an expansive wintering range including areas south of the equator globally. Three subspecies have been described, two of which have occurred in the Pacific: *Numenius phaeopus variegatus* of Asia and *Numenius phaeopus hudsonicus* of North America. Both forms have reached the Hawaiian Islands. There are a minimum of twenty-four individuals recorded on Oʻahu from 1971 to 2023. Many of these were found at James Campbell NWR where they occur with the closely related Bristle-thighed Curlew.

Kahuku, O'ahu (both images).

Bristle-thighed Curlew
Kioea

Numenius tahitiensis

WINTER VISITOR
LENGTH 40–44 cm. (15.7–17.3 in.)
WINGSPAN 82–90 cm. (32.2–35.4 in.)
WEIGHT 310–800 g. (0.6–1.7 lb.)

A large shorebird with a striped head, a long decurved bill, and buffy-brown upper body. The breast is streaked brown and the belly reddish brown. It has a pale, buffy-orange rump, long grayish-blue legs, and bristly feathers at the end of its thighs. Sexes are similar in appearance, and the female is larger.

An estimated 10,000 Bristle-thighed Curlews exist in the world today. They breed in western Alaska near the mouth of the Yukon River and on the Seward Peninsula and winter on islands throughout the central Pacific Ocean. The fossil record indicates their presence in Hawai'i for at least 200,000 years.[40] Winter populations in the Hawaiian Islands declined after the arrival of Polynesians due to hunting, predation, and habitat loss. This is partly because Bristle-thighed Curlews become flightless during their molt in Hawai'i. They were considered a game bird in the territory and hunted until 1939.[41]

In 2014, the estimated population in and around James Campbell NWR was 126 birds.[42] This is the largest concentration in the main Hawaiian Islands. Most of the adult birds depart O'ahu between May 1 and 9 every year. A few sub-adult birds over-summer on O'ahu.

Reykjanes Peninsula, Iceland.

Kogarah Bay, Sydney, Australia. JJ HARRISON

Black-tailed Godwit

Limosa limosa

EXTREMELY RARE VAGRANT

LENGTH 40–44 cm. (15.7–17.3 in.)
WINGSPAN 70–82 cm. (27.5–32.2 in.)
WEIGHT 280–340 g. (9.8–12 oz.)

Black-tailed Godwit is a large, long-billed shorebird. It has a distinctive black and white wingbar, white underwings, black tail, and white coverts. In breeding plumage, it has an orange head, neck, and chest, and the bill is orange-yellow with a black tip. It has a white mark between the eye and beak. The legs are dark gray or black. Sexes look similar but the male is brighter, and the female is bigger, heavier, and has a longer beak. In non-breeding plumage, it is mostly dull gray-brown above and white below. Juvenile has a pale orange neck and breast.

Black-tailed Godwits breed throughout the Palearctic and winter South to eastern Africa and Australia. There is a single record in the Hawaiian Islands for an individual of the Asian subspecies that was first observed on Maui, October 26, 2000. After a few months, it flew to James Campbell NWR and remained there until April 23, 2002.

Hudsonian Godwit

Limosa haemastica

EXTREMELY RARE VAGRANT

LENGTH 36–42 cm. (14.5–16.7 in.)
WINGSPAN 66–76 cm. (26–30 in.)
WEIGHT 195–358 g. (6.8–12.6 oz.)

Hudsonian Godwit is the smallest godwit species. It has a distinctive black underwing only seen in flight, a long upturned reddish-orange bill with a dark tip, a white eyebrow, and long, dark legs. The tail is black and the rump white. In breeding plumage, male has a rich, rufous belly and mottled brown upperparts. Female breeding plumage is duller. In non-breeding plumage, it is overall gray above and whitish below. Juvenile is similar to non-breeding adult but browner.

The Hudsonian Godwit is a long-distance migrant through the Americas, breeding in Alaska and the Hudson Bay region and wintering in southern South America. There are three confirmed records for the Hawaiian Islands, with one on Oʻahu at James Campbell NWR from September 13 to October 3, 2007.

Juvenile, Limosa lapponica baueri,
Kapapapuhi Point Park, Oʻahu.

Bar-tailed Godwit

Limosa lapponica

RARE VAGRANT
LENGTH 37–41 cm. (15–16 in.)
WINGSPAN 70–80 cm. (28–31 in.)
WEIGHT 190–630 g. (0.4–1.3 lb.)

Bar-tailed Godwits of the *baueri* subspecies migrate 9,000 miles nonstop from Alaska to New Zealand, the longest flight of any bird species![43] It is a large shorebird with a long, upturned , pinkish-orange bill with a black tip and relatively short legs. The white tail is barred with brown. Female is larger than male. In breeding plumage, the neck, breast and belly are brownish-red. The upperparts are mottled dark brown. Female breeding plumage is duller than male. In non-breeding plumage, it is plain grayish-brown above and white below. Juvenile is similar to non-breeding adult but more buff with streaks on flanks and breast and a distinct supercilium.

Bar-tailed Godwits breed from western Alaska across north Asia and winter throughout Europe, Africa, south Asia, Australia, and casually along the Pacific North American coast. A minimum of twenty-seven have been recorded in the Southeastern Hawaiian Islands from 1962 to 2023; eleven of these have occurred on Oʻahu.

James Campbell NWR, Oʻahu.

Marbled Godwit

Limosa fedoa

EXTREMELY RARE VAGRANT
LENGTH 40–50 cm. (16–20 in.)
WINGSPAN 70–88 cm. (28–35 in.)
WEIGHT 326–396 g. (11.5–14 oz.)

Marbled Godwit is the largest of the four godwit species. It has a long neck and long blue-gray legs. The slightly recurved, pinkish bill has a dark tip. Upperparts are mottled dark brown notched with buff. It has dark brown barring on the flanks and chest and cinnamon wing linings. In non-breeding plumage the breast is plain buffy. Sexes are similar in appearance. Juvenile looks similar to non-breeding adult.

Marbled Godwits breed in Alaska and in the prairie region of Canada and the northcentral United States and winter along the Pacific North American coast, occasionally to South America. There are three records for the Hawaiian Islands and these are the only records for the Pacific region. The single record for Oʻahu (photo above) was at James Campbell NWR from May 9, 2005 to February 2, 2006.

Ala Moana Beach Park, O'ahu.

James Campbell NWR, O'ahu.

Ruddy Turnstone
'Akekeke
Arenaria interpres

WINTER VISITOR

LENGTH 22–24 cm. (8.7–9.4 in.)
WINGSPAN 50–57 cm. (20–22 in.)
WEIGHT 85–150 g. (3–5.3 oz.)

A small, stocky shorebird with a harlequin face pattern of black and white. The bill is dark, wedge-shaped and slightly upturned. The legs are bright orange. In breeding plumage, the upperparts are chestnut with black markings. The breast is mostly black except for some white on the sides. The rest of the underparts are white. The female is slightly duller than the male. In non-breeding plumage, the face has very little white and is mostly dull brown. The upperparts are dull grayish brown with black mottling. Juvenile is slightly more brownish than non-breeding adult.

Ruddy Turnstones breed in arctic regions around the world and have a circumtropical winter distribution, south to South America, Africa, and Australia. They are the second most common winter migrant in the Hawaiian Islands after the Pacific Golden Plover. Several excellent places to see these colorful shorebirds on O'ahu are Ala Moana Beach Park and Kualoa Regional Park.

Red Knot
Calidris canutus

RARE VAGRANT

LENGTH 23–26 cm. (9.1–10.2 in.)
WINGSPAN 47–53 cm. (19–21 in.)
WEIGHT 125–205 g. (4.4–7.2 oz.)

A medium-sized shorebird with a short, straight bill, a short neck, and olive-yellow legs. In breeding plumage, it is mottled gray, black, and chestnut above and bright rufous below. Female breeding plumage is similar to male but lighter. In non-breeding plumage, it is gray overall except for a white belly and dark barring on the flanks. Juvenile has white-tipped feathers on the wings which gives them a scalloped look.

Red Knots are a Holarctic species, breeding in the tundra around the world and migrating to both sides of the equator and as far south as South Africa, Australia, and the tip of South America. Twenty-five individuals have been recorded in the Southeastern Hawaiian Islands; twelve of these were found on O'ahu.

Ruddy Turnstone, Hilo, Hawai'i.

Southeast coast, O'ahu.

Koros Maros National Park, Hungary (left).
Juvenile, Ohiapilo, Moloka'i (right).

Surfbird

Calidris virgata

EXTREMELY RARE VAGRANT
LENGTH 23–26 cm. (9.1–10.2 in.)
WINGSPAN 59.7–66 cm. (23.5–26 in.)
WEIGHT 133–251 g. (4.7–8.9oz.)

A small, stocky shorebird with a short, dark bill that has a yellow-orange base, a white tail with a black tip, and yellow legs. In breeding plumage, it has mottled gray upperparts with rust coloring on the wings. The head, neck, and breast are heavily streaked. The white underparts have dark chevrons. Sexes look alike, but females are larger. In non-breeding plumage, the upperparts are plain, slate-gray. The flanks have dark spots.

Surfbirds breed in western Alaska and winter from southeast Alaska to Tierra del Fuego. There is a single record for the Hawaiian Islands (above photo) first observed on O'ahu on April 9, 2012.

Homer, Alaska.

Ruff

Calidris pugnax

MIGRANT

LENGTH	*Male* 29–32 cm. (11–13 in.)	
	Female 22–26 cm. (8.7–10.2 in.)	
WINGSPAN	*Male* 54–60 cm. (21–24 in.)	
	Female 46–49 cm. (18–19 in.)	
WEIGHT	*Male* 130–254 g. (4.5–9 oz.)	
	Female 70–170 g. (2.4–6 oz.)	

Ruff is a medium-sized, long-necked shorebird with a medium length bill. The legs are variable in color from pink to orange or reddish-orange. The male is considerably larger than the female. In breeding plumage, the male has brightly colored head tufts, bare, warty orange facial skin, extensive black on the breast, and a large white, black, or chestnut collar. Female in breeding plumage has gray-brown upperparts and mostly white underparts. Juvenile has an unmarked breast, buffy belly, and dark-green legs.

An Old World species that breeds throughout the northern Palearctic and wintering south to Africa, India, and Australia. A minimum of eighty-one Ruffs have been recorded in the Southeastern Hawaiian Islands from 1963 to 2023, with thirty-three of these found on O'ahu.

Sharp-tailed Sandpiper

Calidris acuminata

MIGRANT

LENGTH 17–22 cm. (6.7–8.6 in.)
WINGSPAN 36–43 cm. (14.1–17 in.)
WEIGHT 39–114 g. (1.3–4 oz.)

A medium-sized brown and white shorebird with a distinct chestnut crown, a short black bill, prominent white eyebrow, white eye ring, and olive legs. In breeding plumage, it has rich reddish-brown upperparts with darker feather centers. The breast is buff with brownish speckles and the flanks have dark chevrons. Non-breeding adult is grayish-brown above and has a pale breast. Juvenile is brightly colored above and has a buffy breast with few streaks.

Sharp-tailed Sandpipers breed in northern Russia and winter in southeast Asia, Australia, and New Zealand, and occur as vagrants throughout the world. At least 750 individuals have been recorded in the Southeastern Hawaiian Islands with a minimum of 700 of these being found on Oʻahu.

Stilt Sandpiper

Calidris himantopus

EXTREMELY RARE VAGRANT

LENGTH 20–23 cm. (7.9–9.1 in.)
WINGSPAN 38–41 cm. (15–16 in.)
WEIGHT 50–70 g. (1.8–2.5 oz.)

A medium-sized, long-legged shorebird with a long, slightly downcurved bill. In breeding plumage, the underparts are heavily barred, and it has reddish patches above and below the pale supercilium. The back is brown and white with darker centers. In non-breeding plumage, it is pale gray above and white below. The rump is white, and the tail is gray. The legs are yellow. Juveniles are brownish-gray with lightly streaked breasts.

Stilt Sandpipers breed in the tundra of Alaska and northern Canada and winter from Mexico to South America. There are five records for the Hawaiian Islands including two from James Campbell NWR on Oʻahu.

Pouhala Marsh Wildlife Sanctuary, O'ahu.

Boat Harbour, New South Wales, Australia.
JJ HARRISON

Curlew Sandpiper

Calidris ferruginea

RARE VAGRANT
LENGTH 18–23 cm. (7–9 in.)
WINGSPAN 38–41 cm. (15–16 in.)
WEIGHT 44–117 g. (1.5–4.1 oz.)

A medium-sized shorebird with a down-curved black bill and longish black legs. In breeding plumage, the head, neck and underparts are brick-red. Mantle and scapulars are brown with chestnut and white fringes. In non-breeding plumage, it is pale gray above and white below with a contrasting white supercilium. Juvenile is mottled gray above and has variable buff on breast.

A Eurasian species, the Curlew Sandpiper breeds primarily in the western Palearctic and rarely to extreme northwest Alaska. A minimum of twelve have been recorded in the Hawaiian Islands with five of these from O'ahu.

Red-necked Stint

Calidris ruficollis

RARE VAGRANT
LENGTH 13–17 cm. (5.1–6.7 in.)
WINGSPAN 28–37 cm. (11–15 in.)
WEIGHT 21–51 g. (0.7–1.8 oz.)

A small shorebird with a slightly curved black bill and short legs. In breeding plumage, the head, nape, and breast are un-streaked rufous-orange bordered with dark markings below. In non-breeding plumage, the upperparts are pale gray brown, and the underparts white. The rump and tail are black except for the outer tail-feathers and sides of rump which are white. Immature is similar to non-breeding adult but browner, and the crown is dull rufous.

Red-necked Stints are mainly an Asian species, breeding in Siberia through extreme western Alaska and wintering in South China, southeast Asia, Australia, and New Zealand. A minimum of sixteen Red-necked Stints have been documented in the Hawaiian Islands, with six of these recorded on O'ahu.

James Campbell NWR, Oʻahu (both photos).
Juvenile (bottom).

Sanderling
Haunakai

Calidris alba

WINTER VISITOR
LENGTH 18–20 cm. (7.1–7.9 in.)
WINGSPAN 36–48 cm. (14–19 in.)
WEIGHT 40–100 g. (1.4–3.5 oz.)

A small, pale shorebird with a straight, black bill, short, black legs and a white belly. In breeding plumage, the face, throat, and breast are reddish-brown. In non-breeding plumage, it has very pale gray upperparts except for a dark shoulder patch. Juvenile is spangled black and white on the back.

Sanderlings breed in arctic regions around the world and have a broad wintering range including temperate and tropical regions of both hemispheres. They are fairly common wintering birds on Oʻahu.

James Campbell NWR, Oʻahu (top).
Utqiagvik, Alaska (bottom).

Dunlin

Calidris alpina

WINTER VISITOR
LENGTH 16–22 cm. (6.3–8.7 in.)
WINGSPAN 35.5–48.2 cm. (14–19 in.)
WEIGHT 48–77 g. (1.7–2.7 oz.)

A small shorebird with a slightly down-curved black beak and black legs. In breeding plumage, it has a distinctive black belly patch and a reddish-brown back and wings. The head and breast are white with fine brownish-black streaks. In non-breeding plumage, it is gray above and white below. Juvenile is mostly brown above with black marks on the flanks and belly.

Dunlin breed throughout Holarctic regions and migrate as far south as Central America, North Africa, and South China. A few are found on Oʻahu every winter.

Laguna los Palos, Chile.

Baird's Sandpiper

Calidris bairdii

VERY RARE VAGRANT

LENGTH 14–18 cm. (5.5–7.1 in.)
WINGSPAN 38–45.7 cm. (15–18 in.)
WEIGHT 27–63 g. (0.9–2.2 oz.)

Baird's Sandpiper was named after Spencer Fullerton Baird, a 19th century ornithologist. He was the first curator at the Smithsonian Institution and later became its first secretary.[44] It is a small shorebird that has a short, straight, and thin black bill, long wings with a white wing stripe, and a black patch on the rump and black legs. In breeding plumage, the head is light brown with dark streaks, the wings and back have black spots with pale brown edges, the breast is brown with fine streaks, and the underparts are white. In non-breeding plumage, upperparts are brownish-gray with black feather centers, the breast is finely streaked, and the underparts are white. Juvenile has a buffy breastband. Sexes are similar in appearance.

Baird's Sandpipers breed in arctic North America (Alaska to Greenland) and winter in southern South America. There are twelve records for this species in the Southeastern Hawaiian Islands. Interestingly, ten of these are from O'ahu and all were found between 1968 and 1988. No Baird's Sandpipers have been recorded in the Hawaiian Islands since 2001.

Rheinspitz, Vorarlberg, Austria. KEN BILLINGTON

Little Stint

Calidris minuta

EXTREMELY RARE VAGRANT

LENGTH 12–14 cm. (4.7–5.5 in.)
WINGSPAN 34–37 cm. (13.3–14.5 in.)
WEIGHT 20–40 g. (0.7–1.4 oz.)

A very small shorebird with a short, straight, fine black bill, dark legs, long primary projection, and unwebbed toes. Breeding adult has an orange wash to the breast, face, and neck and a white throat. The back has a distinctive white 'V' when in flight. In winter, adult is brownish-gray above and white underneath.

Little Stints breed in Arctic Eurasia as far east as the Chukotski Peninsula and winter primarily in Africa and India. There are five records for the Hawaiian Islands with three of these being on O'ahu. The first two O'ahu records were from the Waipio Peninsula at closed sugar mill settling ponds in 1985 and 1987. Thirty years later, a Little Stint was discovered at Pearl Harbor NWR less than two miles from the Waipio Peninsula.

Fairbanks, Alaska.

James Campbell NWR, Oʻahu.
Ruddy Turnstone (left) White-Rumped Sandpiper (right).

Least Sandpiper

Calidris minutilla

WINTER VISITOR
LENGTH 13–15 cm. (5.1–5.9 in.)
WINGSPAN 27–28 cm. (10.6–11 in.)
WEIGHT 27–28 g. (0.7–1.1 oz.)

The Least Sandpiper is the world's smallest shorebird. It has a short, thin, black bill with a slight droop at the end and greenish-yellow legs. In breeding plumage, the crown is dark brown and it has a light superciliary. The back and wings are reddish-brown with black, scalloped-shaped markings edged in white. The white breast is finely streaked brown, and the belly is white. In non-breeding plumage, it is brownish-gray above with a white lower breast and belly. Juvenile is brightly patterned above with rusty-colored speckling on the back and white mantle stripes.

Least Sandpiper is an American species that breeds across the Holarctic and winters south to central South America. Seventy-one Least Sandpipers have been recorded in the Southeastern Hawaiian Islands with twenty-five of these sighted on Oʻahu.

Least Sandpiper, James Campbell NWR, Oʻahu.

White-rumped Sandpiper

Calidris fuscicollis

EXTREMELY RARE VAGRANT
LENGTH 15–18 cm. (5.9–7.1 in.)
WINGSPAN 40–44 cm. (15.8–17.3 in.)
WEIGHT 40–60 g. (1.4–2.1 oz.)

A small shorebird with a medium-length, straight bill that has a distinctive orange area on base of lower mandible, long wings, white-rump, and black legs. In breeding plumage, the crown is brown and the face has a brownish tinge. The back is gray and rufous and the breast and flanks are streaked. The underparts are white. In non-breeding plumage, the upperparts are gray with the center of the feathers being darker. The supercilium is white and the pale, gray breast is finely streaked. Sexes are similar in appearance.

White-rumped Sandpipers breed in arctic North America and winter in South America. There is one substantiated record for the Hawaiian Islands and the central Pacific region. A bird was present at James Campbell NWR, Oʻahu September 19 to 28, 2006.

CALEB G. PUTNAM

Buff-breasted Sandpiper

Calidris pugnax

RARE VAGRANT
LENGTH 18.4–23.4 cm. (7.25–9.25 in.)
WINGSPAN 43–47 cm. (17–18.5 in.)
WEIGHT 76–78 g. (1.6–2.8 oz.)

A medium-sized, slender shorebird that has a finely-streaked, dark crown, large dark eyes, a short, dark, straight bill, and a pale, white throat. The nape and breast are buff-colored, and the back and upperwings have a brownish-black scaly pattern. The legs are long and yellow. Juvenile resembles adult. Sexes are similar in appearance.

Buff-breasted Sandpipers breed in northern Alaska and northern Canada and winter in South America. There are fourteen records for the Hawaiian Islands with six of these from Oʻahu.

Fairbanks, Alaska (top).
Pearl Harbor NWR, Oʻahu (bottom).

Pectoral Sandpiper

Calidris melanotos

MIGRANT
LENGTH 19–23.4 cm. (7.4–9.25 in.)
WINGSPAN 38–47 cm. (15-18.5 in.)
WEIGHT 68–94g. (2.4–3.3 oz.)

A medium-sized, brownish shorebird with streaking that ends abruptly at white belly. It has a dark, slightly down-curved bill that has orange at the base of the lower mandible. The back and wings are reddish-brown marked with scalloped-shaped black markings edged in white. The legs are yellow. Non-breeding plumage is grayer. Male and female are similar in appearance. Juveniles are brightly patterned above with rufous coloration.

Pectoral Sandpipers breed in northeast Siberia and across the Holarctic and winter primarily in South America with a smaller wintering population in Australia and New Zealand. They are annual migrants to the Hawaiian Islands.

'Ōhi'apilo Pond Bird Sanctuary, Moloka'i (top).
Fairbanks, Alaska (bottom).

Semipalmated Sandpiper

Calidris pusilla

RARE VAGRANT
LENGTH 13–15 cm. (5.1–5.9 in.)
WINGSPAN 35–37 cm. (13.8–14.6 in.)
WEIGHT 20–32 g. (0.7–1.1 oz.)

A small shorebird with a short neck, a medium length, dark bill that may droop at the tip, and black legs. In breeding plumage, it is gray-brown with little or no rufous coloration on the back. The chest is lightly marked and the belly is white. In non-breeding plumage, it is light gray and has faint streaking on the breast and clean flanks. Immature is similar to adult but the back is more scaled.

Semipalmated Sandpipers breed in Alaska and Canada and winter primarily in eastern South America. Twenty have been recorded in the Hawaiian Islands with eleven of these from O'ahu.

Cattle Point, Uplands, Near Victoria, British Columbia.
ALAN D. WILSON

Western Sandpiper

Calidris pusilla

WINTER VISITOR
LENGTH 14–17 cm. (5.5–6.7 in.)
WINGSPAN 35–37 cm. (13.8–14.6 in.)
WEIGHT 22–35 g. (0.8–1.2 oz.)

A small shorebird with a long bill that slightly droops at the end and long legs. In breeding plumage, it has rusty-brown scaled upperparts, a streaked head with brown wash on face, and a black line on the rump that runs to its tail. The breast and flanks are heavily spotted. In non-breeding plumage, the crown and upperparts are mostly gray and the underparts are white.

Western Sandpipers breed in northeast Siberia and Alaska and winter primarily along both American coasts through central South America. There are a minimum of forty records for this species in the Hawaiian Islands with fourteen of these from O'ahu.

Juvenile, 'Ohi'apilo Pond Bird Sanctuary, Moloka'i (bottom). Homer, Alaska (top).

Short-billed Dowitcher

Limnodromus griseus

RARE VAGRANT
LENGTH 23–32 cm. (9–12.6 in.)
WINGSPAN 46–56 cm. (18–22 in.)
WEIGHT 73–155 g. (2.6–5.5 oz.)

A medium-sized, stocky shorebird with a long bill that is slightly downcurved one third of the way to the tip and long, pale legs. In breeding plumage, upperparts are dark brown and the feathers have dark centers with buffy edges. The neck is orange and heavily spotted. Underparts are mostly rufous-orange. In non-breeding plumage, it has gray upperparts and a gray breast. Juvenile has a buffy chest and flanks.

Short-billed Dowitchers breed in northwest Alaska and northern Canada. Three subspecies have been described. There are fifteen confirmed records for the Hawaiian Islands with six of these from O'ahu.

James Campbell NWR, O'ahu (both photos).

Long-billed Dowitcher

Limnodromus scolopaceus

WINTER VISITOR
LENGTH 28–30.5 cm. (11–12 in.)
WINGSPAN 47–49 cm. (18.5–19.3in.)
WEIGHT 88–131 g. (3.1–4.6 oz.)

A medium-sized shorebird with a long, pale supercilium, long bill, and short tail. In breeding plumage, it has a dark crown and a rufous neck and breast. The back and upper wings are mottled black, brown, and buff. In non-breeding plumage, it is mostly gray with darker upperparts that contrast with a white belly. Juvenile plumage is similar to non-breeding adult but paler.

Long-billed Dowitchers breed in Siberia, Alaska, and northwest Canada, and migrate back to wintering grounds in western North America and Mexico. They occur every winter on O'ahu in small numbers.

Wilson's Snipe
Gallinago delicata

Pearl Harbor, O'ahu.

WINTER VISITOR
LENGTH 23–28 cm. (9.1–11 in.)
WINGSPAN 39–45 cm. (15–18 in.)
WEIGHT 79–147 g. (2.8–5.2 oz.)

Wilson's Snipe is named after Alexander Wilson a Scottish-American ornithologist born in 1766. He is considered the "Father of American Ornithology" and the greatest American ornithologist prior to Audubon.[45] A medium-sized shorebird with brown and black mottled upperparts, heavily streaked head, dark stripe through the eye, buff striped back, and a very long, straight bill. Underparts mostly white with dark bars on sides and flanks and a heavily streaked neck and breast. Sexes are similar in appearance. Juvenile has bolder stripes on the back.

Wilson's Snipes breed across northern Alaska and Canada and winter as far South as northern South America. A minimum of forty-five have been recorded on O'ahu with, one or two reported annually every winter.

Utqiaġvik, Alaska.

Pearl Harbor NWR, Oʻahu

Kihei, Maui.

Common Snipe
Gallinago gallinago

EXTREMELY RARE VAGRANT
LENGTH 25–27 cm. (9.8–10.6 in.)
WINGSPAN 44–47 cm. (17–19 in.)
WEIGHT 80–140 g. (2.8–4.9 oz.)

A small, stocky shorebird with a long, straight bill, alternating pale and dark stripes on the head, mottled back with buffy stripes, and a rusty brown rump. Underparts are white with dark bars on flanks and streaks on breast. They have a diagnostic white stripe at base of the underwing. Sexes are similar in appearance. Juvenile has bolder stripes on the back.

Common Snipes breed across the northern Palearctic and possibly western Alaska, and winter in central Eurasia from the Mediterranean region to the Philippine Islands. There are records for six Common Snipes in the Hawaiian Islands; four of these are from Oʻahu.

Wilson's Phalarope
Phalaropus tricolor

RARE VAGRANT
LENGTH 22–24 cm. (8.7–9.4 in.)
WINGSPAN 39–43 cm. (15.3–19 in.)
WEIGHT 37–111 g. (1.3–3.9 oz.)

Wilson's Phalarope is the largest of the three phalaropes species.

It is a medium-sized shorebird with a black needle-like bill, white rump, and lobed toes. In breeding plumage, the female is more colorful. It is gray and brown above and has a black stripe through the eye and down the cinnamon-colored neck. There are red-brown markings on the white underparts. Breeding male has a similar pattern but is duller. In non-breeding plumage, it is gray above and white below. Juvenile have a dark cap and is brownish above and white below.

Wilson's Phalaropes breed in central and western North America and winter in South America. In the Southeastern Hawaiian Islands there are records for forty-three individuals, with twenty-nine of these from Oʻahu.

Myvatn, Iceland.　　　　　　　　　*Keālia Pond National Wildlife Refuge, Maui.*

Red-necked Phalarope

Phalaropus lobatus

RARE VAGRANT
LENGTH 18–19 cm. (7.1–7.5 in.)
WINGSPAN 32–41 cm. (12.6–16.1 in.)
WEIGHT 27–40 g. (0.9–1.4 oz.)

The Red-necked Phalarope is a small shorebird that has a long-pointed bill, black legs, and lobed toes. In breeding plumage, the female is dark gray above and has a chestnut neck and upper breast, black face, a white spot above the eye, and a white throat. Breeding male is a duller version of the female. In non-breeding plumage, both sexes are gray above and white below. The black eyepatch is present in all plumages. Juvenile is gray and brown above, with a boldly-striped back, and has buff underparts.

Red-necked Phalaropes breed in Holarctic regions and winter in tropical and southern coastal regions around the world. There are only three substantiated records from the Southeastern Hawaiian Islands: one at Mana, Kaua'i during the winter of 1892 to 1893; one at Waipi'o, O'ahu February 27 to March 17, 1985 and the last at Kealia Pond National Wildlife Refuge, Maui from January 7 to February 27, 2012.

Utqiaġvik, Alaska.

Red Phalarope
Phalaropus fulicarius

WINTER VISITOR
LENGTH 20–22 cm. (7.9–8.7 in.)
WINGSPAN 41–44 cm. (16.1–17.3 in.)
WEIGHT 42–60 g. (1.5–2.1 oz.)

Offshore Honolulu, O'ahu.

The Red Phalarope is a small shorebird that has a long, straight bill, black legs, and lobed toes. In breeding plumage, the female is dark brown and black above and has a reddish-brown neck, breast, and belly, a black head, white cheeks, and a yellow bill tipped black. Breeding male is a duller version of the female and has a brown cap. In non-breeding plumage, both sexes are gray above and white below. The black eyepatch is present in all plumages. Juve-nile is light gray and brown above with buff underparts.

Red Phalaropes have a northern circumpolar breeding distribution and winter primarily at sea, as far south as Chile and New Zealand in the Pacific. A few are recorded annually during Hawaiian pelagic trips. Twenty-six have been recorded from O'ahu and its offshore waters from 1941 to 2022.

Offshore Honolulu, O'ahu.

South Polar Skua

Stercorarius maccormicki

RARE MIGRANT

LENGTH 48–53.3 cm. (19–21 in.)
WINGSPAN 122–165 cm. (48–65 in.)
WEIGHT 900–1,600 g. (2 –.5 lb.)

Pomarine Jaeger

Stercorarius pomarinus

WINTER VISITOR

LENGTH 46–67 cm. (18–26 in.)
WINGSPAN 110–138 cm. (43–54 in.)
WEIGHT 540–920 g. (1.19–2.03 lb.)

CALLIE GESMUNDO, USFWS

The South Polar Skua is a large seabird with a barrel chest and has white wing flashes when flying. There are two morphs: light and dark. The light morph has a pale gray head, neck, and underparts. The upperparts are darker and have narrow, whitish streaks and edges. The dark morph is uniformly grayish-brown and has a pale yellowish nape. Juvenile is gray-brown overall.

South Polar Skuas breed in the South Shetland Islands and Antarctica and disperse widely throughout the world's oceans during non-breeding seasons. They are rarely found in O'ahu's offshore waters.

The Pomarine Jaeger is the largest of the three jaegers. "Pomarine," Greek for "lidnosed," refers to the sheath that covers the base of the bill.[46] Breeding adults have two spoon-shaped central tail feathers that are twisted ninety degrees. There are three color morphs. The light morph adult has a blackish cap and dark brown upperparts, white underparts and collar, a yellow wash on the sides of the neck, and a bold, brown band across the breast. Ninety percent of Pomarine Jaegers are light morphs. Dark morph adults are dark brown. Intermediate morph birds are dark and the head, neck, and underparts are paler. All morphs have a diagnostic white wing flash on the underwings.

Pomarine Jaegers have a Holarctic breeding distribution and winter throughout the world's oceans from Florida and California south to South America, South Africa, Australia, and New Zealand. Every year, several Pomarine Jaegers are sighted during pelagics in O'ahu's offshore waters.

Pomarine Jaeger,
Offshore Honolulu, O'ahu.

O'ahu Bird Species Accounts

Raufarhofn, Iceland.

Parasitic Jaeger

Stercorarius parasiticus

RARE MIGRANT

LENGTH 41−48 cm. (16−19 in.)
WINGSPAN 107−125 cm. (42−49 in.)
WEIGHT 300−650 g. (0.6−1.4 lb.)

There are three morphs of Parasitic Jaegers. The light morph breeding adult has brown upperparts, a dark brown cap, light yellowish-white on its head, neck, and back, a white throat and belly, and short, pointed central tail feathers. Dark morph breeding adult is dark brown. Intermediate morph breeding adult is dark with a somewhat paler head, neck, and underparts. All morphs have a white wing flash. Juvenile plumage varies from light to dark.

Parasitic Jaegers breed throughout the Arctic tundra and winter primarily in tropical and temperate coastal waters, south to New Zealand and Australia in the Pacific. There are eleven records from Southeastern Hawaiian Island waters, with three of these from O'ahu.

Old Denali Highway, Alaska.

Long-tailed Jaeger

Stercorarius longicaudus

RARE MIGRANT

LENGTH 38−58 cm. (15−23 in.)
WINGSPAN 102−117 cm. (40−46 in.)
WEIGHT 230−444 g. (8.1−15.7 oz.)

Long-tailed Jaegers are the smallest of the three jaeger species. Breeding adult has long, central tail feathers that extend five to ten inches beyond the rest of the tail, a black cap, gray back, dark primary wing feathers with no white flash, and a light-yellow neck. Dark morphs are very rare in adults. In non-breeding plumage it has a cap with white and gray spots and the underparts are pale gray. The underwing is uniformly dark. Juveniles have light, intermediate, and dark morphs.

Long-tailed Jaegers breed throughout the Arctic tundra and winter primarily in the southern hemisphere, primarily off South Africa, South America, and Australia. There are only three records of this species for O'ahu.

Kachemack Bay, Alaska.

Ancient Murrelet

Synthliboramphus antiquus

EXTREMELY RARE VAGRANT

LENGTH 20–24 cm. (7.9–9.4 in.)
WINGSPAN 45–46 cm. (17.7–18.1in.)
WEIGHT 150–250 g. (5.4–8.8 oz.)

The Ancient Murrelet is a small, pelagic seabird with a short, rounded tail. In breeding plumage, it has a short, stubby yellow bill, a gray back, black face and throat, a white collar and white underparts. In non-breeding plumage, it has a white patch on the sides of the neck, a grayish throat, and gray flanks.

The Ancient Murrelet breeds on rocky seacoasts around the Pacific Rim from northern Japan through coastal British Columbia and winters primarily in the North Pacific, south to Taiwan, the Volcano and Ryukyu Islands, and southern California. There is a single record for the Hawaiian Islands of a first-year male found alive at Ko'olina Beach on November 27, 2003. It died the following day.

Black-legged Kittiwake

Rissa tridactyla

VERY RARE VAGRANT

LENGTH 37–41 cm. (15–16 in.)
WINGSPAN 91–105 cm. (36–41in.)
WEIGHT 305–525 g. (0.6–1.1 lb.)

A medium-sized seagull. Breeding adult has a white head, slate-gray back and wings, white underparts, bright yellow bill and short black legs. Non-breeding adult has a black smudge behind the eye. Juvenile has a black bill, black ear spot, black collar and a black bar on the wings.

The Black-legged Kittiwake breeds in Arctic and Subarctic regions throughout the northern hemisphere and winters in the open ocean, irregularly south to Japan, California, and occasionally farther south. There are eight records for the southeastern Hawaiian Islands with six of these from O'ahu.

Pouhala Marsh, O'ahu.

Bonaparte's Gull
Chroicocephalus philadelphia

VAGRANT

LENGTH 28–38 cm. (11–15 in.)
WINGSPAN 76–84 cm. (30–33 in.)
WEIGHT 180–225 g. (6.3–7.9 oz.)

Bonaparte's Gull is named after Charles Lucien Bonaparte, a French ornithologist and nephew of Napoleon Bonaparte. He spent eight years in the United States contributing to the taxonomy of birds and wrote Synopsis of the Birds of the United States.[47] It is one of the smallest species of gull and has slate-gray upperparts, white underparts, a short, thin, black bill, and pink legs. The wingtips are black above and pale below. In breeding plumage, it has a black head and an incomplete white eye ring. In non-breeding plumage the head is white with a dark ear spot and dark smudges. The sexes are similar in appearance. Juvenile has dark markings on the wings which appear as a narrow, dark 'M' across its back when flying.

Bonaparte's Gulls breed across North America from western Alaska to Quebec, and winter south to central Mexico and the West Indies. There are a minimum of twenty-four records for O'ahu.

Bonaparte's Gull, Kenai River, Alaska.

Lake Balaton, Hungary (above).
Hortobagy National Park, Hungary (right).

Black-headed Gull
Chroicocephalus ridibundus

RARE VAGRANT

LENGTH 37–44 cm. (15–17 in.)
WINGSPAN 94–110 cm. (37–43 in.)
WEIGHT 190–400 g. (6.7–14.1 oz.)

A small gull with an orange-red bill, pale gray upperparts and dark red legs. In breeding plumage, the head is chocolate-brown, not black. There is a distinctive white leading edge to the wing in flight. In non-breeding plumage, the head is mostly white with dark smudges above the eyes and on the ears. The bill has a dark tip. Sexes are similar in appearance. Immature has a black band on the tail and dark inner primaries.

Black-headed Gulls are found across Eurasia, wintering as far south as central Africa, the Philippine Islands, and western Micronesia. They also breed in Greenland and northeast North America (occasionally) and winter regularly along the Atlantic North American coast. There are only three records for the Southeastern Hawaiian Islands with one of these at Waipio, O'ahu December 26 to 28, 1977.

James Campbell NWR, O'ahu.

James Campbell NWR, O'ahu.

Laughing Gull

Leucophaeus atricilla

WINTER VISITOR
LENGTH 36–41 cm. (14–16 in.)
WINGSPAN 98–110 cm. (39–43 in.)
WEIGHT 203–371 g. (7.2–13.1 oz.)

A medium sized gull with very long, dark-gray wings, a long, drooping bill, white throat, white underparts, and black legs and feet. In breeding plumage, the head is black, and the bill is red. In non-breeding plumage, the head is white except for small areas of gray behind the eyes, and the bill is black. Juvenile is dusky-brownish above.

Laughing Gulls breed primarily along the Pacific coast of Mexico and the Atlantic and Caribbean coasts from southern Canada to Venezuela, and they winter south to Peru and the Amazon delta. They are the most common visiting seagull species in the Hawaiian Islands.

Franklin's Gull

Leucophaeus pipixcan

MIGRANT
LENGTH 32–36 cm. (12.6–14.2 in.)
WINGSPAN 85–95 cm. (33.5–37.4 in.)
WEIGHT 230–300 g. (7.2–13.1 oz.)

Franklin's Gull was named after Sir John Franklin, a British Royal Navy officer and arctic explorer.[48] It is a small gull. In breeding plumage, the head is black and the eye arcs are white. The back and upperparts are dark gray. The underparts are white and often tinged in pink. The wings have black tips with an adjacent white band. The bill is red with a black tip, and the legs are red. In non-breeding plumage, the black on the head is reduced to a small area behind the eyes. The bill is black with a red tip. Juvenile has brownish upperparts and a partial grayish-black hood.

Franklin's Gulls breed throughout prairie regions of western North America and winter primarily along the Pacific South American coast. There are a minimum of thirty records for O'ahu.

Westchester Lake Anchorage, Alaska.

Pouhala Marsh, O'ahu.

Short-billed Gull
(Mew Gull)
Larus brachyrhynchus

EXTREMELY RARE VAGRANT
LENGTH 40–45 cm. (16–18 in.)
WINGSPAN 100–120 cm. (39–47 in.)
WEIGHT 410–430 g. (14.4–15.1 oz.)

A small gull with a short, slender bill. In breeding plumage, it has a white head, a dusky iris with a red orbital ring, a yellow bill, dark gray back, and white underparts. The legs are yellow. In non-breeding plumage, the head is marked with brown spots, the bill is duller yellow, and the orbital ring is dark gray. Juvenile is pale brown with white feather edges and has a dark bill.

Short-billed Gulls breed in northwestern North America. A single record exists in the Southeastern Hawaiian Islands. A Short-Billed Gull was observed at Pearl Harbor NWR from January 1 to April 6, 2015.

Ring-billed Gull
Larus delawarensis

WINTER VISITOR
LENGTH 43–54 cm. (16.9–21.3 in.)
WINGSPAN 105–1117 cm. (41.3–46.1 in.)
WEIGHT 300–700 g. (0.6–1.5 lb.)

The Ring-billed Gull is a medium-sized gull. In breeding plumage, the head is white and the irises are pale. The orbital rings are red. The bill is yellow with a black ring near the tip. The back and wings are gray, and the neck and underparts are white. The legs are yellow. In non-breeding plumage, the head has brown streaking. Juvenile is mottled brown and white and has a dark bill that is pink at the base.

Ring-billed Gulls breed across Canada and the northern United States and winter south to Mexico and the West Indies. They are annual winter visitors to O'ahu with a minimum of eighty-eight records from 1944 to 2023.

Coyote Point, California.

Western Gull
Larus occidentalis

EXTREMELY RARE VAGRANT
LENGTH 55–68 cm. (22–27 in.)
WINGSPAN 130–144 cm. (51–57 in.)
WEIGHT 800–1,400 g. (1.8–3.1 lb.)

A large gull with a mostly white head year-round and pale, pink legs and feet. Breeding adult has a large yellow bill with red spot, variable iris color from pale yellow to dark yellow, upperparts are dark gray, and the underparts are white. Non-breeding adult has limited amount of brown streaking on the head. Juvenile are mottled, sooty brown with a dark bill and dark eyes.

Western Gulls breed along the Pacific coast from Baja California, north to Washington and southern British Columbia. There is only one record for the Western Gull in the Hawaiian Islands. A third-winter bird was discovered at Paiko Lagoon, Oʻahu on December 24, 1978. It stayed until late March 1980 and molted into adult plumage during its fifteen-month stay.

Palo Alto Duck Pond, Baylands Nature Preserve, Palo Alto, California. KING OF HEARTS

California Gull
Larus californicus

EXTREMELY RARE VAGRANT
LENGTH 46–55 cm. (18–22 in.)
WINGSPAN 122–137 cm. (48–54 in.)
WEIGHT 430–1,045 g. (0.9–2.3 lb.)

A medium-sized gull. The breeding adult's head is white, and the beak is yellow with red and black marks. The iris is dark, and the eye has a red orbital ring. The wings and back are slate-gray and the primaries are black with white tips. The underparts are white. The legs are yellow-green. The non-breeding adult has a heavily streaked head. Juveniles are mottled brown and white.

California Gulls breed in western North America and winter south to west central Mexico. There are five records for the Hawaiian Islands with four of these from Oʻahu.

Keflavik, Iceland (top).
Ka'a'awa, O'ahu (bottom).

Herring Gull

Larus argentatus

VAGRANT
LENGTH 53–66 cm. (21–26 in.)
WINGSPAN 120–155 cm. (47–61 in.)
WEIGHT 600–1,650 g. (1.3–3.6 lb.)

A large gull with a long bill. Breeding adult has a white head, a yellow bill with red spot, and the irises are yellow with orange-yellow orbital rings. The back and upper wings are pale gray. The rump, tail and underparts are white. The wing tips are black with white spots. Legs are pink. Non-breeding adult has a streaked head and neck. Sexes are similar in appearance. Juvenile is brown and white overall.

Herring Gulls breed throughout arctic and subarctic latitudes and, along the Pacific Rim, they winter south to Mexico and Japan. There are twenty-three confirmed records of Herring Gulls in the Southeastern Hawaiian Islands. They occur infrequently on O'ahu.

Shari, Hokkaido, Japan. E-190

Slaty-backed Gull

Larus schistisagus

EXTREMELY RARE VAGRANT
LENGTH 55–68.5 cm. (21.7–27 in.)
WINGSPAN 132–160 cm. (52–63 in.)
WEIGHT 1–1.7 kg. (2.3–3.7 lb.)

Slaty-backed Gull is a large gull. Breeding adult has a white head, clear or yellow iris with pinkish-red orbital ring and a yellow bill with a red spot on the lower mandible. The back and wings are dark gray. The wings have a white trailing edge, and the tail is white. Non-breeding adult has brown streaking on the head and neck. Juveniles are mottled mostly brown and have a dark bill.

Slaty-backed Gulls breed from the Bering and Pacific coasts of Siberia (occasionally Alaska), south to Japan, and winter south to China. There are five confirmed records from the Southeastern Hawaiian Islands, with three of these from O'ahu.

Anchor Point, Alaska. (top)
Keawaula Beach, Oʻahu. (bottom)

Glaucous-winged Gull

Larus glaucescens

WINTER VISITOR
LENGTH 50–68.5 cm. (20–27 in.)
WINGSPAN 120–150 cm. (47–59 in.)
WEIGHT 900–1,200 g. (2–2.6 lb.)

A large white-headed gull. In breeding plumage, it has a yellow bill with a red spot on the lower mandible, the irises are dark brown, and the gape is pinkish. The neck, breast, belly and tail are white. The wings and mantle are gray. The legs and feet are pink. In non-breeding plumage, it has faint brown streaks on the head and neck. Juvenile has a dark bill and is mottled brown and white.

Glaucous-winged Gulls breed in the Commander Islands off Siberia and along the Pacific North American coast south-northwest Oregon. In winter, this species disperses south to Japan and Baja California. It is the most frequently reported large gull species in the Hawaiian Islands and they are often found on Oʻahu.

Lānaʻi Lookout, Oʻahu.

Glaucous Gull

Larus hyperboreus

RARE VAGRANT
LENGTH 55–77 cm. (22–30 in.)
WINGSPAN 132–170 cm. (52–67 in.)
WEIGHT 960–2,700 g. (2.1–5.9 lb.)

The Glaucous Gull is the second largest gull in the world. In breeding plumage, it has a white head, clear yellow irises with bright yellow orbital rings and a large, yellow bill with a red spot on the lower mandible. The gape is yellow. The back and wings are pale gray with no black on the wings. The tail is white, and the legs and feet are pink. In non-breeding plumage, the adult's head is streaked brown. Juvenile is mostly white with buff markings and has a pink bill with a black tip.

Glaucous Gulls breed throughout arctic regions of North America and Eurasia. There are nine records for the Southeastern Hawaiian Islands, with four of these from Oʻahu.

Offshore Honolulu, Oʻahu.

Hauʻula. Oʻahu.

Brown Noddy
Noio Kōhā
Anous stolidus

BREEDING VISITOR
LENGTH 38–45 cm. (15–18 in.)
WINGSPAN 75–86 cm. (30–34 in.)
WEIGHT 167–190 g. (5.9–6.7 oz.)

A medium-sized dark brown tern that is highly pelagic and seldom seen near land. It is dark-chocolate brown and adult has a whitish-gray forehead and crown. It has a narrow, incomplete, white eye ring. There is a pale band on the upper wing coverts. The tail is long and wedge-shaped. The bill and legs are black. Juvenile may lack white cap.

Brown Noddy is a pantropical species that breeds in the Hawaiian Islands between May and October. An estimated 160 pairs breed on Mānana, Mokumanu, and Mōkōlea islands off the east coast of Oʻahu. They are observed often during pelagic trips in Oʻahu's offshore waters.

*Black Noddy,
Mokumanu, Oʻahu.*

Black Noddy
Noio
Anous minutus

BREEDING VISITOR
LENGTH 35–37 cm. (14–15 in.)
WINGSPAN 66–72 cm. (26–28 in.)
WEIGHT 98–144 g. (3.5–5.1 oz.)

The Black Noddy is a medium sized tern. Adult has sooty black upperparts that contrast with a gray tail and a white cap that blends gradually into the black nape. The long, thin bill is black, and there is a small white crescent under each eye. Male and female are similar in appearance. Juvenile has a dark tail and the white cap is smaller and sharply differentiated from the dark body plumage.

The Black Noddy is most abundant among islands of the central and southwestern Pacific, with smaller populations occurring in the eastern Pacific and in the Atlantic. The orange-legged *melanogenys* subspecies occurs in the Southeastern Hawaiian Islands and the dark-legged *marcusi* subspecies occurs in the Northwestern Hawaiian Islands. An estimated 110 pairs breed on Oʻahu's offshore islands including Mānana, Mokumanu, Mōkōlea and Kāohikaipu. They are best seen at Nuʻupia Ponds near Kailua, Oʻahu and at Kaʻena Point NAP.

Kapiʻolani Park, Oʻahu. *Waikīkī, Oʻahu.*

White Tern
Manu o Kū
Gygis alba

BREEDING VISITOR
LENGTH 23–33 cm. (9–12.9 in.)
WINGSPAN 70–87 cm. (27.5–34.2 in.)
WEIGHT 77–157 g. (2.7–5.5 oz.)

A medium-sized tern. Adult is entirely white except for a black eye ring, a long, black bill with a blue base, and dark shafts on the primaries. The tail is slightly forked. Legs and feet are slate blue. Juvenile has varying amounts of brown on the body and wings and the base of the bill is black.

White Terns occur in the tropical south Atlantic Ocean, the Marquesas and Kiribati Islands, and throughout the remainder of the tropical Pacific and Indian Oceans, including Micronesia, Wake and Johnston atolls, and the Hawaiian Islands. They are present at nesting colonies year-round, and the peak in breeding activity is February to August. The first report on Oʻahu was a specimen collected in 1924. Between 1948 and 1958 there were infrequent reports of singles and pairs along the southeast coast from Mokapu Peninsula to the Mokolua Islets.

The first record of breeding on Oʻahu was on July 15, 1961 at Koko Head. During the next sixty years the population grew to over 3,000 birds and their present breeding range extends from Makapuʻu Point to Pearl Harbor.[49] They are thriving in the most urban area of the Hawaiian Islands. Some of the best places to see this ethereal bird are Kapiʻolani Park, Royal Hawaiian Hotel, Iolani Palace, and Fort DeRussy.

Offshore Honolulu, O'ahu.

DUNCAN WRIGHT, USFWS

Juvenile,
Mokumanu, O'ahu.

Sooty Tern
'Ewa'ewa
Onychoprion fuscatus

BREEDING VISITOR
LENGTH 33–36 cm. (13–14 in.)
WINGSPAN 82–94 cm. (32.5–37 in.)
WEIGHT 150–240 g. (5.2–8.4 oz.)

A medium-sized tern with long, narrow wings and a deeply forked tail. Adult has a black stripe running through the eye to the base of the black bill. The upperparts are black and the underparts are white. The legs are black. Sexes are similar in appearance. Juvenile is dark sooty brown with indistinct white scaling on the back and a white belly.

Sooty Terns are one of the most common birds of tropical oceans worldwide and are the most abundant breeding seabird species in the Hawaiian Islands. Sixty to 60,000 pairs breed on Mānana Islet and 10,000 to 20,000 pairs breed on Mokumanu Islet off the windward coast of O'ahu. One of the most spectacular birding opportunities on O'ahu is to watch the Sooty Terns flying around their breeding colony on Mānana Islet from Makapu'u Beach Park.

Gray-backed Tern
(Spectacled Tern)
Pākalakala
Onychoprion lunatus

BREEDING VISITOR
LENGTH 35–38 cm. (14–15 in.)
WINGSPAN 73–76 cm. (29–30 in.)
WEIGHT 150–240 g. (5.2–8.4 oz.)

A medium-sized tern. The adult plumage is very similar to a Sooty Tern except the wings, back and tail feathers are gray. The head and eye stripe are black. The underparts are white and the legs and feet are black. Sexes are similar in appearance. Juvenile has a less defined head pattern and scaly upperparts.

Gray-backed Terns breed in small, scattered colonies throughout the tropical Pacific Ocean, from the Tuamotu, Samoan, and Mariana Islands, to Johnston and Wake Atoll and in the Hawaiian Islands. The breeding season in Hawai'i is February to September. Between ten and thirty pairs breed on Mokumanu Islet offshore of Kāne'ohe, O'ahu. This is the only breeding colony in the main Hawaiian Islands. Several places to watch for this species from land include La'ie Point, Sandy Beach, and Makapu'u Beach Park.

Adult, 'Ewa Beach, O'ahu.

Least Tern

Sternula antillarum

BREEDING VISITOR
LENGTH 22–24 cm. (8.7–9.4 in.)
WINGSPAN 48–53 cm. (19–21 in.)
WEIGHT 39–52 g. (1.4–1.8 oz.)

Juvenile, James Campbell NWR, O'ahu.

The Least Tern is the smallest North American tern. Breeding adult has a white head with a black cap and a black line through the eye to the base of the yellow-orange bill. The upperparts are pale gray except for two dark primaries. The underparts are white. The non-breeding adult has a less defined black cap, and the bill is black. Juvenile is faintly barred on the back.

Least Terns breed across the southern United States South through Mexico and the Caribbean, and winter in Central and South America. Several pairs of Least Terns have bred on O'ahu recently. Great places to look for this bird are James Campbell and Pearl Harbor NWRs.

DAVE HAMILTON

Lake Wollumboola, New South Wales, Australia.
JJ HARRISON

Gull-billed Tern
Gelochelidon nilotica

EXTREMELY RARE VAGRANT
LENGTH 33–42 cm. (13-17 in.)
WINGSPAN 76–91 cm. (30-36 in.)
WEIGHT 150–292 g. (5.3- 10.3 oz.)

A medium-sized tern with a black cap, thick, black bill, short-notched tail, and black legs. Adult has gray upperparts and white underparts. Non-breeding adult has a white nape and dark patch through the eye. Juvenile has a weak, gray eyepatch and a faint pattern on the upperparts.

Gull-billed Terns breed locally in temperate latitudes throughout North and South America, Eurasia, Africa, and Australia. There is one record for the Hawaiian Islands. A single individual was discovered at Pearl Harbor NWR on January 11, 1988.

Caspian Tern
Hydroprogne caspia

RARE VAGRANT
LENGTH 48–60 cm. (19–24 in.)
WINGSPAN 127–145 cm. (50–57 in.)
WEIGHT 530–782 g. (1.1–1.7 lb.)

The Caspian Tern is the world's largest tern. Breeding adult has a white head with a black cap, a long, thick, reddish-orange bill with a black tip, pale gray wings and back, and a white neck, belly, and tail. The underwings are pale with dark primary feathers. The wingtips are black on the underside. The legs and feet are black. Non-breeding adult has a receding black cap. Juvenile has a dark, streaked crown and pale upperparts that are mottled tan.

Caspian Terns breed locally throughout North America, Eurasia, Africa, Australia, and New Zealand and migrate to warmer subtropical and tropical latitudes during winter months. A minimum of seventeen birds have been recorded in the Southeastern Hawaiian Islands. The best place to see this species on O'ahu is Nu'upia Ponds WMA. An adult Caspian Tern has returned to this location every winter since 2000!

Kaʻelepulu Wetland, Oʻahu.

Pearl Harbor, Oʻahu.

Black Tern

Chlidonias niger

RARE VAGRANT
LENGTH 23–36 cm. (9.1–14.2 in.)
WINGSPAN 57–60 cm. (22.4–23.6 in.)
WEIGHT 50–60 g. (1.8–2.1 oz.)

A small tern with long, pointed wings. Breeding adult has a black body and gray wings. The bill is black. In non-breeding plumage the head is white with a blackish crown that meets a black patch behind the eye. Upperparts are pale gray, and the underparts are white with a dark patch on the sides of the breast. Juvenile similar to non-breeding adult but has pale brown wash on back and wings.

Black Terns of the subspecies *Chlidonias niger surinamensis* breed throughout Canada and the northern United States and winter from southern Mexico to northern South America. The distinct nominate subspecies breeds in Iceland, Europe, and western Asia and winters primarily in Africa. There are twenty records for this species in Southeastern Hawaiian Islands.

Common Tern

Sterna hirundo

VAGRANT
LENGTH 31–35 cm. (12–14 in.)
WINGSPAN 77–98 cm. (30–39 in.)
WEIGHT 110–141 g. (3.9–5 oz.)

A medium-sized tern with a deeply forked tail. In breeding plumage, it has a black cap, orange-red, pointed bill with black tip, gray upperparts and white to very light gray underparts. The rump and tail are white. The legs are orange-red. Non-breeding adult has a white forehead, black bill, and a dark carpal bar on the wings. The legs are dark red or black. Juvenile has ginger and brown upperparts scaled in white.

Common Terns breed from Southeast Canada to the Caribbean and winter from Mexico and South Caribbean to Argentina. They also breed across the Palearctic as far east as northern Siberia, wintering south to Africa, New Guinea, and Australia. A minimum of thirty-nine have been recorded in the Southeastern Hawaiian Islands of which twenty-two were found on Oʻahu.

Common Tern. **Apaj, Hungary.**

Gardur, Iceland.

Tahiti, French Polynesia.

Arctic Tern

Sterna paradisaea

MIGRANT
LENGTH 28–39 cm. (11–15 in.)
WINGSPAN 65–75 cm. (26–30 in.)
WEIGHT 86–127 g. (3.0–4.5 oz.)

A medium-sized tern that has the longest migration of any animal on Earth with an annual 25,000-mile round trip migration from the Artic to Antarctica.[50] Breeding adult has a black crown and nape, white cheeks, and a small, dark, red-orange bill. Upperparts are gray, and the underparts whitish-gray. Non-breeding adult has a paler crown, and the bill is dark. Juvenile has scaly appearing wings and mantle with dark feather tips and a faint carpal bar. The bill is black.

Arctic Terns breed throughout high latitudes in the northern hemisphere and winter at a similar latitudinal range around the Antarctic. They are mostly observed during pelagic trips during a narrow period from April 15 to May 9 when they migrate past the islands. Eight have been recorded from Oʻahu.

Great Crested Tern

Thalasseus bergii

EXTREMELY RARE VAGRANT
LENGTH 46–49 cm. (18–19.5 in.)
WINGSPAN 125–130 cm. (49–51 in.)
WEIGHT 325–397 g. (11.4–14 oz.)

A large tern with long wings. Breeding adult has gray upperparts, white underparts, a long, straight, yellow bill and a shaggy, black crown. The legs are black. Non-breeding adult has a black and white speckled crown. Juvenile has white, gray, and brown mottling on upperparts.

Great Crested Terns breed on tropical oceanic islands throughout the Indian Ocean and from North Australia in the western Pacific to Taiwan, Micronesia, and Kiribati. There are only three records for the Hawaiian Islands, with one of these from Nuʻupia Ponds WMA on October 21, 1988.

Arctic Tern.
Gardur, Iceland.

Merritt Island NWR, Florida.

Morro Strand State Beach, Morro Bay, California.
MIKE BAIRD

Sandwich Tern

Thalasseus sandvicensis

EXTREMELY RARE VAGRANT
LENGTH 37–43 cm. (15–17 in.)
WINGSPAN 85–97 cm. (33–38 in.)
WEIGHT 180–300 g. (6.3–10.6 oz.)

A medium-large tern named after the town of Sandwich, United Kingdom, where it was first identified.[51] Breeding adult has gray upperparts, white underparts, a black, shaggy crest, and a black bill with a yellow tip. In non-breeding plumage, the forehead is white, and the crest is less prominent. Juvenile similar to non-breeding adult and has gray and brown scalloped plumage on the back and wings.

Sandwich Terns breed at southern temperate latitudes in North America, South America, and Eurasia, withdrawing in winter to subtropical latitudes. There is a single record for the Hawaiian Islands. A first-winter bird was observed at Kahuku, Oʻahu on January 10, 1992.

Elegant Tern

Thalasseus elegans

EXTREMELY RARE VAGRANT
LENGTH 39–42 cm. (15.3–16.5 in.)
WINGSPAN 76–81 cm. (30–32 in.)
WEIGHT 190–325 g. (6.7–11.5 oz.)

A medium-large tern with narrow wings and a deeply forked tail. Breeding adult has a long, shaggy, black crest, a white face, and a long, drooping, reddish-orange bill. Upperparts are gray, and the underparts are white. The legs are black. Non-breeding adult has a white forehead and a streaky, faded black cap. Juvenile has a scaly back and wings and a yellowish bill.

Elegant Terns breed in coastal Northwest Mexico and Southwest California and migrate to coastal western South America in the winter. There are two records for the Hawaiian Islands with one being from Oʻahu. A single individual was observed at Heʻeia State Park on February 7, 2019.

Elegant Tern.
Santa Barbara, California.

Vina del Mar, Chile.

Inca Tern

Larosterna inca

EXTREMELY RARE VAGRANT
LENGTH 39–42 cm. (15.3–16.5 in.)
WINGSPAN 76–86 cm. (30–34 in.)
WEIGHT 180–210 g. (6–7.4 oz.)

An unmistakable charcoal-gray tern with a white "Salvador Dali" mustache and a bright, red bill with yellow wattles at the base. The dark wings have a white trailing edge. The tail is moderately forked. Juvenile is uniformly blackish and has slight, gray tufts at the base of the bill.

Inca Terns breed along the western coast of South America. There is a single record for the Hawaiian Islands. An immature Inca Tern appeared at South Point, Hawai'i Island on March 12, 2021. It stayed on the island obtaining food from local fishermen until June 24, 2021, when it flew 200 miles north to O'ahu. After almost five months it flew back to South Point but only stayed five weeks before flying back to O'ahu!

Waikīkī, O'ahu.

Rock Pigeon
(Rock Dove, Feral Pigeon, or Common Pigeon)

Columba livia

NATURALIZED RESIDENT
LENGTH 29–37 cm. (11–15 in.)
WINGSPAN 62–72 cm. (24–28 in.)
WEIGHT 238–380 g. (8.4–13.4 oz.)

Rock Pigeon, also known as Rock Dove, are common in urban areas of O'ahu. They were first introduced to Hawai'i in 1788. Many of the Rock Pigeons in Waikīkī are white morphs. There are over 1,000 different breeds of Rock Pigeon plus multiple hybrids that have wide assortment of plumages.

Adult (top) and juvenile (bottom), Kapiʻolani Park, Oʻahu.

Spotted Dove

Streptopelia chinensis chinensis

NATURALIZED RESIDENT

LENGTH 28–32 cm. (11.2–12.8 in.)
WINGSPAN 43–48 cm. (17–19 in.)
WEIGHT 160–180 g. (5.6–6.3 oz.)

A long-tailed dove that has dark, gray-brown, scaled upperparts except for white tips on the tail feathers. The distinctive characteristic is the dark nape that has small white spots. The irises are orange-yellow. The underparts are pinkish-brown. Juvenile is duller than adult and lacks the white spots.

Spotted Doves, native to India, China, Southeast Asia, the Philippine Islands, and Indonesia, have been successfully introduced to Australia, New Zealand, Fiji, and Southern California. They were introduced to the Southeastern Hawaiian Islands sometime prior to 1855.

Kapiʻolani Park, Oʻahu.

Zebra Dove
(Barred Ground Dove)

Geopelia striata

NATURALIZED RESIDENT

LENGTH 20–23 cm. (7.8–9 in.)
WINGSPAN 24–26 cm. (9.5–10.2 in.)
WEIGHT 50–72 g. (1.7–2.5 oz.)

A small, slender, brownish-gray dove with a long, narrow tail. It has blue skin around the eyes and bill. Upperparts are brownish-gray with black and white barring. Underparts are buff to pink with black stripes on the neck, breast, and belly. Juvenile is paler and has mottled, brown upperparts and brown underparts.

Zebra Doves are native to the Malay Peninsula, the Philippine Islands, and Indonesia. They were introduced to the Hawaiian Islands in 1922.

Henderson Bird Preserve, Nevada.

Mana Plain, Kaua'i.

Mourning Dove

Zenaida macroura

NATURALIZED RESIDENT
LENGTH 22.8–33 cm. (9–13 in.)
WINGSPAN 37–45 cm. (14.5–17.7 in.)
WEIGHT 112–170 g. (3.9–6 oz.)

A medium-sized dove with a round head, short, black beak, a long tail, and short, reddish legs. The eyes are dark with light skin surrounding them. There is a dark-feathered area below each eye. It is light gray-brown above and light brownish-pink below. The wings have black spots, and the outer tail feathers are white. Male's crown is distinctly bluish-gray. Female is similar to male but browner overall. Juvenile is darker and has a scaly appearance.

Mourning Doves breed throughout North America south to Panama and the Caribbean Islands. They were successfully introduced to the Hawaiian Islands in 1962 after a previous introduction in 1929 failed. This species is difficult to find on O'ahu except at Pearl Harbor NWR where it is often observed.

Barn Owl

Tyto alba

NATURALIZED RESIDENT
LENGTH 33–39 cm. (13–15 in.)
WINGSPAN 80–95 cm. (31–37 in.)
WEIGHT 430–635 g. (.95–1.4 lb.)

Barn Owls are the most widely distributed owl species in the world. A medium-sized owl with long wings and legs and a short tail. The pale, heart-shaped face is distinctive. The eyes are black. The ridge of feathers above the bill resembles a nose. The upperparts are tawny-gray and has black and white spots. Underparts are mostly white. Female is slightly larger than male.

Barn Owls are resident in temperate and tropical zones of all continents including the Americas, from southern Canada to Tierra del Fuego. In the Pacific, they occur naturally in Fiji, Tonga, Samoa, Wallace and Futuna, and Niue Island, but not elsewhere. Barn Owls have been introduced successfully only to the Hawaiian Islands in the Pacific area, and they have become established and common in the Southeastern Hawaiian Islands. They were introduced in 1958 to control rats and mice in agricultural areas.

Ocean Shores, Washington.

Snowy Owl

Bubo scandiacus

EXTREMELY RARE VAGRANT
LENGTH 52.5–64 cm. (20.7–25.2 in.)
WINGSPAN 126–145 cm. (49.6–57 in.)
WEIGHT 1,600–2,950 g. (3.5–6.5 lb.)

A large, mostly white owl with bright yellow eyes and a white face. Male is almost entirely white. Female and juvenile have dark brown barring throughout.

Snowy Owls breed throughout the Holarctic tundra and winter irregularly south to mid-latitudes of the United States and Europe through northern China and Korea. A first-fall male was observed at the Honolulu airport on November 24, 2011. It refused to leave the runways after being scared by airport personnel and was shot. This was perhaps the southernmost record ever recorded for this majestic species. A Snowy Owl irruption occurred during 2011, and the Honolulu Airport Owl was accepted as a natural vagrant by the Hawai'i Rare Birds Committee. This is the only record for the Hawaiian Islands.

Palawai Basin, Lāna'i.

Short-eared Owl
Pueo

Asio flammeus sandwichensis

RESIDENT
LENGTH 34–43 cm. (13–17 in.)
WINGSPAN 85–110 cm. (33–43 in.)
WEIGHT 206–475 g. (0.4–1 lb.)

A medium-sized owl with large, yellow eyes, a short neck, and broad wings. The bill is black and hooked. It has short ear tufts on the top of the head and mottled tawny-brown and buff plumage. The breast is heavily streaked. The wings have dark markings at the wrist on the upper and lower surface. Female is larger than male.

Short-eared Owls breed across Eurasia and North America, in South America, and on many islands around the world, including the Galapagos Islands and the Hawaiian Islands. They are rare and endangered on O'ahu. Locations where the Pueo has been observed since 2017 include Ka'ena Point NAR, Nu'upia Ponds WMA, James Campbell NWR, and the Dole Pineapple Plantation!

Merritt Island NWR, Florida.

Belted Kingfisher

Megaceryle alcyon

RARE VAGRANT
LENGTH 28–35 cm. (11–14 in.)
WINGSPAN 48–58 cm. (19–23 in.)
WEIGHT 113–178 g. (4–6.3 oz.)

'Aiea Ridge Trail, O'ahu.

Mariana Swiftlet

Aerodramus bartschi

RARE NATURALIZED RESIDENT
LENGTH 10–12.7 cm. (4–5 in.)
WINGSPAN 20.3–25.4 cm. (8–10 in.)
WEIGHT 5.6–8.5 g. (0.2–0.3 oz.)

The Mariana Swiftlet is dark gray-brown overall except the throat which is grayish-white. The tail is slightly forked.

On May 15, 1962, the Hawai'i Department of Fish and Game released 125 to 175 swiftlets from Guam in lower Niu Valley in east Honolulu, O'ahu. Then on January 29, 1965, about 210 more at Waimea Falls on the north shore of O'ahu. The best locations to look for this rare species are along the 'Aiea Loop Trail and especially the 'Aiea Ridge Trail. They fly low above the treetops and often go back and forth over a small area while hunting for insects.

A medium-sized stocky bird with a shaggy crest, a long black bill, and a white spot by the eyes. The head is slate-blue, and it has a wide, white collar and a large blue band on the chest. The wings and back are slate-blue. The underparts are mostly white. Female has a rufous band across the upper belly that extends onto the flanks. Juvenile male has a mottled, rufous band on the upper belly. Juvenile female has a very thin rufous band on the upper belly.

Belted Kingfishers breed commonly in fresh-water habitats throughout Southern Canada and the United States and withdraw southward to winter in the West Indies and northern South America. In the Southeastern Hawaiian Islands there are reports of twenty-nine to thirty-one Belted Kingfishers from five islands. There are only five records for O'ahu. The first was in 1962 and the last 1998. Locations on where this distinctive species was observed include Pearl City, Kailua, Hale'iwa, Kuilima, and Nu'upia Ponds WMA.

Belted Kingfisher. **Merritt Island NWR, Florida.**

Key Largo, Florida.

Merlin
(Pigeon Hawk)
Falco columbarius

EXTREMELY RARE VAGRANT
LENGTH 24–33 cm. (9.4–13 in.)
WINGSPAN 50–73 cm. (20–29 in.)
WEIGHT 125–300 g. (4.4–10.6 oz.)

A small, robust falcon with long, pointed wings and a long, barred tail. The upperparts are buff and vertically streaked black to reddish-brown. The legs and feet are yellow. Male has a blue-gray back. Juvenile and female are similar.

Merlins are a highly migratory species that breed throughout Holarctic regions and winters south to Venezuela and Peru and southern Japan. There are six records for the Hawaiian Islands, with two of these from Oʻahu. The first was at Nuʻupia Ponds WMA on December 22, 2001, and the second at Pearl Harbor NWR November 15, 2009.

Immature, Falco peregrinus, Waikīkī, Oʻahu.

Adult, Falco peregrinus anatum, Alcan Highway, Alaska.

Peregrine Falcon
(Duck Hawk)
Falco peregrinus

RARE WINTER RESIDENT
LENGTH 34–58 cm. (13–23 in.)
WINGSPAN 74–120 cm. (29–47 in.)
WEIGHT 330–1,500 g. (0.7–3.3 lb.)

The Peregrine Falcon is a medium-sized falcon with long, pointed wings. It is the fastest bird in the world. Adult has a black hood with a "moustache." The cere is yellow, and the beak is black. The sides of the neck and throat are white. The back and wings are slate-gray to bluish-black. The underparts are white to buff with thin bands of black or dark brown. The rounded tail has a thin white band at the tip. Legs and feet are yellow. Female is larger than male. Juvenile has brown streaks on the underparts and a blue cere.

Peregrine Falcons breed throughout the world, including northeast Siberia and northwest Alaska, with northern populations being highly migratory. They are rare annual visitors to the Hawaiian Islands, with two to three individuals reported every winter. Four races have been observed: *F. p. japonensis* of northeast Asia, *F. p. tundrius* of arctic North America, *F. p. pealei* of northwest North America, and *F. p. anatum* of continental North America including central Alaska.

Kāhala, O'ahu.

Immature, Mililani, O'ahu.

Red-masked Parakeet
(Red-headed Conure)

Psittacara erythrogenys

NATURALIZED RESIDENT
LENGTH 30–35 cm. (12–14 in.)
WINGSPAN 50.8–61 cm. (20–24 in.)
WEIGHT 165–200 g. (5.8–7 oz.)

A medium-sized parrot with a bright red head, a pale eye-ring and a pink-hooked bill. Upperparts and underparts are mostly green except for some red on the neck, wings and thighs. It has gray legs and feet. Juveniles are all green until red feathers begin to appear at four months of age.

Red-masked Parakeets are native to western Ecuador and northwest Peru and are a naturalized resident on O'ahu. A flock of approximately fifty Red-masked Parakeets roost along the coast at Black Point. The best way to see this species is to be at Fort Ruger Park on Kāhala Avenue at dawn or dusk and watch for the flock leaving or returning to their roosting area. During the day, you can look for them in Wailupe Valley or 'Āina Haina Valley where they forage.

Red-crowned Parrot
(Red-crowned Amazon)

Amazonia viridigenalis

NATURALIZED RESIDENT
ENDANGERED
LENGTH 28–33 cm. (11–13 in.)
WINGSPAN 61–66 cm. (24–26 in.)
WEIGHT 283–340 g. (10–12 oz.)

A medium-sized parrot that is mostly green. Adult has a red crown, a dark blue streak behind the eyes, and a bluish nape. The color of the iris ranges from red to yellow. The bill is yellowish-pink. The upper surface of the wings has a red patch. It has a broad, yellow tip on the tail. The legs are gray or flesh colored. Juvenile has a red forehead and a bluish crown and nape.

Red-crowned Parrots are native to the slopes of eastern Mexico. The best place to see this parrot is the 'Aiea Loop Trail early in the morning.

Adult Red-crowned Parrot, 'Aiea Loop Trail, O'ahu.

Rose-ringed Parakeet
Psittacula krameri

NATURALIZED RESIDENT
LENGTH 38–43 cm. (15–17 in.)
WINGSPAN 42–48 cm. (16.5–18.9 in.)
WEIGHT 85–140 g. (3–5 oz.)

A medium-sized green parrot with a long, thin tail. Adult male has a black neck ring. The back of the crown and nape are light blue with a narrow pink band on the nape below the black neck ring. The eyes have red orbital ring and the bill is pinkish-red. The upperside of the middle tail feathers are blue with yellow-green tips. Female looks like male except it does not have the black neck ring or pink band on the nape. Juvenile is similar to adult female but has a pale pink bill.

Rose-ringed Parakeets are native to sub-Saharan Africa north of the equator and to India, Pakistan, and Burma. They were introduced to Honolulu in the 1930s. Some good locations to see this species are Waikīkī, Kapiʻolani Park, and the grounds at Central Union Church where as many as 2,500 birds roost.

Adult male (top), adult female (center), Honolulu, Oʻahu.
Blue morph (bottom), Kapiʻolani Park, Oʻahu.

'Aiea Loop Trail (top three photos).
'Aiea Loop Trail, September 20, 2017 (right). ALAN SCHMIERER

O'ahu 'Elepaio

Chasiempis ibidis

RESIDENT ISLAND ENDEMIC ENDANGERED
LENGTH 12.7–17.7 cm. (5–7 in.)
WINGSPAN 17.7–22.8 cm. (7–9 in.)
WEIGHT 8.5–14.1 g. (0.3–0.5 oz.)

The O'ahu 'Elepaio is a small monarch fly-catcher with a long tail. It is dark brown above and white below. The bill is blunt and mostly black. The base of the mandible is blue-gray in adults. Breeding adult has noticeable white wing bars. Male is slightly larger than female and has a blacker throat. The head and back are brown. The wing bars, rump, and tail are white. Juvenile has a reddish-brown head, neck and breast and the wing bars are cinnamon-colored not white like the adult. The base of the lower bill is yellow.

O'ahu 'Elepaios are endemic to the 597 square mile island of O'ahu. Prior to the arrival of people around 1,000 CE, O'ahu 'Elepaio lived from the seacoast to the tree line in the mountains. Their population would have been in the hundreds of thousands. Today, the population is only 1,200, and they are surviving in a few isolated areas that have high numbers of introduced mosquitoes. Many of them have avian malaria and pox. Introduced rats are eating their eggs, nestlings, and even the incubating females. Rat traps have been deployed to help them but they need more assistance and funds to survive. Please consider donating to Pacific Rim Conservation at elepaio.org. The best locations to look for this endangered species are the 'Aiea Loop Trail, Kuli'ou'ou Valley Trail, Pia Valley Trail, Wailupe Valley Trail, and Wili-wili Nui Ridge Trail. Please do not use tape playback to attract the birds, as it causes them stress and an unnecessary waste of energy.

Kailua-Kona, Hawai'i Island.

Eurasian Skylark

Alauda arvensis

NATURALIZED RESIDENT

LENGTH 18–19 cm. (7.1–7.5 in.)
WINGSPAN 30–36 cm. (11.8–14.1in.)
WEIGHT 17–55 g. (0.5–1.9 oz.)

A medium-sized lark with an indistinct crest on the head. The upperparts are streaked dark brown and the underparts are white with streaks on the flanks and breast. The tail and the trailing edge of the wings are edged with white.

The Eurasian Skylark breeds in temperate latitudes from Western Europe and North Africa to Siberia and Japan, withdrawing south in winter to Africa, India, and Burma. They were introduced to the Hawaiian Islands in 1870. The best place to look for this species is at pullover spots on Lagoon Drive at the Honolulu Airport.

Adult, Waikīkī, O'ahu.

Red-vented Bulbul

Pycnonotus cafer

NATURALIZED RESIDENT

LENGTH 21–22 cm. (8.25–8.75 in.)
WINGSPAN 25.4–.4 cm. (10–12 in.)
WEIGHT 26–45 g. (0.9–1.5 oz.)

The Red-vented Bulbul has a black head with a short crest. The back and breast are scaled brownish-black. The rump is white and the vent red. The tail is black tipped in white. Sexes are similar in appearance. Juvenile is duller than adult.

Red-vented Bulbuls are native to the Indian Subcontinent and Southeast Asia, South to the northern Malay Peninsula. They were introduced to O'ahu in 1965 or 1966 and are considered a pest species.

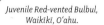

Juvenile Red-vented Bulbul, Waikīkī, O'ahu.

NRIK KIRAN

Kīlauea Point NWR, Kaua'i.

Red-whiskered Bulbul

Pycnonotus jocosus

NATURALIZED RESIDENT
LENGTH 17–23 cm. (6.6–9 in.)
WINGSPAN 25.4–30.4 cm. (10–12 in.)
WEIGHT 23–42 g. (0.8–1.4 oz.)

Adult Red-whiskered Bulbul has a black crest and face with a red patch behind the eye. The cheek and underparts are white. The upperparts are brown. The flanks are buff. The tail is brown with a white tip, and the vent is red. Juvenile lacks the red patch behind the eye and has a rufous-orange vent.

Red-whiskered Bulbuls are native to southern China, with range extensions into India and southeast Asia. They were introduced to Oʻahu in 1965.

Mānoa Valley, Oʻahu.

Japanese Bush-Warbler

Horornis diphone

NATURALIZED RESIDENT
LENGTH 15–18 cm. (5.9–7 in.)
WINGSPAN 10.1–15.2 cm. (4–6 in.)
WEIGHT 14–26 g. (0.5–0.9 oz.)

The Japanese Bush-Warbler has short wings and a long tail. It has a grayish-tan eyebrow and a grayish-black line through the eye. The upperparts are olive-brown and the underparts are gray.

Japanese Bush-Warblers are native to Japan and surrounding islands, with northern populations being slightly migratory. They were introduced to Oʻahu in 1929 to control insects. Recent locations where this species has been found on Oʻahu include the James Campbell NWR, Kaʻena Point NAR, Mānana Ridge Trail, and along the Mokuleʻia Forest Reserve access road.

'Aiea Loop Trail, O'ahu.

Hule'ia, Kaua'i.

Warbling White-eye
(Japanese White-eye)
Zosterops japonicus

NATURALIZED RESIDENT
LENGTH 10–11.4 cm. (4–4.5 in.)
WINGSPAN 16.5–17.5 cm. (6.5–6.9 in.)
WEIGHT 9.75–12.75 g. (0.3–0.4 oz.)

The Warbling White-eye is a small bird with rounded wings and a long, slender tail. It has a distinctive white eye ring. The head, neck and back are olive-green. The wings are dark brownish outlined in green. The throat is yellow, and the breast is gray. The belly is white. The bill, legs, and feet are black. Juvenile is similar to adult.

Warbling White-eye is native to eastern China, Taiwan, Japan, and surrounding islands. They were introduced to the Hawaiian Islands in 1929 and are now the most abundant and widespread land bird in the Southeastern Hawaiian Islands. They can be found along the coast in urban areas and in the mountain forests.

'Aiea Loop Trail, O'ahu.

Hwamei
(Melodious Laughingthrush)
Garrulax canorus

NATURALIZED RESIDENT
LENGTH 21–24 cm. (8.2–9.4 in.)
WINGSPAN 35.5–38 cm. (14–15 in.)
WEIGHT 50–75 g. (1.7–2.6 oz.)

A medium-sized reddish-brown songbird that has a distinctive bluish-white eye ring that extends backward as a white stripe. The bill is yellowish. It has rounded wings and a fan-shaped tail. The crown, throat, and back have dark streaks. Juvenile has less streaking on the head and breast.

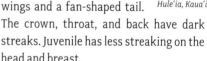

Hule'ia, Kaua'i.

Hwameis are native to central and southeast China. They were introduced to the Southeastern Hawaiian Islands sometime before 1900. They are scarce and declining on O'ahu. Places to look for this secretive bird include Koko Crater Botanical Garden, Mānana Trail, Mānoa Cliffs Trail, and the 'Aiea Loop Trail.

O'ahu Bird Species Accounts

Kuliʻouʻou Valley Trail, Oʻahu. (both photos)

Red-billed Leiothrix
(Peking Nightingale)
Leiothrix lutea

NATURALIZED RESIDENT
LENGTH 14–15 cm. (5.5–5.9 in.)
WINGSPAN 15–20 cm. (6–8 in.)
WEIGHT 18–28 g. (0.6–0.9 oz.)

The Red-billed Leiothrix has a bright red bill and a dull yellow ring around the eyes. The cheeks and the sides of the neck are bluish-gray. The throat is bright yellow-or-ange, and the chin is yellow. The breast is orange, and the back is olive green. The edges of the wing feathers are brightly colored in orange, red, yellow, and black. The tail is olive-brown. The female is a lot duller than the male. Juvenile is duller than adult male and has a black bill with varying amounts of red near the tip.

Red-billed Leiothrix are native to the Himalayan region from Nepal and north-ern India to southern China and Myanmar. They were introduced to Oʻahu in 1928. Places to look for this very colorful bird include the Kuliʻouʻou Trail, Koko Crater Botanical Garden, ʻAiea Loop Trail, Wahi-awa Botanical Gardens, and the Mokuleia Forest Reserve Access Road.

Male (above) and female (opposite page), Tantalus Drive, Oʻahu.

Juvenile (right), Lyon Arboretum, Oʻahu.

White-rumped Shama

Copsychus malabaricus

NATURALIZED RESIDENT

LENGTH 23–28 cm. (9–11 in.)

WINGSPAN 25.4–30.4 cm. (10–12 in.)

WEIGHT 28–34 g. (1–1.2 oz.)

A medium-sized songbird with a long tail, black bill, and pink legs. Adult male is glossy-black with a chestnut belly. The outer tail and rump are white. Female is similar but is paler and has a duller breast. The head and neck are gray, not black. Juvenile is a dull gray-brown with two cinnamon wingbars and many buffy spots on the head, breast, and back.

White-rumped Shamas are found from South India (including Sri Lanka) and Southwest China to Southeast Asia and western Indonesia, and they have been introduced only to the Southeastern Hawaiian Islands and nowhere else in the world. They were introduced to Oʻahu in 1940. They are common on Oʻahu and can be seen in most forested areas.

Sand Island, Oʻahu.

Kailua-Kona, Hawaiʻi Island.

Northern Mockingbird

Mimus polyglottus

NATURALIZED RESIDENT

LENGTH 20.5–28 cm. (8.1–11 in.)
WINGSPAN 31–38cm. (12–15 in.)
WEIGHT 40–58 g. (1.4–2 oz.)

A medium-sized bird with a long tail and conspicuous white wing patches in flight. The iris is yellow, and the bill is black. Upperparts are gray, and the underparts are whitish-gray. Legs and feet are black. Sexes are similar in appearance. Juvenile has a spotted breast.

The Northern Mockingbird is found throughout the United States, Mexico, and the Caribbean, withdrawing from northern regions in winter. It was introduced to Oʻahu in 1928. It is declining on the island but can be found in drier areas: Sand Island Recreation Area, Lānaʻi Lookout, Kapiʻolani Park, and the Makapuʻu Lighthouse Trail.

Common Myna

Acridotheres tristis

NATURALIZED RESIDENT

LENGTH 23–26 cm. (9–10.2 in.)
WINGSPAN 35.5–40.6 cm. (14–16 in.)
WEIGHT 82–143 g. (2.8–5.0 oz.)

A stocky, dark brown bird with a black head, yellow bill, and conspicuous yellow-orange wattle behind and below the eye. Upperparts, lower breast, and flanks are brown. The lower belly is white. It has very noticeable white patches in the underwing when flying. Sexes are similar in appearance. Juvenile is duller and browner than adult.

Common Mynas are native to India, the Middle East, and the Himalayan region. They were introduced into the Hawaiian Islands in 1866.

Adult (top) and juvenile (bottom), Kapiʻolani Park, Oʻahu.

Puʻu Anahulu, Hawaiʻi Island.

Red-crested Cardinal

Paroaria coronata

NATURALIZED RESIDENT

LENGTH 12.7–22.8 cm. (5–9 in.)
WINGSPAN 25–31 cm. (10–12 in.)
WEIGHT 30–45 g. (1.5 oz.)

A medium-sized bird that is in the tanager family. Adult has a bright red head, neck, and crest. It has an incomplete white collar. The back, tail, and wings are gray. The underparts are white. Juvenile is similar to adult but has a rusty brown head.

The Red-crested Cardinal is a monotypic species inhabiting northern Bolivia and southern Brazil through North Argentina. They were introduced to Oʻahu in 1928.

Saffron Finch

Sicalis flaveola

NATURALIZED RESIDENT

LENGTH 15.2–20.3 cm. (6–8 in.)
WINGSPAN 20.3–25.4 cm. (8–10in.)
WEIGHT 17–22.6 g. (0.6–0.8 oz.)

Adult has a yellow head with orange on the crown and throat, a gray upper mandible, and an ivory lower mandible, yellow-green upperparts and yellow underparts. Female is duller than male. Juvenile has a grayish head, dark-streaked light brown upperparts and throat, and underparts are grayish.

Pearl Harbor NWR Honouliuli.

Saffron Finches are native to South America. They were introduced to Oʻahu in 1965. Good places to see this bird on Oʻahu include Salt Lake, Kapiʻolani Park, Kaʻena Point NAR, and James Campbell NWR.

Adult male (left) and adult female (right), Palikea, O'ahu.

Yellow-faced Grassquit

Tiaris olivaceous

NATURALIZED RESIDENT
LENGTH 10–10.7 cm. (3.9–4.2 in.)
WINGSPAN 15–17.7 cm. (6–7 in.)
WEIGHT 8–10 g. (0.28–35oz.)

The Yellow-faced Grassquit is a small bird and a member of the tanager family. Adult male has a black face with an orange-yellow supercilium, chin, and throat. The back is olive-green, and the underparts grayish-olive. The eyes and the pointed beak are dark. Legs and feet are dark gray. Adult female is similar, and the face pattern is much weaker and duller and may be almost invisible. Juvenile is very similar to adult female with a dull whitish superciliary and chin.

Yellow-faced Grassquits are native to eastern Mexico and the Caribbean through northern South America. They were introduced to O'ahu sometime before 1974. Best places to look for this rare species are: Wa'ahila Ridge Trail, Kuli'ou'ou Ridge Trail, Lyon Arboretum, Palehua Road, and Ka'ena Point State Park.

Adult male, Honolulu, O'ahu.

Northern Cardinal

Cardinalis cardinalis

NATURALIZED RESIDENT
LENGTH 21–23 cm. (8.3–9.1 in.)
WINGSPAN 25–31 cm. (9.8–12.2 in.)
WEIGHT 42–48 g. (1.5–1.7 oz.)

A mid-size songbird with a distinctive crest. Adult male is bright red. It has a black mask and chin which contrast with the thick, red bill. Adult female is light brown overall and has a red bill and reddish tinges in the wings and tail. Juvenile is similar to female but has a black to gray bill.

Northern Cardinals are resident throughout the east and arid southwest United States through southern Mexico. They were introduced to O'ahu in 1929.

Adult female Northern Cardinal, Honolulu, O'ahu.

(clockwise starting from top left) Adult, Pihea Trail, Kaua'i;
Adult, Hosmer's Grove, Haleakalā National Park, Maui;
Adult, Pihea Trail, Kaua'i; Juvenile, Waikamoi Preserve, Maui.

'Apapane

Himatione sanguinea

RESIDENT
LENGTH 12–14 cm. (4.8–5.6 in.)
WINGSPAN 12–15.2 cm. (5–6 in.)
WEIGHT 11.3–17 g. (0.4–0.6 oz.)

Immature, Haleakalā
National Park, Maui.

A bright crimson honeycreeper with a medium-length, decurved, black bill. Adult has a white underbelly and vent. The tail and wings are black. Sexes are similar in appearance. Juvenile is brownish-gray and buff and has white undertail-coverts.

The 'Apapane is the most abundant native Hawaiian honeycreeper today and is found on six of the eight main Hawaiian islands. It is omnivorous; mostly a nectar feeder but also eats insects and spiders. In pre-contact Hawai'i they could be found along the coastlines. The population on O'ahu is declining. Best places to see this species include the Wiliwilinui Trail, 'Aiea Loop Trail, Mānana Ridge Trail, and the Palikea Trail.

Hosmer's Grove, Haleakalā NP, Maui (all photos).

'I'iwi

Drepanis coccinea

RESIDENT ENDANGERED

LENGTH 14–15 cm. (5.5–5.9 in.)
WINGSPAN 17.7–20.3 cm. (7–8 in.)
WEIGHT 16–20 g. (0.5–0.7 oz.)

The adult 'I'iwi is bright scarlet and has a long, curved, salmon-colored bill. The wings and tail are black. It has a small patch of white on the inner secondary feathers. Juvenile are buff colored with black spots and a dusky-brown bill.

The 'I'iwi population on O'ahu is either extinct or very close to extinction. The last recorded obser-

vation was on January 17, 2013 of a single adult in the Wai'anae Mountains. A small population of perhaps six to eight birds was located in the central Ko'olau Mountains on December 5, 1995.[52] This population had disappeared by 2000. The iconic 'I'iwi is now endangered and declining throughout their range due to avian malaria.

Waikamoi Preserve, Maui.

'Aiea Loop Trail, O'ahu (top left).
Kalāwahine Trail, O'ahu (top right and bottom right).

O'ahu 'Amakihi

Chlorodrepanis flava

RESIDENT ISLAND ENDEMIC

LENGTH 10–12.7 cm. (4–5 in.)
WINGSPAN 15–18 cm. (5.9–7 in.)
WEIGHT 8.5–14.1 g. (0.3–0.5 oz.)

Adult male is yellow-green above and yellow below. The lores are black. The gray bill is decurved. Female and immature are grayish-green above and grayish-white below and have two white wingbars.

Good places to look for this island endemic honeycreeper include the 'Aiea Loop Trail, Mānana Trail, Tantalus-Round Top Drive, Wa'ahila Ridge Recreation Area, and the Wiliwilinui Ridge Trail.

Adult female.
Kalāwahine Trail, O'ahu.

Kapi'olani Park, O'ahu.

Kapi'olani Park, O'ahu.

House Finch

Haemorhous mexicanus

NATURALIZED RESIDENT
LENGTH 12.5–15 cm. (5–6 in.)
WINGSPAN 20–25 cm. (8–10 in.)
WEIGHT 16–27 g. (0.5–0.9 oz.)

A small finch with a conical bill and a notched tail. Adult male has red on the head, neck, and upper breast. The back, belly, and tail are streaky brown. Adult female and juvenile have brown upperparts with indistinct streaks on the breast and belly.

The House Finch is native to western North America and Mexico. It was introduced the Hawaiian Islands in the mid-1800s.

Yellow-fronted Canary

Crithagra mozambica

NATURALIZED RESIDENT
LENGTH 11–14 cm. (4.3–5.5 in.)
WINGSPAN 21–22 cm. (8.3–8.7 in.)
WEIGHT 8.5–16 g. (0.29–0.56 oz.)

Adult male has a yellow head, a gray crown and nape, a dark malar stripe, and a yellow eyebrow and cheek. The back, wings, and tail are green. The legs and feet are gray. Female is duller. Juveniles are duller than female.

Yellow-fronted Canaries are found throughout most of Africa south of the Sahara Desert. They were introduced to O'ahu in 1965. Places to look for this species include Kapi'olani Park, Ala Moana Park, Pearl Harbor NWR, Waimea Valley, and White Plains Beach.

Las Vegas, Nevada.

Male, Kapi'olani Park, O'ahu.

Wailupe Valley, O'ahu.

House Sparrow

Passer domesticus

NATURALIZED RESIDENT
LENGTH 14–18 cm. (5.5–7.1 in.)
WINGSPAN 19–25 cm. (7.5–9.8 in.)
WEIGHT 24–39 g. (0.85–1.39 oz.)

Adult male has a gray crown flanked by chestnut brown. It has black around its bill and on its throat. There are small white stripes behind the lores and eyes and a small white spot behind the eyes. The cheeks and underparts are gray. The upper back and mantle are brown with broad, black streaks. The lower back and rump are grayish-brown. Adult female has a brown head and upperparts. It has a distinct pale supercilium. The underparts are pale, gray-brown. Juvenile is similar to adult female but deeper brown below and paler above with a less defined supercilium.

The House Sparrow was originally native to Europe and the Middle East but has become introduced throughout North and South America and extensively around the world, wherever human inhabitation occurs. The first documented introduction of this species into the Hawaiian Islands was in 1871.

Lavender Waxbill

Estrilda caerulescens

NATURALIZED RESIDENT
LENGTH 10–12.7 cm. (4–5 in.)
WINGSPAN 12.7–14 cm. (4.7–5.5 in.)
WEIGHT 6–10 g. (0.21–0.35 oz.)

A very small, gray finch with a black eye stripe and blackish-red bill. The rump and tail are red. There are a few small white spots on the flanks. Adult male has a pale gray throat and chest. Adult Female is similar but is darker below. Juvenile is paler than female and has no black eye stripe. The rump, tail, and undertail-coverts are less bright red, and the flanks lack white spots.

The Lavender Waxbill is native to West Africa from Senegal and Nigeria to southwest Chad and northeast Cameroon. It was introduced to O'ahu in 1965. Today they are extremely rare. The best place to look for this species is Wailupe Valley.

Female House Sparrow.
Kapi'olani Park, O'ahu.

Kealia Pond NWR, Maui.

Adult, 'Aiea Loop Trail, O'ahu.

Orange-cheeked Waxbill

Estrilda melpoda

NATURALIZED RESIDENT

LENGTH 9–11 cm. (3.5–4.3 in.)
WINGSPAN 12.7–14 cm. (4.7–5.5 in.)
WEIGHT 6.5–9.6 g. (0.21–0.34 oz.)

A very small, mostly gray finch with a bright red bill and distinctive orange cheek. The back and wings are brown and the rump is red. Sexes are similar in appearance. Juvenile is similar to adult, but the rump is reddish brown and the face patch is paler. The bill is black.

Orange-cheeked Waxbills are native to West Africa, from Senegal and Gambia to Chad and Zambia. They were introduced to O'ahu in 1965. This species has extremely low populations on O'ahu and the few birds that remain are located on the windward side of the island near Kāne'ohe.

Common Waxbill

Estrilda astrild

NATURALIZED RESIDENT

LENGTH 9.5–13 cm. (3.7–5.1 in.)
WINGSPAN 12–14 cm. (4.7–5.5 in.)
WEIGHT 5–11 g. (0.17–0.38 oz.)

A very small finch with short, rounded wings and a long tail. Adult is mostly gray-brown, finely barred with dark brown. It has a bright red-orange bill and a red stripe through the eye. The throat and cheeks are whitish. The rump is brown, and the vent and tail are dark. Female is similar to male but paler. Juvenile is similar to adult, but underparts are buffier, and the red eye stripe is paler and narrower. The bill is black.

The Common Waxbill is a native of Africa south of the Sahara. They were introduced to O'ahu in 1973.

Juvenile Common Waxbill.
Ala Moana Beach Park, O'ahu.

Breeding adult male, Hawai'i Kai, O'ahu (top left).
Breeding adult female, Pu'uanahulu, Hawai'i Island
(top right and bottom right).

Red Avadavat
(Strawberry Finch)

Amandava amandava

NATURALIZED RESIDENT
LENGTH 9.5–10 cm. (3.7–3.9 in.)
WINGSPAN 11–14 cm. (4.5–5.5 in.)
WEIGHT 7.2–9.5 g. (0.25–0.33 oz.)

A small finch with a rounded tail. Breeding adult male is mostly red with many rows of white spots. The bill is red. The upperwing and tail are brownish. The lores and line through the eye are black. There are narrow white streaks under the eyes. Breeding female is grayish-brown above. The rump and uppertail coverts are red with a few indistinct white spots. The lores are black and the throat whitish. The breast and belly are pale buff with an orange tinge. Non-breeding male looks like female but has some white spots on the red uppertail coverts. Juvenile is dull grayish-brown and has a dark bill.

Red Avadavats are native to Pakistan, India, Nepal, and Indonesia. They were introduced to O'ahu between 1900 and 1910 and are scarce on the island. Best places to look for this very colorful species include Pearl Harbor NWR, Kawainui Marsh, Nu'upia Ponds WMA, Ka'ena Point NAR, and James Campbell NWR.

Puʻuanahulu, Hawaiʻi Island.

African Silverbill
(Warbling Silverbill)
Euodice cantans

NATURALIZED RESIDENT
LENGTH 11–11.5 cm. (4.3–4.5 in.)
WINGSPAN 20–22 cm. (7.8–8.7 in.)
WEIGHT 10–14 g. (0.35–0.49 oz.)

A small finch with a long, black, pointed tail. Adult has a stubby, bluish-silver bill and finely vermiculated buff brown upperparts. The wings and rump are brownish-black. Underparts are whitish. Sexes are similar in appearance. Juvenile lacks the vermiculations, and the bill is gray.

African Silverbills are native to Africa south of the Sahara Desert. They were introduced to the Hawaiian Islands in the mid-1960s and were first observed on Oʻahu in February 1984. Places to look for this species include Kaiwi State Scenic Shoreline, Kapiʻolani Park, Makapuʻu Point Lighthouse Trail, Kapapapuhi Point Park, and Kaʻena Point NAR.

Adult, Ala Moana Beach Park, Oʻahu.

Java Sparrow
Lonchura oryzivora

NATURALIZED RESIDENT
LENGTH 15–17 cm. (5.9–6.7in.)
WINGSPAN 21–23 cm. (8.2–9 in.)
WEIGHT 22.5–27.8 g. (0.79–0.98 oz.)

A small finch that is mostly bluish-gray. Adult has a black head with a distinctive white patch below the eye, a red eye-ring, and a thick red bill. The upperparts and breast are gray and the belly pinkish. The tail is black. Legs and feet are pale pink. Sexes are similar in appearance. Juvenile is pale grayish-buff.

Java Sparrows are native to Java and Bali Islands in Indonesia. They were introduced to Oʻahu in the 1960s and can be found in many locations on the island.

Juvenile Java Sparrow.
Ala Moana Beach Park, Oʻahu.

Pu'u Anahulu, Hawai'i Island.

Adult, Waipahu, O'ahu.

Scaly-breasted Munia

Lonchura punctulata

NATURALIZED RESIDENT
LENGTH 11–12 cm. (4.3–4.7 in.)
WINGSPAN 15–18 cm. (6–7 in.)
WEIGHT 12–16 g. (0.42–0.56 oz.)

A small songbird that eats mostly grass seeds. Adults are brown above with a darker face and they have scale-like feather markings on the breast and belly. The bill is dark and conical. The outer primaries and tail are blackish. The rump is black. Juvenile is plain brown with slightly paler underparts.

Scaly-breasted Munias are native to India and Southeast Asia. They were introduced to O'ahu in June 1866 by William Hillebrand. Best locations to look for this finch include Pouhala Marsh Wildlife Sanctuary, 'Aiea Ridge Trail, Kapi'olani Park, Fort Derussy Beach Park and Ka'elepulu Wetland.

Chestnut Munia

Lonchura atricapilla

NATURALIZED RESIDENT
LENGTH 11–12 cm. (4.3–4.7 in.)
WINGSPAN 15–18 cm. (6–7 in.)
WEIGHT 11–16 g. (0.38–0.56 oz.)

A tiny chestnut-brown finch with a large silver-blue, conical bill. The head, breast and abdomen are black. Immature is uniformly lighter brown with a blue-gray bill and a chestnut tail.

Chestnut Munias are native to India, Nepal, South China, Southeast Asia, Taiwan, the Philippine Islands, Indonesia, and the Malaysian Penninsula. They are popular in the pet trade and were first observed on O'ahu at Honouliuli National Wildlife Refuge in 1959. The initial group of twenty-five birds expanded rapidly and by 2000, this species range included most of the island. Look for this distinctive species at James Campbell NWR, Turtle Bay Resort, Kawainui Marsh, Ho'omaluhia Botanical Garden, Lyon Arboretum and 'Iolani Palace.

Juvenile Chestnut Munia.
Waipahu, O'ahu.

O'AHU'S EXTINCT NATIVE BIRD SPECIES

The following O'ahu bird species are extinct. They are either on the official list or went extinct before 1778 and are not included on the official list. The pre-1778 extinctions are based on subfossil remains. For more information about Hawai'i's extinct birds please see *Extinct Birds of Hawai'i* by Michael Walther, illustrated by Julian Hume.

Pre-1778 Extinctions

O'ahu Moa-nalo
Thambetochen xanion

Ziegler's Crake
Zapornia ziegleri

Ralph's Crake
Zapornia ralphorum

Hawaiian Eagle
Haliaeetus albicilla ssp.

Hawaiian Harrier
Circus dossenus

O'ahu Stilt Owl
Grallistrix orion

Deep-billed Crow
Corvus impluviatus

Robust Crow
Corvus viriosus

Narrow-billed Kioea
Chaetoptila sp.

Laysan Finch
Telespiza cantans
Extinct on Oʻahu

Makawehi Finch
Telespiza persecutrix

Palila
Loxioides bailleui
Extinct on Oʻahu

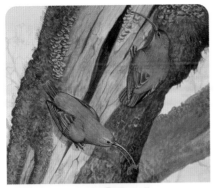

Hoopoe-billed 'Akialoa
Akialoa upupirostris

Straight-billed Gaper
Aidemedia chascax

Sickle-billed Gaper
Aidemedia zanclops

O'ahu Koa Finch
Rhodacanthis litotes

Wahi Grosbeak
Chloridops wahi

King Kong Grosbeak
Chloridops regiskongi

Ridge-billed Finch
Xestospiza fastigialis

Post-1778 Extinctions

'Amaui (O'ahu Thrush)
Myadestes woahensis

O'ahu 'Ō'ō
Moho apicalis

'Ō'ū
Psittirostra psittacea

O'ahu 'Akialoa
Akialoa ellisiana

O'ahu 'Alauahio
Paroreomyza maculata

O'ahu Nukupu'u
Hemignathus lucidus

O'ahu 'Ākepa
Loxops wolstenholmei

O'ahu's Extinct Introduced and Established Bird Species

Saddle Road, Hawai'i Island.

Tennoji Park in Osaka. LAITCHE

California Quail
Callipepla californica

NATURALIZED RESIDENT

Varied Tit
Japanese Tit, Japanese Tumbler
Parus varius

NATURALIZED RESIDENT

Introduced Species
That Are Not Established on Oʻahu,
Not on the Official List
and Present on Oʻahu in 2023

The following sixteen introduced bird species are seen occasionally on Oʻahu and are recorded on ebird but they are all considered non-established and are not on Oʻahu's official checklist. Some of them escaped from captivity, some were purposely introduced and one was ship assisted.

The information below is derived from: Pyle, R.L., and P. Pyle. *The Birds of the Hawaiian Islands: Occurrence, History, Distribution, and Status.* Honolulu, HI: B.P. Bishop Museum, 2017. Version 2 (1 January 2017) http://hbs.bishopmuseum.org/birds/rlp-monograph

Szeged, Hungary.

Graylag Goose

Anser anser
Escaped. First report 1984.

Koʻolina, Oʻahu.

Black Swan

Cygnus atratus
Escaped or Introduced. First report 1987.

ʻAina Haina, Oʻahu.

Muscovy Duck

Cairina moschata
Introduced. First report 1970s.

Lyon Arboretum, Oʻahu.

Tanimbar Corella

Cacatua goffiniana
Escaped. First report 1987.

Oʻahu's Extinct Native Bird Species

Lyon Arboretum, O'ahu.

Salmon-crested Cockatoo

Cacatua moluccensis
Escaped. First report 1972.

White Cockatoo

Cacatua alba
Escaped. First report 1991.

Cockatiel

Nymphicus hollandicus
Escaped. First report 1979.

Budgerigar

Melopsittacus undulates
Escaped. First report 1933.

Lyon Arboretum, O'ahu.

Eclectus Parrot

Eclectus roratus
Escaped. First report 1972.

Lilac-crowned Parrot

Amazona finschi
Escaped. First Report 2022.

Kihei, Maui.

Rosy-faced Lovebird

Agapornis roseicollis
Escaped. First report 1973.

Kahuku, O'ahu.

Blue-crowned Parakeet

Thectocercus acuticaudata
Escaped. First report 1986.

Kotu Creek, Western Division, The Gambia. STEVE GARVIE

Northern Red Bishop

Euplectis franciscanis
Escaped. First report 1965.

Ala Moana Beach Park, O'ahu.

Great-tailed Grackle

Quiscalus mexicanus
Ship-assisted.

Waimānalo, O'ahu

Helmeted Guineafowl

Numida melagris
Introduced. First report 1901.

ANDY MORFFEW

Northern Bobwhite

Colinus virginianus
Introduced. First report 1962.

Extirpated on Oʻahu and Never Established

White-faced Whistling Duck
Common Shelduck
Wood Duck
Mandarin Duck
Maned Duck
Chiloe Wigeon
Rosy-billed Pochard
Mountain Quail
Crested Partridge
Gray Partridge
Blue-breasted Quail
Reeves Pheasant
Copper Pheasant
Golden Pheasant
Lady Amherst Pheasant
Silver Pheasant
Greater Prairie Chicken
Savanah Hawk
Purple Swamphen
Ringed Turtle-Dove
Eurasian Collared Dove
Island Collared Dove
Asian Emerald Dove
Common Bronzewing
Crested Pigeon
Diamond Dove
Peaceful Dove
Bar-shouldered Dove

Palm Cockatoo
Galah
Yellow-crested Cockatoo
Sulphur-crested Cockatoo
Monk Parakeet
Orange-chinned Parakeet
White-fronted Parrot
Red-lored Parrot
Blue-fronted Parrot
Yellow-headed Parrot
Orange-fronted Parakeet
Nanday Parakeet
Jandaya Parakeet
Blue-and-yellow Macaw
Scarlet Macaw
Plum-headed Parakeet
Red-crowned Parakeet
Yellow-collared Lovebird
Senegal Parrot
Red-billed Blue Magpie
Dark-throated Oriole
Black-naped Oriole
Willie Wagtail
Magpie-Lark
Asian Fairy-bluebird
Sunbird
White-crested Laughingthrush

Black-throated Laughingthrush
Oriental Magpie-Robin
Blue-and-white Flycatcher
Japanese Robin
Ryuku Robin
Narcissus Flycatcher
Hill Myna
Black-collared Starling
Bali Myna
Red-cowled Cardinal
Red-capped Cardinal
Yellow Cardinal
Indigo Bunting
Orange-breasted Bunting
Painted Bunting
White-rumped Seedeater
Baya Weaver
Yellow-crowned Bishop
Southern Cordonbleu
Blue-capped Cordonbleu
Red-billed Firefinch
African Firefinch
Diamond Firetail
Zebra Finch
Tricolored Munia
Pin-tailed Whydah
Village Indigobird

Species on Hypothetical List

Fulvous Whistling-Duck
European Starling
Buffy Laughingthrush

PLACES TO SEE BIRDS ON O'AHU

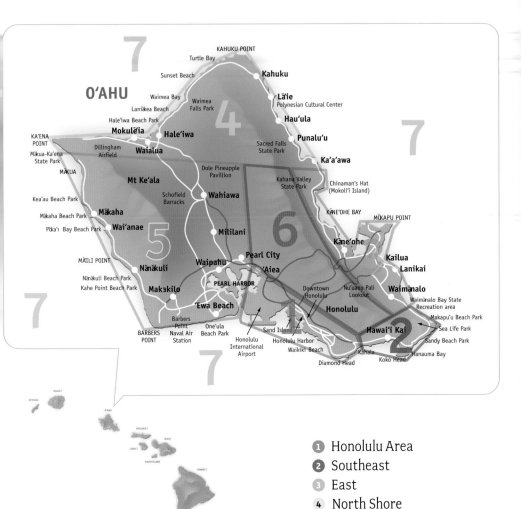

1. Honolulu Area
2. Southeast
3. East
4. North Shore
5. Central
6. Ko'olau Range
7. Pelagics

Salt Lake Community Park.

Salt Lake and Ala Puʻumalu Community Park

DISTANCE ¼-mile

TIME 30 minutes

HIGHLIGHTS Migratory ducks, resident endangered waterbirds, and Saffron Finch.

POTENTIAL SPECIES 34

DIRECTIONS From H2 Freeway West take exit 3 (Puʻuloa Rd/Tripler Hospital). Turn left onto Puʻuloa Road then turn right Salt Lake Boulevard. Turn right on Ala Lilikoi Boulevard.

Situated in an ancient volcanic area of Honolulu, Salt Lake is a good place to visit for migrating waterfowl between November and April. **Lesser Scaup, Ring-necked Duck, Northern Pintail**, and **Northern Shoveler** have all been observed here. On December 17, 1972, an extremely rare **Loon** (not confirmed to species but either Pacific or Arctic) was reported. A rare **Caspian Tern** was observed at the lake on January 3, 1979, and a very rare **Hooded Merganser** was there on March 7, 2003. This is a great location to check for rarities.

The lake can only be viewed from the baseball field at Ala Puʻumalu Park and requires a spotting scope to view the birds on the 500-yard-wide shallow lake. This is also a very good place to look for **Saffron Finch, Chestnut Munia,** and a variety of introduced species. Check the grass areas for introduced species and walk to the fence to view Salt Lake.

Eurasian Skylark can occasionally be found at the nearby Honolulu Airport along Lagoon Drive. The larks are often seen foraging in the grass areas on the right side of the road as you drive toward Keʻehi Lagoon. It is best to pull over onto the grass shoulder to look for them due to heavy traffic on Lagoon Drive.

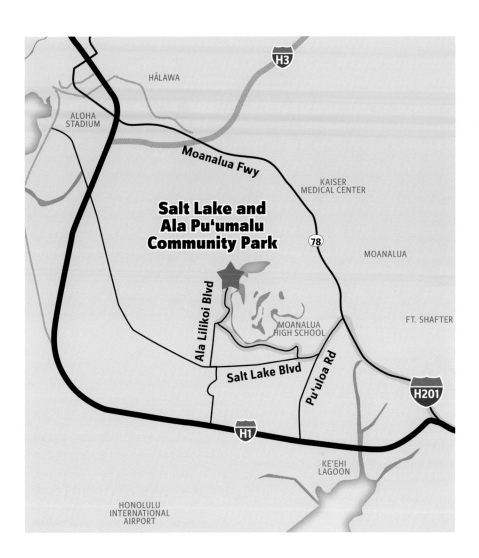

Salt Lake and
Ala Puʻumalu
Community Park

HĀLAWA

ALOHA
STADIUM

H3

Moanalua Fwy

KAISER
MEDICAL CENTER

78

MOANALUA

Ala Lilikoi Blvd

MOANALUA
HIGH SCHOOL

FT. SHAFTER

Salt Lake Blvd

Puʻuloa Rd

H201

H1

KEʻEHI
LAGOON

HONOLULU
INTERNATIONAL
AIRPORT

Ala Moana Beach Park. MKOJOT

Ala Moana Beach Park

DISTANCE 1-mile

TIME 1 hour

HIGHLIGHTS Ruddy Turnstone, Wandering Tattler, Brown Booby, and an excellent variety of introduced species.

POTENTIAL SPECIES 45

DIRECTIONS Located on Ala Moana Boulevard. From Waikīkī drive toward Honolulu. Turn left at Ala Moana Park Drive. From Honolulu, drive toward Waikīkī and turn right at Ala Moana Park Drive / Kamakeʻe Street.

Ala Moana Beach Park is a 100-acre urban park located across from Ala Moana Shopping Center. It is best to arrive early to find a parking place especially on weekends. This is the best place near Waikīkī to find the migratory **Ruddy Turnstone** and **Wandering Tattler**. To completely check the park for birds, walk along the beach all the way to the end at the boat harbor then walk inland and check the ponds along the walkway back to the south end of the park. This is a loop that should take about one hour. From September through April, fifteen to thirty Ruddy Turnstones, mostly in small groups, can be found feeding along the shoreline or on the raised limestone reefs. Several solitary Wandering Tattlers are also usually present.

The southeast corner of the park is called Magic Island. Next to the saltwater pool is a rock jetty which provides a great place for some sea watching. **Brown Booby, Red-footed Booby, Sooty Tern,** and **Wedge-tailed Shearwater** are all possible especially in the early morning and with a spotting scope.

Several rare species have been found in the park including **Bristle-thighed Curlew, Peregrine Falcon, Ring-billed Gull,** and a one-legged **Great-tailed Grackle** that is believed to have been assisted to Hawaiʻi by a container ship.

Magic Island. PATRICK EVANS

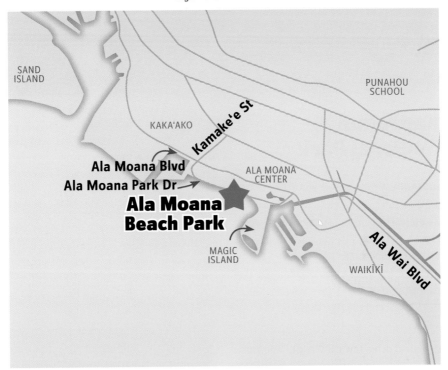

SAND ISLAND

PUNAHOU SCHOOL

KAKA'AKO

Kamake'e St

Ala Moana Blvd
Ala Moana Park Dr

ALA MOANA CENTER

Ala Moana Beach Park

MAGIC ISLAND

Ala Wai Blvd

WAIKĪKĪ

Ruddy Turnstone

Wandering Tattler

Kapiʻolani Regional Park

DISTANCE ¼-mile

TIME 1 hour

HIGHLIGHTS White Tern, Pacific Golden Plover, and many introduced bird species.

POTENTIAL SPECIES 71

DIRECTIONS Located in Honolulu on the east end of Waikīkī just beyond Kūhiō Beach Park and the Honolulu Zoo.

Kapiʻolani Park is the largest and oldest public park in the state. The 300-acre park was named after Queen Kapiʻolani, the wife of Hawaiʻi's last king, David Kalākaua. It opened on June 11, 1877. The Park is a great place to watch the graceful and elegant **White Tern**. Be sure to check the branches of the giant Indian Banyan trees for both adults and young chicks. The entire population of over 3,000 birds lives in southeast Oʻahu and they are rarely observed on the other islands in Hawaiʻi.

Look for the beautiful **Pacific Golden-Plover** in the grassy areas. This incredible bird migrates every year back and forth between Hawaiʻi and their breeding grounds in the Arctic. They are present from late July until late April and spend about nine months of their life every year in Hawaiʻi.

This location is a great place to see what I call the "United Nations" of Hawaiian birds. Introduced species from four continents reside here. Two varieties of dove from Asia, the **Spotted Dove** and **Zebra** or **Barred Dove,** can easily be found. Several parakeet species have been observed in and around the park area. The **Rose-ringed Parakeet** naturally occurs in Africa and Asia. They were first

noticed on Oʻahu in the 1930s and the flock today has increased to over 700 birds. **Red-masked Parakeets**, native to South America, roost at the Doris Duke Estate and occasionally fly over the park as they search for food.

Asian Red-vented Bulbuls are very common at Kapiʻolani Park. This species is considered an agricultural pest and were first observed on Oʻahu in 1966. Several other birds introduced from Asia are seen in the park often. These include

Scaly-breasted Munia, Java Sparrow, Chestnut Munia and Common Myna. The North American House Finch and English Sparrow both thrive here. This is one of the best places on Oʻahu to see the Yellow-fronted Canary from Africa.

Beginning in the late 1920s, a group of affluent citizens in Honolulu formed a bird society called Hui Manu ("hui" is the Hawaiian word for group, and "manu" is the Hawaiian word for bird). They brought in species from around the world to repopulate the island with singing birds after the native birds had declined and to help control insects. Many species of exotic birds were recorded in the park area during the 1960s that had been released from cages onto the slopes of Diamond Head Crater. These included the Pin-tailed Whydah, African Firefinch, Red Bishop, White-rumped Seedeater, Baya Weaver, Blue-capped Cordonbleu, and Red-cheeked Cordonbleu. Most of these species last-

ed only ten or twenty years before they disappeared from the area. Two other species that were included in these introductions, the Lavender Waxbill and Orange-cheeked Waxbill, persisted in the Kapiʻolani Park area until the late 1980s. Today, the Lavender Waxbill can sometimes be found in Wailupe Valley in southeast Oʻahu, and the Orange-cheeked Waxbill still exists and has a very small population in Kāneʻohe.

If visiting the park at night, it's possible to see the few resident Barn Owls that live in the area. The owls were introduced to Hawaiʻi in 1958 to control rats and mice that were causing damage on agricultural land. The park has many acres of grass that are excellent for the exotic species.

Be sure to check all the branches of the huge Indian Banyan trees for nesting White Terns and Rose-ringed Parakeets.

Lyon Arboretum

DISTANCE ¼-mile

TIME 2 hours

HIGHLIGHTS Oʻahu ʻAmakihi, White-rumped Shama, Japanese Bush Warbler, Red-billed Leothrix, and several introduced parrot species.

POTENTIAL SPECIES 45

DIRECTIONS From Waikīkī, proceed on Ala Wai Boulevard to McCully Street and turn right on McCully Street. Turn right on Kapiʻolani Boulevard then left on University Avenue. Veer slightly right on Oʻahu Avenue then right on Mānoa Road. Continue to the end of the road. Continue past the parking area at the old Paradise Park until you see the Lyon Arboretum sign on the

left. Drive up the narrow road to the arboretum parking lot.

Located in Mānoa Valley, Lyon Arboretum is a 200-acre tropical garden situated in a lush rainforest that has an average of 165 inches annual rainfall! Most of the vegetation is non-native and the tall trees were planted a hundred years ago to counteract the erosion caused by free-ranging cattle. A variety of introduced and a few native bird species are attracted to the flowers of almost 6,000 tropical plants.

This is one of the best places to search for the **O'ahu 'Amakihi** with easy access close to Honolulu and Waikīkī. The **White-rumped Shamas**, used to seeing people on the trails, provide great photo opportunities. Watch and listen for **Japanese Bush-Warblers** and **Red-billed Leiothrix** hiding in the dense understory. Occasionally scan the sky near the cliffs above the arboretum for possible **White-tailed Tropicbirds.**

Several exotic parrot species inhabit the area including **Tanimbar Corella, Salmon-crested Cockatoo,** and **Eclectus Parrot**. The birds escaped from aviaries that were once part of a tourist attraction called Paradise Park as early as 1972. None of these species are considered fully established by the Hawai'i Bird Records Committee.

When you arrive at the arboretum you will need to sign in at the gift shop. Docents might be able to provide recent bird observations and where to see the parrots. There are many trails that often are muddy so it's best to wear closed-toe shoes and bring a walking stick. This area has mosquitoes, so repellent is important to have with you.

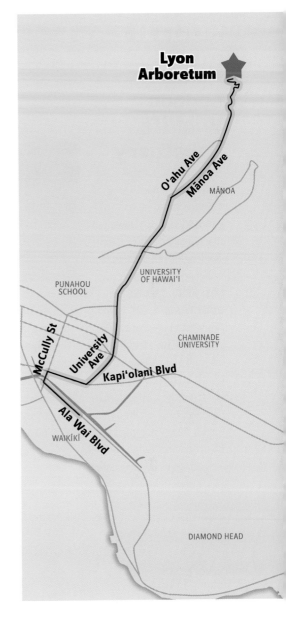

Paikō Lagoon Wildlife Sanctuary

DISTANCE None

TIME 20 minutes

HIGHLIGHTS Hawaiian Black-necked Stilt, Pacific Golden Plover, and Black-crowned Night Heron

POTENTIAL SPECIES 40

DIRECTIONS From Waikīkī, proceed on Ala Wai Boulevard to McCully Street and turn right on McCully Street. Turn right on Kapiʻolani Boulevard and continue to the H1 East freeway onramp. Continue on the freeway until Kalanianaʻole Highway. Proceed East on Kalanianaʻole Highway for 3.8 miles then turn right on Kuliʻouʻou Road and proceed to the end.

Paiko Lagoon Wildlife Sanctuary was created in 1981 to protect the **Hawaiian Black-necked Stilt** and migratory birds. The 39.42-acre preserve consists of a salt water tidal lagoon and surrounding areas. No one is permitted to enter the sanctuary unless they have a special permit, but most of the lagoon can be viewed from the

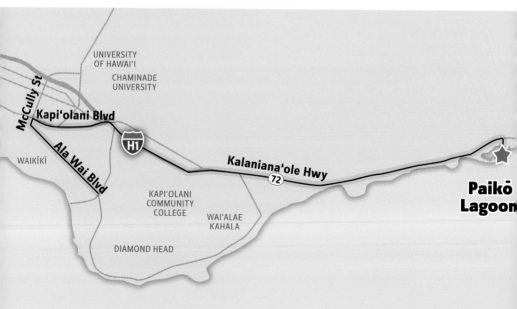

end of Kuli'ou'ou Road. A spotting scope is very helpful at this location.

It is best to time a visit at low tide when the tidal flats are visible. **Pacific Golden-Plovers, Ruddy Turnstones,** and **Wandering Tattlers** congregate on the flats to feed daily. On most days several Hawaiian Black-necked Stilts are present. Several rare species for Hawai'i have been observed at the Lagoon including **Great Egret, Red Phalarope, Western Gull, Caspian Tern,** and **Greater Yellowlegs**. It is always worth checking this easily accessible location to check for any rarities.

A regular flock of **Hawaiian Duck/Mallard** hybrids lives at the lagoon and they are regularly fed by visitors and residents. A recent DNA study sampled some of these birds and found them to be about 80 percent Mallard. The same study concluded that the only pure form of Hawaiian Duck exists on Kaua'i, and there are no pure Koloa on O'ahu currently although some ducks sampled at James Cambell NWR were 80 percent Hawaiian Duck.

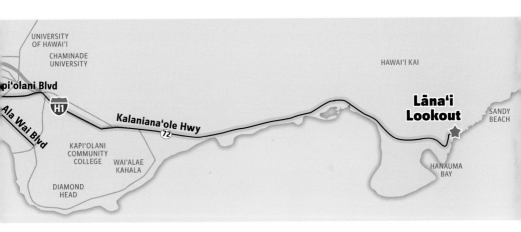

Lāna'i Lookout to Sandy Beach

DISTANCE 1 mile

TIME 1 hour

HIGHLIGHTS Red-tailed Tropicbird, White-tailed Tropicbird, Red-billed Tropicbird, Brown Booby, Wandering Tattler, and rare migratory species.

POTENTIAL SPECIES 40

DIRECTIONS From Waikīkī proceed on Ala Wai Boulevard to McCully Street and turn right on McCully Street. Turn right on Kapi'olani Boulevard and continue to the H1 East freeway onramp. Continue on the freeway until Kalaniana'ole Highway. Proceed east on Kalaniana'ole Highway until you arrive at the Lāna'i Lookout just past Hanauma Bay.

Red-tailed Tropicbird.

Red-billed Tropicbird.

White-tailed Tropicbird.

This is one of the most scenic coastlines on Oʻahu and was created by volcanic explosions as recently as 50,000 years ago. The best way to bird this area is to stop at some or all the lookouts and parking spots along Kalanianaʻole Highway between the Lānaʻi Lookout and Sandy Beach. There are three parking areas between the Lānaʻi Lookout and Sandy Beach. The first has enough space for four vehicles, the second for one, and the third area, near the Japanese fishing shrine, can accommodate six vehicles. The highway is very busy so please exercise caution when going back on the highway after parking. All of these locations allow for great views of the ocean, volcanic cliffs, and surrounding sky.

Red-tailed Tropicbirds are the most spectacular and noticeable birds along this section of the coast especially between February and October. The best time to see them is between 11:00 AM and 3:00 PM when they are most active and occasionally you might see their amazing courtship display flights. The colony consisted of about twelve breeding pairs in 2005 and has grown to around seventy-five pairs. It is now the fourth biggest Red-tailed Tropicbird colony in the Southeastern Hawaiian Islands.[2]

This is one of the only places in the world where you might see all three species of Tropicbird. **White-tailed Tropicbirds** are frequent visitors to this section of coastline. **Red-billed Tropicbirds** are rare in Hawaiʻi. I first discovered this species in the area on March 3, 2006 and one or two birds were present between March and July 2006 to 2008. After a ten-year absence they have been annual visitors since 2018.

Check the offshore waters for **Brown Booby, Red-footed Booby, Wedge-tailed Shearwater,** and **Sooty Terns**. Look for solitary **Wandering Tattlers** on the lava rock shoreline. This section of Oʻahu coast has been the location where several Hawaiʻi first records have occurred including **Surfbird** and **Inca Tern** so it is worthwhile to allocate a few hours looking for birds along this spectacular coast. Watch for Humpback whales in the fall and winter.

O'ahu Islets, Hawaiian Islands, Breeding Seabird Populations (Pairs)

COMMON NAME	MOKU-AUIA	MOKOLI'I	KAPAPA	KEKEPA	MOKU-MANU	MOKO-LEA	POPOIA	MOKULUAS	MANANA	KAOHI-KAIPU
Bulwer Petrel			10	10	100	10	125	150	10	10
Wedge-tailed Shearwater	2,500	200	300		2,000		1,500	10,000	12,000	400
Christmas Shearwater					50			5		
White-tailed Tropicbird		2								
Red-tailed Tropicbird									15	
Masked Booby					50					
Brown Booby					100					
Red-footed Booby					200					
Great Frigatebird					B					
Brown Noddy					2,000	10			20,000	
Black Noddy					75	20			10	5
Sooty Tern					15,000				75,000	
Gray-backed Tern					25					
TOTALS	2,500	202	310	10	19,590	40	1,625	10,155	107,025	415

Breeding seabird chart courtesy of: Pyle, R.L., and P. Pyle. 2017. The Birds of the Hawaiian Islands: Occurrence, History, Distribution, and Status. B.P. Bishop Museum, Honolulu, HI, U.S.A. Version 2 (1 January 2017) http://hbs.bishopmuseum.org/birds/rlp-monograph

Red-billed Tropicbird.

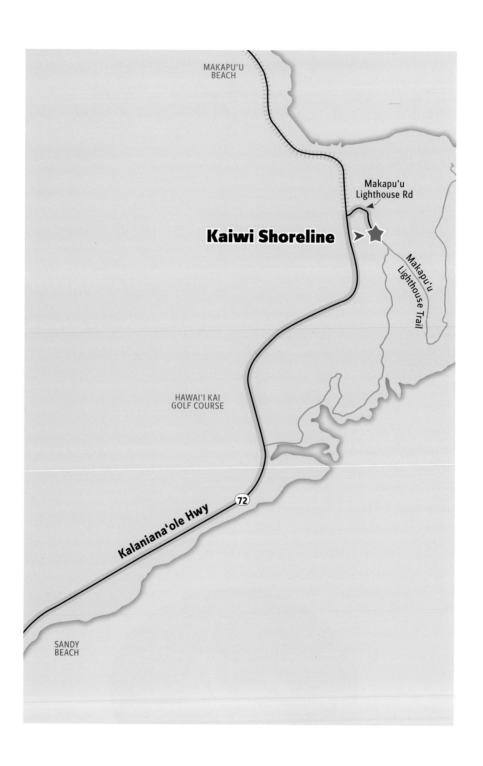

MAKAPU'U
BEACH

Makapu'u
Lighthouse Rd

Kaiwi Shoreline ⭐

Makapu'u
Lighthouse Trail

HAWAI'I KAI
GOLF COURSE

72

Kalaniana'ole Hwy

SANDY
BEACH

Kaiwi State Scenic Shoreline

DISTANCE 1 mile

TIME 2 hours

HIGHLIGHTS African Silverbill, Sooty Tern, Wedge-tailed Shearwater, and Red-footed Booby.

POTENTIAL SPECIES 50

DIRECTIONS Driving from Honolulu proceed east on Kalaniana'ole Highway past Sandy Beach. Continue driving until the driveway on the right with a gate. This is the entrance to the parking lot. If arriving before 7 AM you can park along the highway. If driving from Kāne'ohe or Kailua proceed on Kalaniana'ole Highway past Waimānalo and Sea Life Park, continue past the top of the hill and the Makapu'u Lookout until you see the driveway the on the left.

Lava flows from Kalama Crater covered much of this area about 30,000 years ago. Subsequent wave action reshaped this shoreline and deposited sand and cobble beaches. Look for the dirt trail located on the right at the end of the parking lot which goes to the coastal area below. The main road/trail leads up the hill to the Makapu'u lighthouse. Walk along the coast to the other side of this area by turning right at the ocean. The trail meanders around Ka'ili'ili Bay and Kaloko Inlet and ends near the highway past Kaloko Point.

African Silverbills (*Lonchura cantans*), previously called the **Warbling Silverbill,** inhabit this area. This species was introduced to Hawai'i in the mid 1960s and the first birds were observed at Kaiwi in 1984. The **'Iwa** or **Great Frigatebird** (*Fregata minor*), one of Hawai'i's largest birds with a seven-foot wingspan, can occasionally be spotted soaring over the area usually flying from west to east. These incredible birds have some of the lightest bones of any bird species on Earth. All of the 'Iwa breed in the northwestern Hawaiian Islands with the exception of two historical nests at Mokumanu islet off Kāne'ohe; one in the summer of 1970 and the other in the summer of 2008. Over 1,000 birds of this species roost on the same islet. A extremely rare **Red-breasted Merganser** (*Mergus serrator*) was observed feeding on small fish in the tide pools along this shoreline in 2011.

Makapuʻu Beach Park and Mānana Island

DISTANCE 200 yards

TIME 1 hour

HIGHLIGHTS Offshore seabird sanctuaries, Red-footed Boobies, Masked Booby, Gray-backed Tern, Brown Noddy, and Wedge-tailed Shearwaters.

POTENTIAL SPECIES 53

DIRECTIONS Driving from Honolulu proceed east on Kalanianaʻole Highway past Sandy Beach. Continue driving past the Makapuʻu lookout at the top of the hill. Here is a spectacular view of windward Oʻahu. Continue to the bottom of the hill and then turn right to a Makapuʻu Beach Park. The entrance is on the ocean side of the highway across from Sea Life Park

entrance. Best to park in the lot and walk the area to the north along the coast going in the opposite direction of the lighthouse and Makapuʻu Point. If driving from Kāneʻohe or Kailua proceed on Kalanianaʻole Highway past Waimānalo until the beach park on the left.

This is an excellent place to contemplate the different types of volcanic events that were included in the Honolulu volcanic series. Two offshore islands, Mānana, a tuff cone, and Kāohikaipu, a cinder cone, are seabird preserves and are closed to the public. The land you are walking on is part of the Kaupo lava flow which has been dated to only 30,000 years ago. The lava emerged from a vent 250 feet above sea level on the cliff behind Sea Life Park.

If you are able visit this location at dawn in April to June you will witness one of Hawaiʻi's most incredible bird displays.

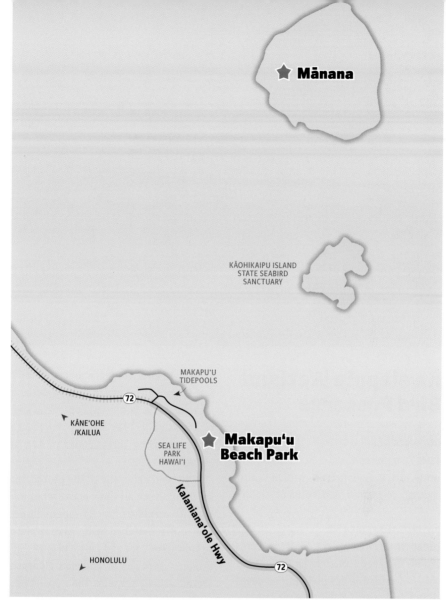

Bring binoculars or a spotting scope to watch a continuous movement of tens of thousands of birds as they fly from Mokumanu Islet, Ulupou Crater, Mānana Islet and other locations past the ocean side of Mānana and around Makapuʻu point into the Kaiwi Channel which separates Oʻahu from Molokaʻi. The great majority of birds are **Wedge-tailed Shearwaters, Red-footed** and **Brown Boobies, Brown Noddies,** and **Sooty Terns** but likely some **Masked Boobies, Black Noddies,** and **Gray-backed Terns** are among the multitudes. In the spring and early summer these species and others are nesting on the offshore islands. On most days during the year, you can relax along this coast and watch a steady procession of year-round resident Red-footed Boobies passing close to shore as they fly towards their fishing grounds off Molokaʻi. It is best to be there early in the morning.

Kaʻelepulu Wetland Bird Preserve

DISTANCE None
TIME 30 minutes
HIGHLIGHTS Endangered wetland bird species. Migratory and resident waterfowl.
POTENTIAL SPECIES 53
DIRECTIONS From Waimānalo and Kalanianaʻole Highway, turn right on Keolu Drive going towards the ocean. Continue down the hill to the second left which is also Keolu Drive. Continue to Kiukeʻe Street and turn right. On the left side of the street, you will see Kaʻelepulu Pond.

Kaʻelepulu Pond, also known as Enchanted Lake, includes about 95 acres of water, wetlands, and several small, low islands. The water is brackish and connected to the ocean near Kailua Beach. Before development of the Enchanted Lake subdivision in 1960, the lake covered nearly 190 acres with an additional marsh area of 90 acres. A privately-owned 5.8-acre wetland located at the southwest end of the lake was created in 1995 and was purchased by two local conservationists in August 2004.

This wetland is one of the best places on Oʻahu to see all three endangered Hawaiian water birds. The Hawaiian subspecies of **Black-necked Stilt**, **ʻAlae keʻokeʻo** or **Hawaiian Coot** and **ʻAlae ʻula**, the Hawaiian subspecies of **Common Moorhen** are all usually present. The populations of Black-necked Stilt fluctuate between 1,200 to 2,000 statewide with as many as 600 on Oʻahu. The cryptic Moorhen's population is estimated at only 750 birds in Hawaiʻi, and the Coot has the highest populations of 1,500 to 3,000 birds, with as many as 1,000 birds on Oʻahu. All three of these endangered species have declined due to severe loss of habitat, hunting, and predation by rats, mongoose, housecats, dogs, and introduced bullfrogs.

Additional species that have been

observed include the **'Aukuʻu**, or **Black-crowned Night-Heron**, **Koloa mapu** or **Northern Pintail**, **Koloa mohā** or **Northern Shoveler, Lesser Scaup**, and **Cackling Goose.** An extremely rare pair of **Ruddy Duck** were at Kaʻelepulu December 23, 1945. Occasionally **hybrid Koloa** or **Hawaiian Ducks** are also present at this wetland. Several rare species have been observed here and include **Black Tern, Tufted Duck,** and **Semipalmated Plover**.

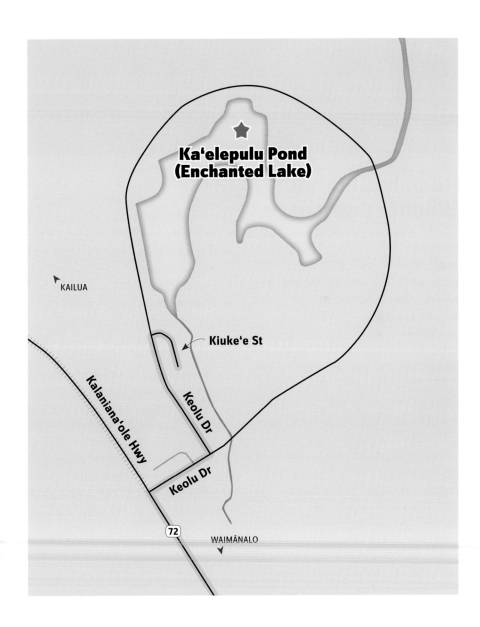

Hāmākua Marsh Wildlife Sanctuary

DISTANCE ¼-mile

TIME 1 hour

HIGHLIGHTS Endangered wetland bird species. Migratory shorebirds.

POTENTIAL SPECIES 56

DIRECTIONS From Honolulu take the Pali Highway to Kailua. Continue on Kalaniana'ole Highway towards Kailua which turns into Kailua Road. Turn right on Hāmākua Drive and look for Hāmākua Marsh on your right. You can park at several locations along Hāmākua Drive including behind the Down to Earth Natural Foods store.

NOTES Please do not feed the birds.

The 22.7-acre Hāmākua preserve is conveniently located in downtown Kailua, and you can drive right to the edge of the marsh; drive-up birding at its best! It was once part of a larger wetland complex that included Ka'elepulu Pond and Kawai Nui Marsh which, at over 800 acres, is the largest remaining wetland in Hawai'i. Unfortunately, in the early 1960s a flood control levee was built that cut off the flow of water from Kawai Nui Marsh into Hāmākua. As a result, Hāmākua Marsh is completely dependent on rainfall. Current and future projects intend to restore habitat and protect the native flora and fauna.

All of the endangered wetland birds that can be observed at Ka'elepulu are also found at Hāmākua. In addition, during wet years when suitable mud flats and shallow pools develop, several less common migratory shorebirds have been sighted here during the fall and winter. On March 5, 1978, a rare **Greater Yellowlegs** was recorded. A single, **Black-bellied Plover** was found on April 9, 2012. A **Lesser Yellowlegs** was visiting Hāmākua Marsh on November 23, 2012. The following year, an uncommon, **Asian Sharp-tailed Sandpiper** was documented at this location on December 29, 2013. One of the greatest satisfactions of bird watching is finding rare species...so good luck!

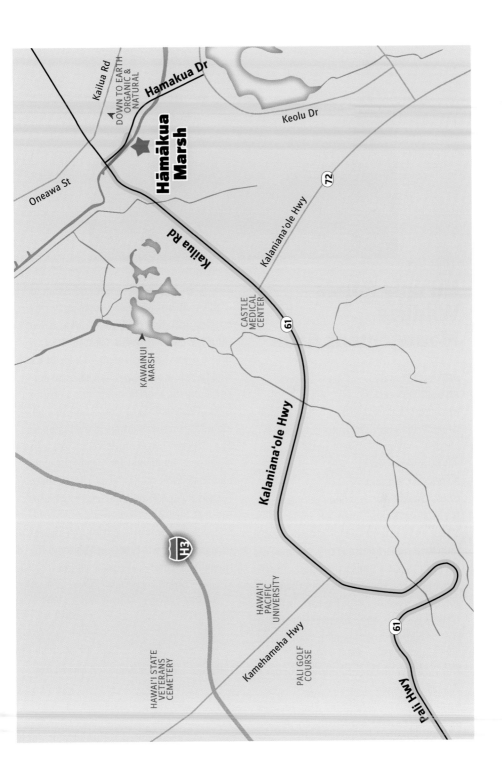

Nu'upia Ponds Wildlife Management Area

DISTANCE ⅛-mile

TIME 30 minutes

HIGHLIGHTS Caspian Tern, Black Noddy, Great Frigatebird, Migratory waterfowl, resident endangered waterbirds, and rare migratory species.

POTENTIAL SPECIES 78

DIRECTIONS From Honolulu take the Pali Highway to Kailua. Turn left on Oneawa Street and continue to Mokapu Boulevard then turn right. Continue to Kāne'ohe Bay Drive for several miles then park on the side of the road before the right turn that goes to the Marine Corps Base. Walk ten to twenty yards to the northwest until you see the bike path on the right. Walk on the bike path until you reach a four-foot-high block wall. Walk up onto this wall to get a view of the ponds.

NOTE If you have a military pass you can drive into the Kāne'ohe Marine Corps base for better viewing of all of the ponds.

This is one of the best wetland areas on O'ahu that has produced some very rare species including **Gull-billed Tern, Great Blue Heron,** and **Great Crested Tern.** It is also a very good place to look for **Black Noddy.** A few of these small seabirds forage along the shore of the ponds. Look for **Great Frigatebirds** to the left of the high mountain on the coastline in the distance. The Greater Frigatebirds roost just offshore on Mokumanu islet. One of the most amazing birds on O'ahu is the **Caspian Tern** at Nu'upia Ponds that has returned to the area for twenty-two years as of 2022. It leaves O'ahu at the end of March and returns in January to enjoy the Winter in the Hawaiian Islands ... a true snowbird.

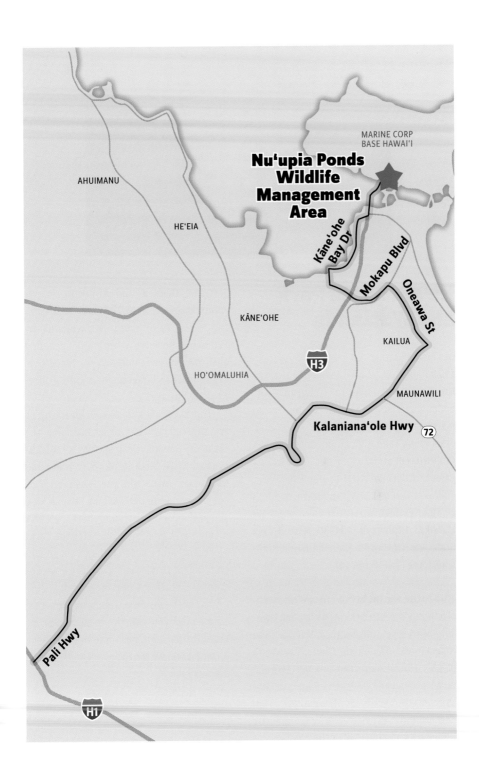

Nu'upia Ponds Wildlife Management Area

MARINE CORP BASE HAWAI'I

AHUIMANU

HE'EIA

Kāne'ohe Bay Dr

Mokapu Blvd

Oneawa St

KĀNE'OHE

KAILUA

H3

HO'OMALUHIA

MAUNAWILI

Kalaniana'ole Hwy 72

Pali Hwy

H1

He'eia State Park and Wetlands

DISTANCE ¼-mile

TIME 1 hour

HIGHLIGHTS Possible rare migrants and endangered Hawaiian waterbirds.

POTENTIAL SPECIES 25

DIRECTIONS Take Ala Wai Boulevard to McCully Street and turn right on McCully Street. Continue to H-1 Freeway West. Follow H-1 W, H-201 W, and H-3 E to HI-63 N. Take exit 9 from H-3 E. Take HI-83 W/Kahekili Highway to HI-830 N to He'eia State Park (46-465 Kamehameha Highway, Kāne'ohe, HI 96744).

This entire area is in the process of extensive habitat restoration that is a partnership of Nature Conservancy, Kako'o 'Oiwi Ko'olaupoko Hawaiian Civic, Papahana Kuaola, Hui Kū Maoli Ola, Paepae O He'eia, State of Hawai'i Division of Aquatic Resources, University of Hawai'i, U.S. Fish and Wildlife Service (USFWS), and the National Oceanic and Atmospheric Administration (NOAA). They are transforming 405 acres of overgrown wetlands by removing invasive vegetation, including the widespread non-native Mangrove. Eight streams converge here into a once-healthy estuary.[1]

This is a great area to look for Hawai'i's endangered wetland birds including the **'Ae'o** or Hawaiian subspecies of **Black-necked Stilt, 'Alae ke'oke'o** or **Hawaiian Coot,** and **'Alae 'ula**, the Hawaiian subspecies of **Common Moorhen.** Several rare species have been found here recently including Hawai'i's second **Elegant Tern.** More migratory shorebird species should be found at this location as more development of suitable habitat is created.

To check this area completely it is recommended you ask the local non-profit organizations for permission and advice on when and where to go. Organized tours are available.

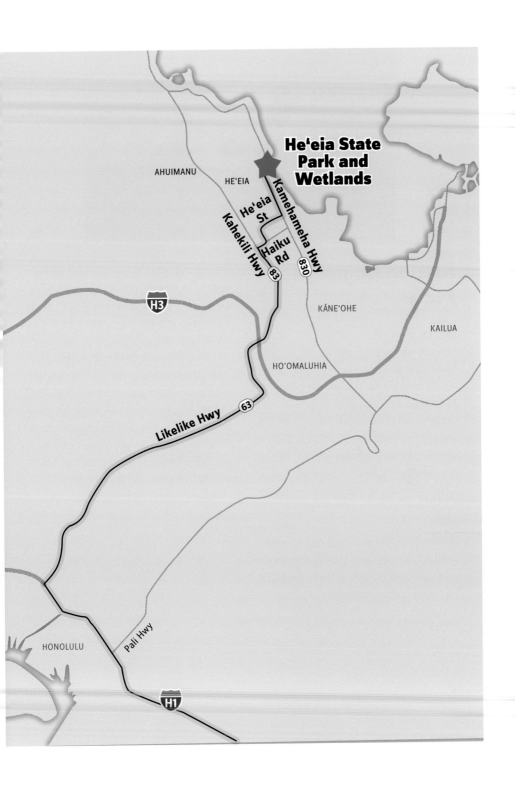

He'eia State Park and Wetlands

AHUIMANU

HE'EIA

He'eia St

Kahekili Hwy

Kamehameha Hwy

Haiku Rd

830

83

H3

KĀNE'OHE

KAILUA

HO'OMALUHIA

Likelike Hwy

63

HONOLULU

Pali Hwy

H1

Kualoa Regional Park

DISTANCE ¼-mile

TIME 30 minutes

HIGHLIGHTS Black-necked Stilt, Ruddy Turnstone, and Pacific Golden Plover.

POTENTIAL SPECIES 50

DIRECTIONS Take the H-1 Freeway west to the Likelike Highway, Route #63. Proceed up the Likelike Highway and go through the Wilson Tunnel. Descend toward Kāneʻohe and exit onto Kahekili Highway, Route #83, going north. Continue along Kahekili Highway; note that the road becomes Kamehameha Highway. Continue until you see the entrance to Kualoa Regional Park on the left. You will see Moko-liʻi Island (Chinaman's Hat).

This is a good location to check on your way to or from the North Shore of Oʻahu. Depending partly on if the grassy areas have been cut you might find large flocks of **Ruddy Turnstones** and significant numbers of **Pacific Golden-Plovers**. This is a staging ground for the plovers and they gather in large numbers here in mid-April before migrating to their Arctic breeding grounds. It is also a good area to search for a variety of introduced species including **Scaly-breasted Munia, Saffron Finch, Chestnut Munia,** and **Java Sparrow.**

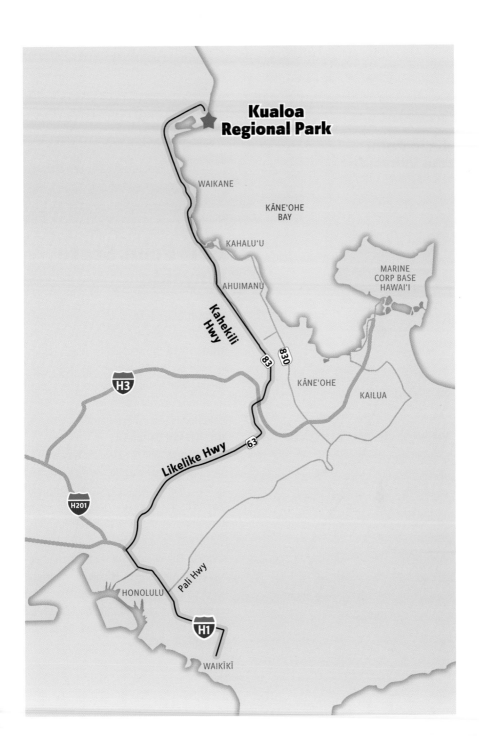

La'ie Point
State Wayside

Lā'ie Point State Wayside

DISTANCE 50 yards

TIME 30 minutes

HIGHLIGHTS Brown Noddy, Black Noddy, Masked Booby, Brown Booby, Red-footed Booby, Wedge-tailed Shearwater, Sooty Tern, and possibly rare migratory seabirds including Black-winged Petrel.

POTENTIAL SPECIES 50

DIRECTIONS Take the H-1 Freeway west to the Likelike Highway, Route #63. Proceed up the Likelike Highway and go through the Wilson Tunnel. Descend toward Kāne'ohe and exit onto Kahekili Highway, Route #83, going north. Continue along Kahekili Highway; note that the road becomes Kamehameha Highway. Continue north to Lā'ie and turn right on Anemoku Street. Turn right on Naupaka Street and proceed to the end of the road. Be careful not to block other cars or driveways.

This is a very scenic location that is ideal for a dawn sea watch. Between January and October, large numbers of **Brown Noddies** pass close to the point if wind conditions are favorable to push the birds close to shore. A good variety of seabird species is possible if you arrive at or before sunrise.

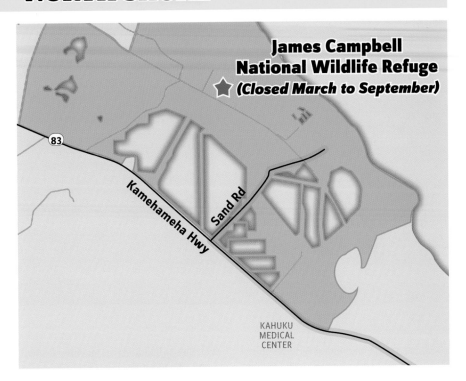

James Campbell
National Wildlife Refuge
★ (Closed March to September)

83

Kamehameha Hwy

Sand Rd

KAHUKU
MEDICAL
CENTER

James Campbell National Wildlife Refuge

DISTANCE ¼-mile

TIME 1 hour

HIGHLIGHTS Endangered wetland bird species. Migratory and resident waterfowl, shorebirds, birds of prey, seagulls, and terns.

POTENTIAL SPECIES 124

DIRECTIONS From Honolulu take H1 west to Highway 63 Likelike Highway then take Highway 83 Kahekili which becomes Kamehameha Highway. Turn right on Sand Road just after passing Kahuku.

NOTES Wear sunscreen and hat. Please check if open before visiting.

James Campbell National Wildlife Refuge is currently open to the public for guided tours every Saturday at 9:00 AM during October to February. The rest of the year it is closed. It is hoped a planned visitor center and additional access trails will be developed soon. Oʻahu is the most populated and visited island in Hawaiʻi and it would be great if the national wildlife refuges on Oʻahu had the same visitor opportunities as the refuges at Kīlauea Point on Kauaʻi and Kealia Pond on Maui.

James Campbell National Wildlife Refuge is the premier wetland bird watching location on the Oʻahu. The 240-acre refuge was created in 1976 to provide habitat for endangered Hawaiian water birds. In

2005, the refuge expanded with the purchase of 1,100 acres, including the shrimp ponds, to be used for providing additional habitat for endangered water birds, migratory waterfowl, shorebirds, seabirds, native plant species, the endangered 'lioholo-i-ka-uaua (Hawaiian monk seal), and threatened honu (Hawaiian green turtle).

More bird species have been observed on the refuge than any other location on O'ahu. Waterfowl species seen almost every year include **Canada Geese, Eurasian Wigeon, American Wigeon, Green-winged Teal, Ring-necked Duck,** and **Bufflehead**. Rare vagrant waterfowl species observed here include **Greater White-fronted Goose, Snow Goose, Brant, Gadwall, Garganey, Redhead, Canvasback, Hooded Merganser, Pied-billed Grebe,** and **Eared Grebe**.

Rare shorebirds seen on the refuge have included **Spotted Sandpiper, Whim-** brel, **Bar-tailed Godwit, Marbled Godwit, Red Knot, Semipalmated Sandpiper,** and **Short-billed Dowitcher.** Extremely rare birds in Hawai'i that could be found in this area in the future include **Tundra Swan, Red-necked Phalarope,** and **Common Snipe.**

Several rare birds of prey have also been observed on the refuge. These include **Peregrine Falcon, Osprey,** and **Northern Harrier.** A **Great Blue Heron** was recorded at James Campbell NWR in 2006 and a **White-faced Ibis** in 2009. Seagulls are very rare in Hawai'i and do not breed in the state but every year a handful of gulls arrive in Hawai'i. The refuge is a great place to look for vagrant gulls. The **Laughing Gull** is the most likely species to be seen followed by **Franklin's Gull, Bonaparte's Gull,** and **Ring-billed Gull.** The ponds and marshy areas are attractive to a variety of terns that have included **Common Tern,**

Black Tern, and **Least Tern**. The **Red Ava-davat**, a beautiful introduced bird from Asia, feeds on grass seed in the area.

On September 19, 2006, I discovered a **White-rumped Sandpiper** feeding in the mud of a drained shrimp pond on land that is now part of the refuge. This amazing bird was supposed to be spending the winter in South America after leaving its breeding areas in Northern Canada but somehow wandered for thousands of miles off course. In birding terms this is called vagrancy and every fall and spring birdwatchers all over the planet watch for any rare species that might arrive in their local area. I will never forget that special day when the rare bird I found was added to the list of Hawaiian bird species.

Turtle Bay Resort to Kahuku Point Walk

DISTANCE 7 miles roundtrip
TIME 4 to 5 hours
HIGHLIGHTS Native plants, Bristle-thigh-ed Curlew, Hawaiian Monk Seal, Green Sea Turtle, excellent coastal scenery.
POTENTIAL SPECIES 70

DIRECTIONS From Honolulu take H1 west to Highway 63 Likelike Highway then take Highway 83 Kahekilli which becomes Kamehameha Highway. Turn right on Kuilima Drive and proceed to the public parking beach access area.
NOTES Leave no valuables in car; start early in morning. Please do not walk on native plants. Maintain adequate distance from both Monk Seals and Green Sea Turtles. Wear sunscreen and hat. Do not trespass on private land above high tide mark. Keep dogs on a leash.

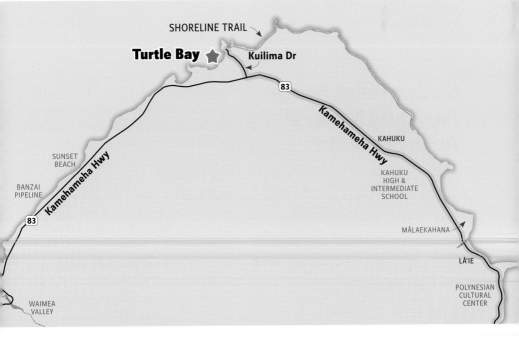

Walking this section of Oʻahu coastline is a great way to enjoy nature on the island. It has everything; spectacular scenery, resting Hawaiian Monk Seals and Green Sea Turtles, beautiful native coastal plants and birds and a feeling of wildness that is difficult to find on Oʻahu. It is best to park at the beach access parking lot at the Turtle Bay Resort and walk north as far as the Kahuku Golf Course and then walk back or have someone pick you up and drive back. Please be sure to use only the public beach access trails in this area. Several areas require crossing shallow water ways so be prepared with proper shoes, etc.

After leaving Turtle Bay, look for endangered Hawaiian Monk Seals on the beach. Please be sure to stay away from them so they can get the rest they need. At Kahuku Point look for several species of native coastal plants. Migratory shorebirds that forage along this coast include the **Wandering Tattler, Sanderling,** and **Ruddy Turnstone.** Look for these species between August and April. Sometimes the **Great Frigatebird, Masked Booby, Black-footed** and **Laysan Albatross** can also be seen.

Watch for **Ring-necked Pheasants** in the pasture areas inland from the shoreline. The best find for birdwatchers along this coast is seeing the rare **Kioea** or **Bristle-thighed Curlew.** The wintering flock on Oʻahu varies in number from year to year but averages around fifty birds. Most of these are found around the ponds at James Campbell NWR but a few visit the tidepools and beaches along this wild coast. These amazing birds fly round trip from the Yukon to Oʻahu every year.

Kaʻena Point State Park and Natural Area Preserve

DISTANCE 6 miles roundtrip

TIME Minimum 3 to 4 hours

HIGHLIGHTS Laysan Albatross (November to July), Humpback Whales (November to April) , Monk Seals, Native plants, excellent coastal scenery.

POTENTIAL SPECIES 73

DIRECTIONS Take H-2 to Kaukonahua Road (Route 803) to Farrington Highway (Route 930) pass Waialua and go about one mile past Camp Erdman. The trailhead to Kaʻena Point begins where the paved road ends and a rough four-wheel drive road begins.

NOTES Bring plenty of water, leave no valuables in car, start early in morning. Do not disturb birds or leave trails inside Natural Area Reserve, please clean footwear before hike and before entering Natural Area Reserve, best to leave dogs at home. Bring cellular phone and sunscreen.

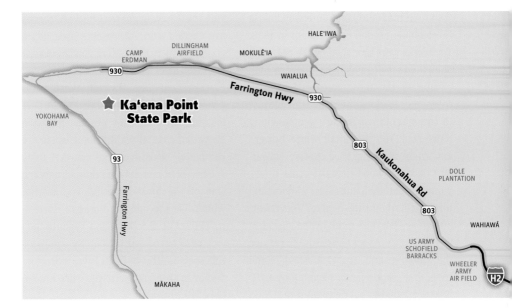

Ka'ena Point State Park and the Natural Area Reserve at the very tip of the point are some of the best places to experience nature on O'ahu. The narrow strip of land and shore line that lies just below the towering cliffs of the ancient Waianae volcano is one of the islands' most rugged and best-preserved coastal areas. It is also an excellent location to see conservation in action.

The trail begins at the parking area where the road ends. You will see many large black lava rocks. Be sure to leave nothing of value in the car and leave nothing on the seats, etc. that might be perceived as valuables.

The trail is a dirt road that is used by 4WDR vehicles but do not drive a non-4WDR on this road. If you have a 4WDR be very careful if it has rained since many 4WDR vehicles get stuck. There are several trails/roads in the area. The main one is the dirt road which is inland from and parallel to the coast. Some minor trails/roads that spur off the main road will take you closer to the ocean.

In the Hawaiian language, Ka'ena means "the heat" and is a reference to either a brother or cousin of Pele the Hawaiian volcano goddess. Several archaeological sites have been discovered in the area. This location is considered very sacred to the Hawaiian people because they believe the large rock near the end of the point is the where their souls departing-place, leina-a-ka-uhane, or leap of the soul is situated.

Just offshore of the very end of the point is a rock called Pohaku O Kaua'i, which according to tradition was once a part of Kaua'i. The boulder was brought to O'ahu when Māui, the Hawaiian superhero demigod, attempted to bring Kaua'i closer to O'ahu. Māui used his supernatural hook "Mana'ia-ka-lani" to snag Kaua'i and pull it closer to O'ahu. During this effort, a part of Kaua'i—Pohaku O Kaua'i—suddenly broke-off and catapulted to the tip of Ka'ena Point. This is the extreme western most place on O'ahu.

For many years livestock was grazed along in this area. Walter Dillingham's

O'ahu Railroad and Land Company built a railroad line around Ka'ena point in 1898. The tracks were damaged by the 1946 tsunamis and service ended the following year.

One of the most conspicuous small trees you see along the road/trail (closest to the mountains) is the sweet-smelling Naio. Look for the small white flowers and enjoy the fragrance. Native Hawaiians used the wood to make house posts, gunwales for their outrigger canoes and torches for night time fishing. This tree is known as "bastard sandalwood" because it was used as a poor substitute to replace the valuable and aromatic sandalwood trees that were quickly depleted by 1840 in Hawai'i due to over exploitation. Naio wood was occasionally sent to the Chinese merchants instead of sandalwood but they rejected this species.

While walking to and from the point between November and April it is a good idea to stop occasionally to look for Humpback whales. Sometimes you might see them spouting, tail or fin flapping or the most spectacular of all: a breach. Adults can weigh 80,000 pounds and are over fifty feet long and they make a huge splash! Watch for small, grouse-size brown birds feeding near the brush or perhaps in the open. Most likely these are **Gray Francolin** which are native to the Middle East and India. They were first recorded on O'ahu in 1980. Two other game bird species, the **Erckel's Francolin** and the **Black Francolin,** have been observed at Ka'ena but are less common.

As you approach the end of the State Park you will see a sign and large boulders which is the entrance to the Natural Area Reserve. Here you will find the recently constructed predator-proof fence that includes two double door entry gates. Be sure to clean your shoes so no weedy seeds are carried into the reserve area. It's a good idea to do this before you begin your walk and also here.

Once you pass through these gates you have entered the reserve and the best location on O'ahu for observing native Hawaiian coastal plants. Some areas are completely weed-free and you can enjoy the perfection of nature's floral creations. One of the most beautiful is the Ohai which has stunning red-orange flowers. In 2003, the U.S. Fish and Wildlife Service designated critical habitat areas for this species after only fifty-five individual plants in three occurrences were known to be left on O'ahu.

If you visit between November and July, you most likely will see the magnificent **Laysan Albatross,** or **Moli** in Hawaiian, flying very close as they glide effortlessly on huge wings. This is the only accessible Laysan Albatross colony on O'ahu. These incredible birds can live to be over sixty-five years old and sometimes fly thousands of miles to Alaska from Ka'ena Point in order to bring food back to their growing chicks.

Special predator-proof entry gate.

The work being done at Ka'ena Point is one of O'ahu's best examples of conservation to save and restore Hawai'i's native flora and fauna. The 2,000-foot fence protects fifty-nine acres of land and was completed in March 2011. In 2006, dogs killed twenty-one **Wedge-tailed Shearwater** or **'Ua'u kani** chicks in a single night at Ka'ena Point. One evening in 2007, more than 125 native seabirds were killed, most likely by one or more dogs. Rats kill and eat nestling chick and also eat seeds of native plants, preventing the growth and spread of new plants.

Once the fence was finished intensive efforts began to remove predatory animals from the reserve by using traps for larger animals and bait boxes for rodents. In 2018, 106 pairs of Laysan Albatross were present compared to zero pairs in 1989. The **Wedge-tailed Shearwaters** at Ka'ena Point are also starting to increase as are the native plants.

Brown Boobies can be seen along this coast and Ka'ena Point is one of the best places on O'ahu to see the introduced **Northern Mockingbird.** Watch for the elegant **White-tailed Tropicbird** or **Koa'e kea** riding the warm air thermals above the cliffs. These graceful flyers are rare on O'ahu and are the smallest of the world's three tropicbird species.

On December 27, 2009 a **Glaucous-winged Gull** was photographed in the area. This was one of only ninty-six recorded sightings of this species in the southern Hawaiian islands ever recorded. An even rarer species, a **Black-legged Kittiwake** with only five historical records in Hawai'i was reported in the vicinity of Ka'ena Point on February 11, 2012. Seagulls do not breed in the islands and are considered rare.

Brown Booby.

Pearl Harbor National Wildlife Refuge

DISTANCE 100 yards

TIME 30 minutes

HIGHLIGHTS Migratory waterfowl and shorebirds, rare vagrants, and resident Mourning Doves.

POTENTIAL SPECIES 98

DIRECTIONS From downtown Honolulu take the H-1 Freeway west. After Pearl City, the freeway forks, as the H-2 goes north. From the Pearl City fork, remain on the H-1 for another four miles, then exit onto Fort Weaver Road southbound. About a mile down this road, turn left onto Laulaunui Street. Take the second right onto Kapapapuhi Street, and go 0.3 miles to its dead-end, which is a small parking area for Kapapapuhi Point Park. The Bet-

ty Bliss Observation Deck is a half-mile walk south of this parking area.

The closest spot to the ponds where streetside parking is usually available is Haiea Place in West Loch Estates. To reach this spot from the H-1, exit onto Fort Weaver Road southbound, as above, but do not turn onto Laulaunui Street. Instead, continue an additional three-quarters of a mile and turn left onto A'awa Drive. After a half-mile, turn left onto Hamana Street. The take the second left onto Aipo'ola Street, then the first right onto Haiea Place. The cul-de-sac gives access to a paved bike path, where it is a 300-yard walk north to the observation deck. Parking on the cul-de-sac itself is prohibited, but otherwise streetside parking is generally allowed. Please be respectful of the residents by walking to and from the refuge quietly and do not block any driveways.

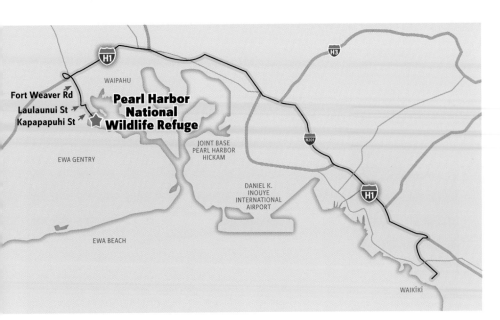

This is the second most important birding location on Oʻahu after the James Campbell National Wildlife Refuge. Unfortunately, both the thirty-six-acre Honouliuli and the twenty-five-acre Waiawa units are closed to the public. Hopefully, someday both refuges will have visitor centers and be open to birdwatchers and everyone interested in nature. An overlook was constructed at Honouliuli in 2016 that provides limited views of a portion of the refuge. Tall vegetation along the fence line blocks closer views of the ponds from the dirt access road.

Many extremely rare bird species for Hawaiʻi have been found at Honouliuli including **Merlin, Slaty-backed Gull, Short-billed Gull, Little Stint, Gull-billed Tern,** and **Common Snipe.**

This refuge is also the most reliable location on Oʻahu to find **Mourning Doves.** During fall migration it is a great place to check for a good assortment of waterfowl and shorebird species.

Pouhala Marsh Wildlife Sanctuary

DISTANCE 100 yards

TIME 30 minutes

HIGHLIGHTS Resident populations of **Black-necked Stilts**, **Hawaiian Coot**, and **Common Gallinule**. During fall migration this is a good place to check for rare or uncommon migratory waterfowl and shorebird species.

POTENTIAL SPECIES 75

DIRECTIONS Exit the H-1 in Pearl City, immediately before the freeway forks. Take Exit 8-B toward Waipahu. The exit ramp merges into the Farrington Highway westbound. Remain on Farrington Highway for 1.5 miles, then turn left onto Waipahu Depot Street. Streetside parking is generally available about a quarter-mile south, where this street crosses the Pearl Harbor Bike Path. Please be sure to pull off the road completely. Viewing birds is only possible from the road as this state waterbirds refuge is also closed to the public.

Pouhala Marsh is an important eighty-four-acre tidal wetland to check before or after your visit to Honouliuli. Many of the birds travel between these two wetland areas. Pouhala Marsh is a mostly seasonal wetland that is highly affected by rainfall. After winter storms, the water levels might be too high for shorebirds but still good for waterfowl. During the summer most of the wetland dries up. Several very rare species in Hawai'i have been found at this location including **Marsh Sandpiper, Curlew Sandpiper, Red Knot,** and **Short-billed Dowitcher.**

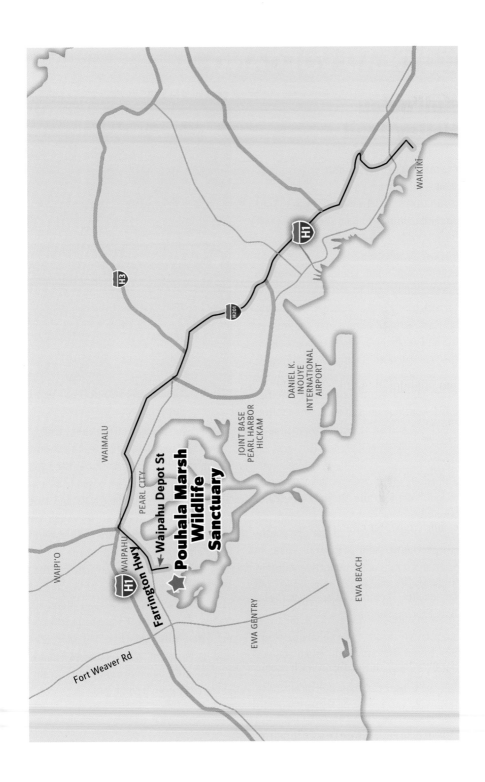

KOʻOLAU VOLCANO

Kuliʻouʻou Valley Trail

DISTANCE 2.8 miles roundtrip

TIME 1.5 to 2 hours

HIGHLIGHTS Oʻahu ʻElepaio, Oʻahu ʻAmakihi, White-rumped Shama, Japanese Bush-Warbler, Red-billed Leothrix

POTENTIAL SPECIES 20

DIRECTIONS From Waikīkī proceed on Ala Wai Boulevard to McCully Street and turn right on McCully Street. Turn right on Kapiʻolani Boulevard and continue to the H1 East freeway onramp. Continue on the freeway until Kalanianaʻole Highway. Proceed east on Kalanianaʻole Highway. After 3.8 miles turn left onto Kuliʻouʻou Road. Continue on Kuliʻouʻou Road to Kalaʻau Place and turn right . Drive to the end of the cul-de-sac and park.

Kuliʻouʻou Valley Trail is a good choice to look for the **Oʻahu ʻElepaio and Oʻahu ʻAmakihi.**

The trail is located in the dry southeast section of Oʻahu, so the trail is usually drier and less muddy than the mountain trails. You can drive to the parking area where the trail begins in twenty-five to thirty minutes from Waikīkī. After parking proceed through the yellow gate and stay to the left. Stay right when you see the Na Ala Hele trail sign. At 0.1 mile you will see a sign that has Kuliʻouʻou Ridge Trail right and Kuliʻouʻou Valley Trail left.

Stay left and proceed on the Valley trail.

A small population of Oʻahu ʻElepaio live in this valley and with patience you might find several birds, possibly a family group. Listen for their calls and stop frequently along the trail to watch for movement in the trees around you. Both the Oʻahu ʻAmakihi and **ʻApapane** are occasionally observed in the valley but they are found easier on some of the higher elevation trails in the Koʻolau Mountain Range. This is a great place to see the colorful **Red-billed Leiothrix** and to observe and listen to the **White-rumped Shama**. You will see a sign that says, "End of Trail!" at the turn around point.

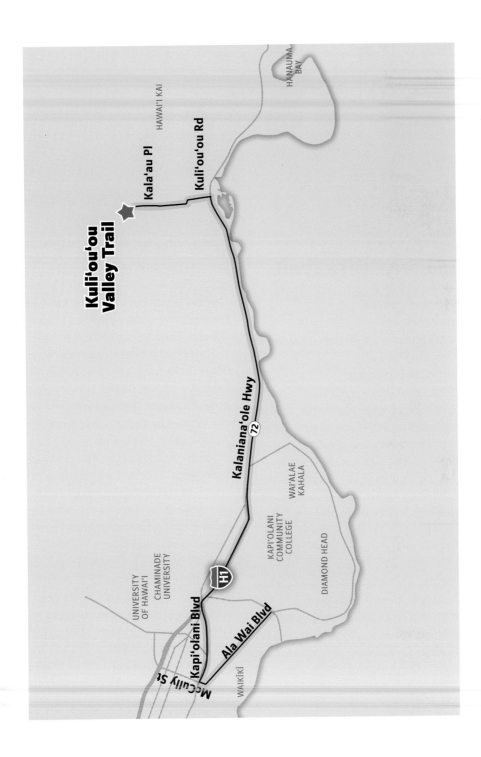

Mānoa Cliffs Trail

DISTANCE 2.8 miles

TIME 2 hours

HIGHLIGHTS Oʻahu ʻAmakihi, ʻApapane, and great views

POTENTIAL SPECIES 40

DIRECTIONS Drive on Ala Wai Boulevard. Turn right on Kalākaua Avenue. Proceed north to King Street and turn right. Then turn left on Punahou Street. Continue on Punahou then turn left on Nehoa Street. Turn right on Makiki Heights Drive. Then proceed on Round Top Drive all the way to the small dirt parking area across from the Mānoa Cliffs Trail entrance. Do not leave any valuables in your vehicle.

The trail begins in an introduced swamp mahogany forest. Near the top of the steps, you reach a strawberry guava section that is often muddy. After another fifty yards the trail descends, and you have a spectacular view of Mānoa Valley. Be careful in this section due to slippery conditions. The trail contours the cliffs above Mānoa Valley, and around Tantalus Crater to Pauoa Valley. Look for several waterfalls in the back of the valley on rainy days.

Perhaps the most beautiful native tree on this trail is the Oʻahu endemic hibiscus Kokiʻo keʻokeʻo. Watch for **Oʻahu ʻAmakihi** feeding on the nectar by piercing a hole in the stem. These trees grow from fifteen to thirty feet tall and have spectacular white flowers with pink or red staminal columns. The Mānoa Cliff trail is a good place to view **ʻApapane**. If you see any of the exotic Octopus or Umbrella tree flowering, wait and watch for the birds to visit.

As you walk farther on the trail, eventually you will find a bench. This is an excellent place to rest and enjoy the tremendous views of the upper Mānoa Valley. Far below is Lyon Arboretum operated by the University of Hawaiʻi.

Continuing further you will reach the entry gate of the Mānoa Cliff Restoration Area. This is a great place to see how a small area of native forest is being restored through the efforts of dedicated volunteers and the state of Hawaiʻi. The project began in 2005, and a fence to keep out feral pigs was constructed around six acres of the site in 2009.

In this sanctuary you can see several species of lobelias including *Clermontia kakeana* and *Cyanea angustifolia*. These plants are the most

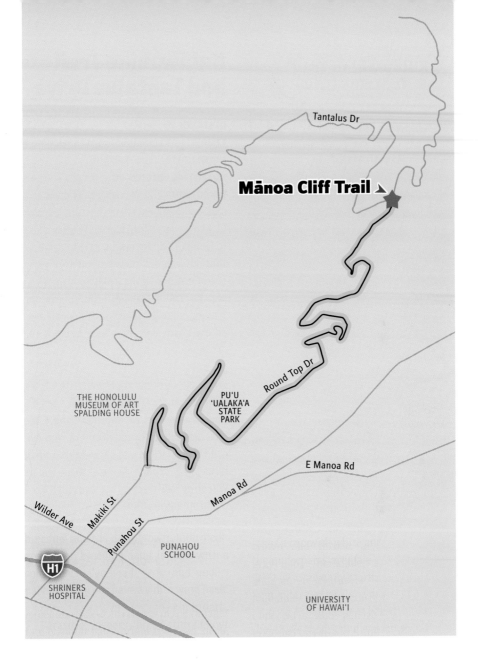

Tantalus Dr

Mānoa Cliff Trail ⏶

Round Top Dr

THE HONOLULU
MUSEUM OF ART
SPALDING HOUSE

PUʻU
ʻUALAKAʻA
STATE
PARK

E Manoa Rd

Manoa Rd

Wilder Ave

Makiki St

Punahou St

PUNAHOU
SCHOOL

H1

SHRINERS
HOSPITAL

UNIVERSITY
OF HAWAIʻI

accessible in the Honolulu area. Clermontia are branched shrubs or small trees, up to twenty feet tall, with fleshy fruits. Cyanea is the largest and most diverse group of Hawaiian lobelias with more than seventy species. Many of them are now extinct.

This trail intersects two other trails.

The first intersection is the Puʻu ʻŌhiʻa Trail on the left. The second intersection is the Pauoa Flats Trail on the right. It is best to turn around and walk back the same way rather than continuing unless you know the trail system well. Unfortunately, many hikers have become lost in this area.

Kalāwahine Trail and Tantalus Drive

Kalāwahine Trail & Tantalus Drive

DISTANCE 25 feet
TIME 30 to 45 minutes
HIGHLIGHTS Oʻahu ʻAmakihi
POTENTIAL SPECIES 40
DIRECTIONS This is a very easy drive to a location that is excellent for Oʻahu ʻAmakihi and several introduced species close to Honolulu and Waikīkī. As you drive up Tantalus you will pass a number of turnouts. Continue on the windy road until you see the trail entrance to the Kalāwahine Trail on your left. Park in the small area on the right. Be careful not to block the driveway.

From the parking area, watch the trees around you for **Oʻahu ʻAmakihi.** Pay particular attention to any flowering trees including Hibiscus and Scefflera. You will need to be patient and check all the small birds flying around. Some of these will be **Warbling White-eyes** but eventually the Oʻahu ʻAmakihi will arrive.

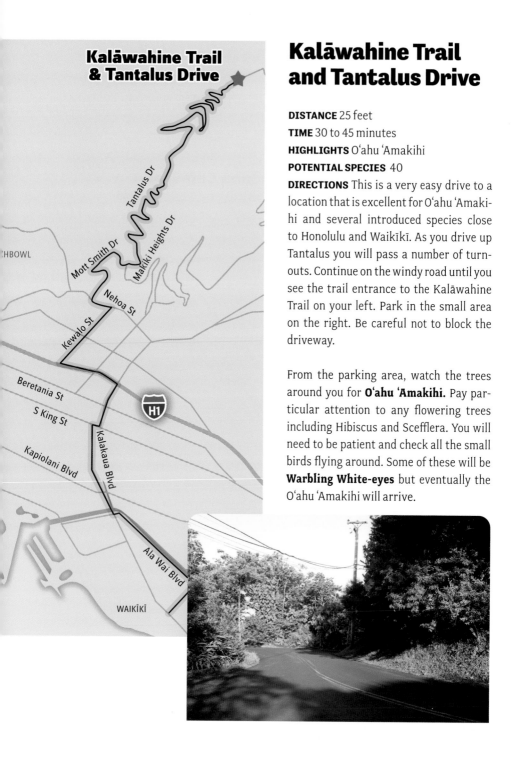

'Aiea Loop and Ridge Trail

DISTANCE 5 miles round trip

TIME Minimum 3 to 4 hours

HIGHLIGHTS O'ahu 'Amakihi, O'ahu 'Elepaio, 'Apapane, Marianas Swiftlet, Sandalwood, remnant native forest, mountain scenery, and Hawaiian Heiau.

POTENTIAL SPECIES 37

DIRECTIONS Follow H-1 to Moanalua Highway (Highway 78). Take the 'Aiea cutoff to the third traffic light, make a right turn at 'Aiea Heights Drive and follow it about 3 miles up to the end of the road. After you drive through the gate continue forward and then stay right at the fork. Continue to the top of the road where you will see the parking lot for the 'Aiea Trail.

NOTES Bring plenty of water, leave no valuables in car, start early in morning, bring cellular phone, and sunscreen. Be careful on the slippery, wet, and muddy trail that has exposed roots in some areas.

The 'Aiea Loop Trail is located in a forested area high above Pearl Harbor. From several lookout points you can see the southern coastline of O'ahu and the Wai'anae Range. This area was replanted by foresters in the late 1920s after uncontrolled grazing by cattle and goats destroyed almost all of the native vegetation. Eucalyptus, Strawberry Guava, and stands of Norfolk Island pine trees are common along the entire trail. You can walk the 4.8-mile loop or turn around at the half way point where a short spur trail leads to an overlook of the H-3 freeway and Hālawa Valley. Experienced hikers can walk up the 'Aiea Ridge trail which has the best remaining native forest in the area and offers great opportunities to see native birds.

'Apapane.

As you walk up the path you occasionally will see the surviving, endemic Acacia Koa trees. This species is the second most common tree in the native forest. Koa means brave, bold, fearless warrior in Hawaiian. They have sickle shaped phyllodes which are not leaves but flattened stems. The true leaves are very small and the flowers are pale yellow. Hawaiians used Koa to make surfboards and outrigger canoes. Today the valuable wood is used to make bowls, boxes, cabinets, and counter tops. Hawai'i's only endemic butterfly species, Kamehameha butterfly and Blackburn's little blue butterfly both use sap of the Koa for

O'ahu 'Amahiki.

food and the endemic Koa bugs eat the seeds.

The most common native tree is the 'ōhi'a lehua. Look for the bright red flowers. The **'Apapane** and **O'ahu 'Amakihi** will visit the flowers when they are producing nectar. If you find the honeycreepers in a particular tree you can wait for them to return again to get more nectar every twenty to thirty minutes. Be careful you don't confuse the abundant alien Japanese White-eye for the similar looking 'Amakihi. Hawaiians used the wood to make idols, weapons, tool handles, and boards for making poi. These trees have very tiny seeds and are wind dispersed.

Look for the small red berries of the Pūkiawe along the mid-section of the trail. This species is indigenous to Hawai'i and the Marquesas Islands. A few remnant 'Iliahi or Sandalwood trees also occur on the 'Aiea Loop Trail. Notice the drooping leaves and very small reddish-yellow flowers. Hawaiians used various parts of the trees for medicine, perfume, firewood and musical instruments. Great quantities of Sandalwood trees were cut down on O'ahu and the other Hawaiian islands and sent to China from 1791 to 1839. In Asia the dried heartwood was used to make idols and sacred utensils for shrines, carvings, boxes, and incense. By 1840 most of the easily accessible Sandalwood had been removed and the industry collapsed.

Several hundred years ago many extinct species of endemic Hawaiian birds, including the **'Ō'ū, O'ahu 'Akialoa, O'ahu Nukupu'u, O'ahu 'Ākepa,** and **O'ahu 'Ō'ō** and others, would have been present in the trees along this trail but today only old field notes and fading museum skins remain as witness to their former existence.

Two other bird species have been observed on O'ahu in recent years and could be found on the 'Aiea trail and surrounding areas with exceptionally luck. One is extremely rare and the other most likely extinct. **'I'iwi** have been sighted in the Wai'anae range in 2008, 2009, and 2013 and a small population of six birds were documented in the northern Ko'olau range in 1996. The **O'ahu 'Alauahio** or Creeper last well-documented sighting was of two birds in 1985 not far from the 'Aiea trail.

Sadly, most of O'ahu's endemic forest birds have been devastated. The few species that have survived this avian catastrophe cling to a precarious existence in forests that are declining. One of the best places to look for the O'ahu 'Amakihi, 'Apapane, and the endangered **O'ahu 'Elepaio** is on the 'Aiea Trail. The 'Amakihi and 'Apapane are survivors partly because they have adapted to feeding on introduced species including *Lantana camara, Schefflera actinophylla*, many Eucalyptus species, and others. The island wide populations of the only remaining honeycreepers on O'ahu are unknown due to a lack of recent surveys. The O'ahu 'Elepaio is an endangered species and fewer than 1,200 birds remain. Their numbers have plummeted because of avian diseases, predation, loss of habitat, and competition with introduced birds.

One other bird to watch for on the 'Aiea Loop Trail is the rare **Mariana Swiftlet**. In May 1962, 125 to 175 birds were introduced from Guam into a valley in southeast O'ahu. Seven years later a population was documented in North Hālawa Valley. In 1978 their nesting site was discovered in the same valley. In 2000, forty-nine active nests were counted. The swiftlets are very fast and most of the observations last only a few seconds as the birds race by. Look for this endangered species where you have good vantage places along the trail with a lot of open sky. Several other rare introduced birds have been seen on the 'Aiea trail. The **Melodious Laughingthrush** or **Hwamei** is native to China and was introduced to Hawai'i sometime before 1900. They are very secretive and are rarely seen. The **Yellow-faced Grassquit** has occurred in this area in the past but is extremely rare today.

Mariana Swiftlet.

The Keaīwa Heiau was used by kāhuna lapa'au, highly regarded ancient practitioners, who used plants to cure illnesses. Many of the species used in traditional herbal medicines still grow in the area. It was built in the 16th century by Kakuhihewa, an ali'i or chief of O'ahu. The rock walled heiau or temple is four feet tall, 100 feet wide and 160 feet long.

PELAGIC

Offshore Honolulu

DISTANCE 40 to 50 miles

TIME 6 to 8 hours

HIGHLIGHTS Spectacular coastal scenery from offshore perspective. Migratory and resident seabirds. Marine mammals including whales, dolphins, and sharks occasionally.

POTENTIAL SPECIES 30

DIRECTIONS Most boats leave from the Kewalo Basin boat Harbor next to Ala Moana Beach Park on Ala Moana Boulevard.

NOTES Wear sunscreen and hat. Have medicine for sea sickness if needed.

In order to escape the frustrations caused by all of the closed and restricted access refuges, preserves, and other areas on Oʻahu, there is nothing better than a exhilarating six to eight hour boat trip twenty-five miles offshore of Oʻahu. No fences, no trespassing or closed signs, no barbed wire just the wild, open and inviting ocean. Traveling at dawn toward the distant, glowing horizon searching for rare seabirds and marine mammals is a great experience you should definitely try.

On many days after reaching the twenty-mile mark Oʻahu is barely visible. The far-off Waiʻanae and Koʻolau volcanoes' shield shape becomes more apparent from this long-distance vantage point. Using your imagination, you can visualize what Captain Cook observed just after daybreak on January 18, 1778 when he discovered Oʻahu for the outside world.

Many species of migrating seabirds fly every year from their breeding colonies in the southern hemisphere across the equator all the way to the waters off the western United States, Alaska, and Siberia. These epic journeys usually begin in March with April being the highpoint. After spending late Spring and Summer in their northern feeding grounds, the birds fly rapidly thousands of miles back home in the Fall. Details about the precise timing of their movements and their migration routes are still being learned. Every time you venture offshore searching for these rare and unusual species is a opportunity to discover something new and to contribute as citizen scientists toward a better understanding of these birds' uncharted pathways. For the most part, they are deep ocean wanderers and only rarely fly close to the coastline of Oʻahu.

Red-tailed Tropicbird

One of the most impressive groups of birds to be found on a pelagic trip off Honolulu are the graceful and agile petrels. Species that occasionally are observed include the mid-sized, trans-equatorial migrating **Mottled, Black-winged, Cook's,** and **Stejneger's Petrels**. They feed on food items picked from the surface but when flying by the Hawaiian Islands they are usually going very fast without stopping.

The larger **Hawaiian petrels** are residents and nest on Kauaʻi, Molokaʻi, Maui, Lānaʻi and Hawaiʻi. This endangered species has been recorded off Oʻahu occasionally. Another state breeding bird is the small **Bulwer's Petrel** which nests on Oʻahu but is rarely seen close to shore. The very rare **Kermadec Petrel** has only been seen once in the Oʻahu's offshore waters.

Several species of diminutive **Storm Petrels** including **Leach's** and **Band-rumped** can be encountered during a day trip off Oʻahu but sightings are rare. On April 21, 2013, an astonishing thirty-five

storm-petrels were recorded between ten to twenty-five miles offshore of Waikīkī during a unusually calm day when the Kona winds were less than five knots and the ocean surface was smooth as glass.

Sooty Shearwaters, Pomarine Jaegers, Red Phalaropes, Red-tailed Tropicbird, and the very rare **Red-billed Tropicbird** in addition to many resident seabird species can all be found on these exciting trips. Every so often flying fish will break the surface or a group of Short-finned Pilot whales will be sighted. One of the most thrilling experiences is encountering a pod of performing Spinner Dolphins who seem to thoroughly enjoy riding the bow wave and showing off their incredible swimming abilities. Altogether forty different species of seabirds have been observed in the waters surrounding Oʻahu so these are great places to go if you want to enjoy nature at its best while visiting or living on the island.

Pomarine Jaegers

Leach's Storm-Petrel

Sooty Tern

O'AHU SPECIES OFFICIAL CHECKLIST

Displayed in taxonomic order

R - **Resident** (Endemic or Indigenous; see acount for status)

N - **Naturalized** (non-native) **resident** (established and breeding)

n - **Naturalized** (non-native) **visitor** (from another island or island group)

B - **Breeding visitor** (occurs seasonally and breeds)

M - **Migrant** through the islands (some may winter) or non-breeding visitor (often seabirds)

W - **Winter visitor** (some may migrate through the islands or breed occasionally)

V - **Vagrant** (visitor that does not occur regularly)

X - **Extinct** or almost certainly Extinct

x - **Extirpated** from that island or island group (Resident or Naturalized populations)

	Greater White-fronted Goose	**V**		Garganey	**V**
	Emperor Goose	**V**		Green-winged Teal	**W**
	Snow Goose	**V**		Canvasback	**V**
	Brant	**V**		Redhead	**V**
	Cackling Goose	**W**		Ring-necked Duck	**W**
	Canada Goose	**V**		Tufted Duck	**V**
	Hawaiian Goose	**R**		Greater Scaup	**W**
	Gadwall	**W**		Lesser Scaup	**W**
	Eurasian Wigeon	**W**		Surf Scoter	**V**
	American Wigeon	**W**		Long-tailed Duck	**V**
	Mallard	**W**		Bufflehead	**W**
	Hawaiian Duck	**R**		Common Goldeneye	**V**
	Blue-winged Teal	**W**		Hooded Merganser	**V**
	Cinnamon Teal	**V**		Common Merganser	**V**
	Northern Shoveler	**W**		Red-breasted Merganser	**V**
	Northern Pintail	**W**		Ruddy Duck	**V**

Chukar	**N**	
Gray Francolin	**N**	
Black Francolin	**N**	
Erckel's Francolin	**N**	
Japanese Quail	**N**	
Red Junglefowl	**x**	
Kalij Pheasant	**N**	
Ring-necked Pheasant	**N**	
Indian Peafowl	**N**	
Wild Turkey	**N**	
Pacific Loon	**V**	
Pied-billed Grebe	**W**	
Eared Grebe	**V**	
Laysan Albatross	**B**	
Black-footed Albatross	**B**	
Northern Fulmar	**W**	
Kermadec Petrel	**M**	
Murphy's Petrel	**M**	
Mottled Petrel	**M**	
Juan Fernandez Petrel	**M**	
Hawaiian Petrel	**M**	
White-necked Petrel	**M**	
Bonin Petrel	**M**	
Black-winged Petrel	**M**	
Cook's Petrel	**M**	
Stejneger's Petrel	**M**	
Bulwer's Petrel	**B**	
Wedge-tailed Shearwater	**B**	
Buller's Shearwater	**M**	
Sooty Shearwater	**M**	
Christmas Shearwater	**B**	
Newell's Shearwater	**M**	
Leach's Storm-Petrel	**W**	

Band-rumped Storm-Petrel	**M**
Tristram's Storm-Petrel	**B**
White-tailed Tropicbird	**B**
Red-billed Tropicbird	**V**
Red-tailed Tropicbird	**B**
Great Frigatebird	**B**
Lesser Frigatebird	**V**
Masked Booby	**B**
Nazca Booby	**V**
Brown Booby	**B**
Red-footed Booby	**B**
American Bittern	**V**
Great Blue Heron	**V**
Great Egret	**V**
Snowy Egret	**V**
Little Blue Heron	**V**
Cattle Egret	**N**
Green Heron	**V**
Black-crowned Night-Heron	**R**
White-faced Ibis	**V**
Osprey	**W**
Northern Harrier	**V**
Sora	**V**
Common Gallinule	**R**
Hawaiian Coot	**R**
Sandhill Crane	**V**
Black-necked Stilt	**R**
Black-bellied Plover	**W**
Pacific Golden-Plover	**W**
Semipalmated Plover	**W**
Killdeer	**V**
Terek Sandpiper	**V**
Spotted Sandpiper	**V**

Solitary Sandpiper	**V**	
Gray-tailed Tattler	**V**	
Wandering Tattler	**W**	
Greater Yellowlegs	**V**	
Willet	**V**	
Lesser Yellowlegs	**M**	
Marsh Sandpiper	**V**	
Whimbrel	**W**	
Bristle-thighed Curlew	**W**	
Black-tailed Godwit	**V**	
Hudsonian Godwit	**V**	
Bar-tailed Godwit	**M**	
Marbled Godwit	**V**	
Ruddy Turnstone	**W**	
Red Knot	**V**	
Surfbird	**V**	
Ruff	**M**	
Sharp-tailed Sandpiper	**M**	
Stilt Sandpiper	**V**	
Curlew Sandpiper	**V**	
Red-necked Stint	**V**	
Sanderling	**W**	
Dunlin	**W**	
Baird's Sandpiper	**V**	
Little Stint	**V**	
Least Sandpiper	**W**	
White-rumped Sandpiper	**V**	
Buff-breasted Sandpiper	**V**	
Pectoral Sandpiper	**M**	
Semipalmated Sandpiper	**V**	
Western Sandpiper	**W**	
Short-billed Dowitcher	**V**	

Long-billed Dowitcher	**W**	
Wilson's Snipe	**W**	
Common Snipe	**V**	
Wilson's Phalarope	**V**	
Red-necked Phalarope	**V**	
Red Phalarope	**W**	
South Polar Skua	**M**	
Pomarine Jaeger	**W**	
Parasitic Jaeger	**M**	
Long-tailed Jaeger	**M**	
Ancient Murrelet	**V**	
Black-legged Kittiwake	**V**	
Bonaparte's Gull	**V**	
Black-headed Gull	**V**	
Laughing Gull	**W**	
Franklin's Gull	**M**	
Short-billed Gull	**V**	
Ring-billed Gull	**W**	
Western Gull	**V**	
California Gull	**V**	
Herring Gull	**V**	
Slaty-backed Gull	**V**	
Glaucous-winged Gull	**W**	
Glaucous Gull	**V**	
Brown Noddy	**B**	
Black Noddy	**B**	
White Tern	**B**	
Sooty Tern	**B**	
Gray-backed Tern	**B**	
Least Tern	**B**	
Gull-billed Tern	**V**	
Caspian Tern	**V**	

Black Tern	**V**	
Common Tern	**V**	
Arctic Tern	**M**	
Great Crested Tern	**V**	
Sandwich Tern	**V**	
Elegant Tern	**V**	
Inca Tern	**V**	
Rock Pigeon	**N**	
Spotted Dove	**N**	
Zebra Dove	**N**	
Mourning Dove	**N**	
Barn Owl	**N**	
Snowy Owl	**V**	
Short-eared Owl	**R**	
Mariana Swiftlet	**N**	
Belted Kingfisher	**V**	
Merlin	**V**	
Peregrine Falcon	**W**	
Red-masked Parakeet	**N**	
Red-crowned Parrot	**N**	
Rose-ringed Parakeet	**N**	
Oʻahu ʻElepaio	**R**	
Eurasian Skylark	**N**	
Red-vented Bulbul	**N**	
Red-whiskered Bulbul	**N**	
Japanese Bush-Warbler	**N**	
Japanese White-eye	**N**	
Hwamei	**N**	
Red-billed Leiothrix	**N**	
White-rumped Shama	**N**	

Northern Mockingbird	**N**
Common Myna	**N**
Red-crested Cardinal	**N**
Saffron Finch	**N**
Yellow-faced Grassquit	**N**
Northern Cardinal	**N**
ʻApapane	**R**
ʻIʻiwi	**R**
Oʻahu ʻAmakihi	**R**
House Finch	**N**
Yellow-fronted Canary	**N**
House Sparrow	**N**
Lavender Waxbill	**N**
Orange-cheeked Waxbill	**N**
Common Waxbill	**N**
Red Avadavat	**N**
African Silverbill	**N**
Java Sparrow	**N**
Scaly-breasted Munia	**N**
Chestnut Munia	**N**

Extinct

Oʻahu ʻŌʻō	**X**
Oʻahu Nukupuʻu	**X**
Oʻahu ʻAkialoa	**X**
Oʻahu ʻĀkepa	**X**
ʻŌʻū	**X**
ʻAmaui	**X**
Oʻahu ʻAlauahio	**X**
Varied Tit	**X**
California Quail	**X**

The information above was derived from:

Pyle, R.L., and P. Pyle. "The Birds of the Hawaiian Islands: Occurrence, History, Distribution, and Status." B.P. Bishop Museum, Honolulu, HI, U.S.A. Version 2 (1 January 2017) http://hbs.bishopmuseum.org/birds/rlp-monograph

GLOSSARY

Archipelago: sometimes called an island group or island chain, is a chain, cluster or collection of islands.

Alien: Animals, plants or other organisms introduced by man into places out of their natural range of distribution, where they become established and disperse, generating a negative impact on the local ecosystem and species.

Avifauna: The birds of a particular region, habitat, or geological period.

Co-evolved: The change of a biological object triggered by the change of a related object.

Culmen: The upper ridge of a bird's beak.

Deforestation: The conversion of forested areas to non-forest land use. It can be the result of the deliberate removal of forest cover for agriculture or urban development, or it can be a consequence of grazing animals, wild or domesticated.

Divergence: The evolutionary tendency or process by which animals or plants that are descended from a common ancestor evolve into different forms when living under different conditions.

Ecological: Relating to or concerned with the relation of living organisms to one another and to their physical surroundings.

Ecosystem: The community of living organisms in a particular place, together with the non-living physical environment in which they live.

Endemic: Confined to a particular geographic area and with a specific distribution; found nowhere else.

Evolution: The process by which different kinds of living organisms are thought to have developed and diversified from earlier forms during the history of the earth. Consists of changes in the heritable traits of a population of organisms as successive generations replace one another. It is populations of organisms that evolve, not individual organisms.

Fauna: All of the animal life of any particular region or time

Flora: The plant life occurring in a particular region or time, generally the naturally occurring or indigenous—native plant life.

Genus: A principal taxonomic category that ranks above species and below family, and is denoted by a capitalized Latin name.

Herbivore: An animal anatomically and physiologically adapted to eating plant material, for example foliage, for the main component of its diet. As a result of their plant diet, herbivorous animals typically have mouthparts adapted to rasping or grinding.

Infestation: To overrun in large numbers, usually so as to be harmful.

Irides: The colored part of the eye surrounding the pupil and controlling the latter's size by expanding or contracting according to light intensity.

Invasive species: Introduced species (also called "non-indigenous" or "non-native") that adversely affect the habitats and bioregions they invade economically, environmentally, and/or ecologically.

Microrganism: Any organism too small to be viewed by the unaided eye, as bacteria, protozoa, and some fungi and algae.

Native: An organism that originated in an area which it lives.

Naturalized: Thoroughly established and replacing itself by vegetative or sexual means, but originally coming from another area. As used here, introduced, intentionally or un-intentionally, by man or his activities.

Organism: An organism is any contiguous living system, such as an animal, insect, plant or bacterium. All known types of organism are capable of some degree of response to stimuli, reproduction, growth and development and self-regulation.

Pest: Any animal, plant or disease that is injurious to agriculture, commerce, human health or the environment.

Phylogenetic analysis: The means of inferring or estimating these relationships. The evolutionary history inferred from phylogenetic analysis is usually depicted as branching, treelike diagrams that represent an estimated pedigree of the inherited relationships among molecules ("gene trees"), organisms, or both.

Sub-fossil: A term applied to the remains of a once-living organism in cases where the remains are not considered to be fully fossil for one of two possible reasons: that not enough time has elapsed since the animal died, or that the conditions in which the remains were deposited were not optimal for fossilization.

Tarsus: Part of the leg of a bird below the thigh.

Taxonomy: The science dealing with the description, identification, naming, and classification of organisms.

ENDNOTES

INTRODUCTION

1. Sinton, J. M., D. E. Eason, M. Tardona, D. Pyle, I. van der Zander, H. Guillou, D. Clague, and J. J. Mahoney. "Ka'ena Volcano: A Precursor Volcano of the Island of O'ahu, Hawai'i." *Geological Society of America Bulletin.* 2014. Published online May 2.

2. MacDonald, Gordon Andrew. *Volcanoes in the Sea: The Geology of Hawaii.* Honolulu: University of Hawai'i Press, 1983.

3. Tibbitts, T. Lee, Daniel R. Ruthrauff, Jared G. Underwood, Vijay P. Patil. "Factors promoting the recolonization of Oahu, Hawaii, by Bristle-thighed Curlews." *Global Ecology and Conservation,* Volume 21 (2020), 7.

4. https://pacificrimconservation.org/wp-content/uploads/2021/03/Pacific-Rim-Conservation-Annual-Report-2020.pdf, 5.

SPECIES

1. Lavretski, et al. "Genetic admixture supports an ancient hybrid origin of the endangered Hawaiian duck." *Journal of Evolutionary Biology.* (2015). 28 (5): 1005–1015. doi:10.1111/jeb.12637. PMID 25847706. Abstract.

2. Wells, C. P., P. Lavretsky, M. D. Sorenson, J. L. Peters, J. M. DaCosta, S. Turnbull, K. J. Uyehara, C. P. Malachowski, B. D. Dugger, J. M. Eadie, and A. Engilis, Jr. "Persistence of an endangered native duck, feral mallards, and multiple hybrid swarms across the main Hawaiian Islands." *Molecular Ecology,* (2019). 28(24), 5203-5216. 5209.

3. https://en.wikipedia.org/wiki/Chukar_partridge

4. Caum, E.L. "The exotic birds of Hawaii." *Occas. Pap. B. P. Bishop Mus.* 1933. 10(9): 1-55. Honolulu, HI

5. Swedberg, G. "Hawaiian bird introductions." Unpublished report. Div. of Fish and Game, DLNR, Honolulu, HI, 1967. Copy on file B.P. Bishop Museum, Honolulu.

6. https://indiabiodiversity.org/species/show/33707

7. http://www.oiseaux-birds.com/card-black-francolin.html

8. Hawaii Audubon Society. *Hawaii's birds. Seventh Edition.* Honolulu, HI: Hawaii Audubon Society, 2020. 77.

9. Jobling, James A. *The Helm Dictionary of Scientific Bird Names.* London: Christopher Helm, 2010. 148.

10. Denny, Jim. *A photographic guide to the birds of Hawaii: The main islands and offshore waters.* Honolulu, HI: University of Hawaii Press, 2010. illus. 51.

11. Swedberg, 1967.

12. Munroe, Gregory. Report of the director for 1930. *B.P. Bishop Mus. Bull.* (1931) 82: 1-36.

13. Schwartz, C.W. and E.R. Schwartz. "The game birds in Hawaii." Unpub. report. Honolulu, Hawaii: Hawaii Board of Agric. and Forestry, 1949.

14. Pyle, R.L., and P. Pyle. *The Birds of the Hawaiian Islands: Occurrence, History, Distribution, and Status.* Honolulu, HI: B.P. Bishop Museum, Version 2 (1 January 2017) http://hbs.bishopmuseum.org/birds/rlp-monograph

15. American Ornithologists' Union (AOU). Checklist of North American birds. Seventh ed. Washington, D.C.: American Ornithologists' Union, 1998. 829 pp.

16. Schwartz, C.W. and E.R. Schwartz. "The game birds in Hawaii." Unpub. report. Honolulu, Hawaii: Hawaii Board of Agric. and Forestry, 1949.

17. Denny, J. *The birds of Kauai.* Honolulu: University of Hawaii Press, 1999.

18. Gering, E., M. Johnsson, P. Willis, T. Getty, D. Wright. "Mixed ancestry and admixture in Kauai's feral chickens: invasion of domestic genes into ancient Red Junglefowl reservoirs." *Mol. Ecol.* 2015 May; 24(9): 2112-24. doi: 10.1111/mec.13096. Epub 2015 Mar 6. PMID: 25655399 2122.

19 Pyle, R.L., and P. Pyle. *The Birds of the Hawaiian Islands: Occurrence, History, Distribution, and Status*. Honolulu, HI: B.P. Bishop Museum, 2009. Version 1 (31 December 2009) http://hbs.bishopmuseum.org/birds/rlp-monograph

20 https://manoa.hawaii.edu/hpicesu/DPW/HCC-2010/Mosher_et_al_2010_Kalij_Oahu_HCC%20Poster.pdf

21 Sibley, David. *Sibley Birds West: Field Guide to Birds of Western North America*. New York: Alfred A. Knopf, 2016. 41.

22 Caum, E.L. "The exotic birds of Hawaii." Honolulu, HI: Occas. Papers B. P. Bishop Mus, 1933. 10 (9): 1-55.

23 https://pacificrimconservation.org/wp-content/uploads/2019/05/Young-et-al-2019-NESH-HAPE-Oahu.pdf

24 https://pacificrimconservation.org/conservation/project-coordination/

25 https://www.staradvertiser.com/2021/08/03/breaking-news/1st-wild-bonin-petrels-fledged-from-their-nests-on-oahus-north-shore/

26 https://en.wikipedia.org/wiki/Leonhard_Stejneger

27 https://en.wikipedia.org/wiki/James_Bulwer

28 https://en.wikipedia.org/wiki/Walter_Buller

29 Henshaw, H. W. (1900). Description of a new shearwater from the Hawaiian Islands. Auk 17:246–247

30 https://www.antwiki.org/wiki/Leach,_William_Elford_(1790-1836)

31 https://www.birdpop.org/docs/pubs/Pyle_et_al_2016_Leachs_vs_Band-rumped_Storm_Petrels.pdf

32 https://en.wikipedia.org/wiki/Henry_Baker_Tristram

33 VanderWerf, E. A., L. C. Young, and C. Blackburn. "First record of Tristram's Storm-petrel in the Southeastern Hawaiian Islands." *'Elepaio* 71, 2011 (7): 41-43.

34 https://pacificrimconservation.org/conservation/bird-translocations/

35 https://www.marineornithology.org/PDF/49_2/49_2_215-222.pdf

36 https://abcbirds.org/bird/hawaiian-common-gallinule/

37 http://hbs.bishopmuseum.org/birds/rlp-monograph/pdfs/03-PHAE-GRUI/SACR.pdf

38 James, H. F. "A late Pleistocene avifauna from the island of Oahu, Hawaiian Islands." *Documents Labs. Geol. de Lyon* 99 (1987): 121-128.

39 https://en.wikipedia.org/wiki/Terek_sandpiper#:~:text=The%20Terek%20sandpiper%20(Xenus%20cinereus,first%20observed%20around%20this%20area.

40 James, H.F. "A late Pleistocene avifauna from the island of Oahu, Hawaiian Islands." *Documents Labs. Geol. de Lyon* 99 (1987): 121-128.

41 https://themolokaidispatch.com/tagging-kioea-learning-about-molokais-rare-shorebirds/

42 Tibbitts, T. Lee, Daniel R. Ruthrauff, Jared G. Underwood, Vijay P. Patil. "Factors promoting the recolonization of Oahu, Hawaii, by Bristle-thighed Curlews." *Global Ecology and Conservation*, Volume 21, 2020.

43 Gill, R.E., T.L. Tibbitts, D.C. Douglas, C.M. Handel, D.M. Mulcahy, J.C. Gottschalck, N. Warnock, B.J. McCaffery, P.F. Battley, T. Piersma. "Extreme endurance flights by landbirds crossing the Pacific Ocean: ecological corridor rather than barrier?" Proceedings of the Royal Society B. (2009). 276 (1656): 447–457.

44 https://en.wikipedia.org/wiki/Spencer_Fullerton_Baird

45 https://en.wikipedia.org/wiki/Alexander_Wilson_(ornithologist)

46 https://www.birdweb.org/birdweb/bird/pomarine_jaeger

47 https://en.wikipedia.org/wiki/Bonaparte%27s_gull

48 https://en.wikipedia.org/wiki/Franklin%27s_gull

49 https://pacificrimconservation.org/wp-content/uploads/2018/06/VanderWerf-and-Downs-2018-White-Terns-WJO.pdf

50 https://www.allaboutbirds.org/guide/Arctic_Tern/overview

51 https://en.wikipedia.org/wiki/Sandwich_tern

52 VanderWerf E.A., J.L. Rohrer. "Discovery of an 'I'iwi population in the Ko'olau Mountains of O'ahu." *'Elepaio* 56 (1996): 25–28.

LOCATIONS

1 https://www.nature.org/en-us/get-involved/how-to-help/places-we-protect/heeia/

2 VanderWerf, E. A. 2021. "Status and monitoring methods of a Red-tailed Tropicbird colony on O'ahu, Hawai'i." Marine Ornithology 49: 215-222.

PHOTO CREDITS

Pg. 2 (Emperor Goose): Lisa Hupp, USFWS.

Pg. 6 (Eurasian Wigeon): Laitche, https://commons. wikimedia.org/wiki/File:Eurasian_wigeon_in_ Sakai,_Osaka,_February_2016.jpg

Pg. 8 (Blue-winged Teal): Tom Koerner, USFWS.

Pg. 10 (Garganey): Charles J. Sharp, https://commons. wikimedia.org/wiki/File:Garganey_(Spatula_ querquedula)_male.jpg

Pg. 12 (Ring-necked Duck, bottom): P. Davis, USFWS.

Pg. 20 (Japanese Quail): Ingrid Taylor, https://commons. wikimedia.org/wiki/File:Japanese_Quail.jpg

Pg. 21 (Red Junglefowl): Francesco Veronesi, https:// commons.wikimedia.org/wiki/File:Red_Junglefowl_ (male)_-_Thailand.jpg

Pg. 24 (Pacific Loon, top): Karen Lebbing, USFWS.

Pg. 24 (Pacific Loon, bottom): USFWS.

Pg. 24 (Pied-billed Grebe): Dori, https://commons. wikimedia.org/wiki/File:Pied-billed_Grebe_0561.jpg

Pg. 26 (Black-footed Albatross): Wieteke Holthuijzen, USGS.

Pg. 27 (Murphy's Petrel): Robbie Kohley, USFWS.

Pg. 28 (Motted Petrel): JJ Harrison, https://commons. wikimedia.org/wiki/File:Mottled_Petrel_0A2A3403. jpg

Pg. 28 (Juan Fernandez Petrel): Annie B. Douglas, Cascadia Research Collective.

Pg. 29 (White-necked Petrel, right): JJ Harrison, https:// commons.wikimedia.org/wiki/File:White-necked_ Petrel_0A.jpg

Pg. 30 (Bonin Petrel): USFWS.

Pg. 31 (Cook's Petrel): J.J. Johnson, https:// commons.wikimedia.org/wiki/File:Cook%27s_ Petrel_0A2A7458.jpg

Pg. 33 (Buller's Shearwater): Gregory "Slobrdr" Smith, https://commons.wikimedia.org/wiki/ File:Buller%27s_Shearwater_(Puffinus_bulleri)_ (10573504913).jpg

Pg. 34 (Christmas Shearwater): Duncan Wright USFWS.

Pg. 37 (Tristram's Storm-Petrel): USFWS.

Pg. 41 (Lesser Frigatebird): Ron Knight, https://commons. wikimedia.org/wiki/File:Lesser_Frigatebird.jpg

Pg. 42 (Nazca Booby): Floodmfx, https://commons. wikimedia.org/wiki/File:Nazca_booby2.jpg

Pg. 43 (American Bittern): Sandra Uecker, USFWS.

Pg. 49 (Sora): Elaine R. Wilson, https://commons. wikimedia.org/wiki/File:Sora_(Porzana_carolina).jpg

Pg. 55 (Terek Sandpiper): Vedant Raju Kasambe, https:// commons.wikimedia.org/wiki/File:Terek_Sandpiper_ Xenus_cinereus_by_Vedant_Kasambe_01.jpg

Pg. 58 (Greater Yellowlegs): Mike Baird, https://commons. wikimedia.org/wiki/File:Greater_Yellowlegs2.jpg

Pg. 59 (Marsh Sandpiper): gilgit2, https://commons. wikimedia.org/wiki/File:Marsh_Sandpiper_(Tringa_ stagnatilis).jpg

Pg. 62 (Hudsonian Godwit): JJ Harrison, https://commons. wikimedia.org/wiki/File:Limosa_haemastica_-_ Kogarah_Bay.jpg

Pg. 66 (Stilt Sandpiper): Lisa Hupp, USFWS.

Pg. 67 (Red-necked Stint): JJ Harrison, https://commons. wikimedia.org/wiki/File:Red-necked_Stint_-_Boat_ Harbour.jpg

Pg. 69 (Little Stint): Ken Billington, https://commons. wikimedia.org/wiki/File:Little_Stint_(Calidris_ minuta)_(1).jpg

Pg. 71 (Buff-breasted Sandpiper): Caleb Putnam, https:// commons.wikimedia.org/wiki/File:Buff-breasted_ Sandpiper_(5430006758).jpg

Pg. 72 (Western Sandpiper): Alan D. Wilson, https:// commons.wikimedia.org/wiki/File:Western_ Sandpiper.jpg

Pg. 78 (South Polar Skua): Callie Gesmundo, USFWS.

Pg. 80 (Ancient Murrelet): Eric Ellingson, https:// commons.wikimedia.org/wiki/File:Ancient_ Murrelet_-_Semiahmoo_Spit.jpg

Pg. 84 (California Gull): King of Hearts, https://commons. wikimedia.org/wiki/File:Larus_californicus_Palo_ Alto_May_2011_009.jpg

Pg. 85 (Slaty-backed Gull): E-190, https://commons. wikimedia.org/wiki/File:Ooseguro-kamome.jpg

Pg. 89 (Gray-backed Tern): Duncan Wright, USFWS.

Pg. 91 (Gull-billed Tern): USFWS.

Pg. 91: (Caspian Tern): JJ Harrison, https://commons.
wikimedia.org/wiki/File:Caspian_Tern_1_-_Lake_
Wollumboola.jpg

Pg. 94 (Elegant Tern): Mike Baird, https://commons.
wikimedia.org/wiki/File:Elegant_Tern_(Thalasseus_
elegans).jpg

Pg. 103 (lower right O'ahu 'Elepaio): Alan Schmierer,
https://commons.wikimedia.org/wiki/File:Oahu_
Elepaio_(9-19-2017)_Aiea_Loop_trail,_Keaiwa_
Heiau_recreation_area,_Honolulu_co,_Hawaii_-02_
(23717988448).jpg

Pg. 105 (Red-whiskered Bulbul): Nrik kiran, https://
commons.wikimedia.org/wiki/File:Red_whiskered_
Bulbul_(Pycnonotus_jocosus).jpg

Pg. 127 (Varied Tit): Laitche, https://commons.wikimedia.
org/wiki/File:Varied_tit_at_Tenn%C5%8Dji_Park_
in_Osaka,_January_2016.jpg

Pg. 129 (White Cockatoo): Valerie Everett, https://
commons.wikimedia.org/wiki/File:Umbrella_
Cockatoo_(Cacatua_alba)_-upper_body.jpg

Pg. 129 (Cockatiel): Jim Bendon, https://commons.
wikimedia.org/wiki/File:Cockateil_2_(20125670450).
jpg

Pg. 129 (Budgerigar): Josh Berglund, https://commons.
wikimedia.org/wiki/File:Budgerigar_(Melopsittacus_
undulatus)-6.jpg

Pg. 129 (Lilac-crowned Parrot): Cédric Allier, https://
commons.wikimedia.org/wiki/File:Amazona_
finschi_-perching_on_branch-8.jpg

Pg. 130 (Northern Red Bishop): Steve Garvie, https://
commons.wikimedia.org/wiki/File:Euplectes_
franciscanus_-Kotu_Creek,_Western_Division,_The_
Gambia_-male-8.jpg

Pg. 130 (Northern Bobwhite): Andy Morffew, https://
commons.wikimedia.org/wiki/File:Northern_
Bobwhite_(34922287366)_(cropped).jpg

Pg. 136 (Ala Moana Beach): Mkojot | Dreamstime.com

Pg. 137 (Magic Island): Patrick Evans | Dreamstime.com

BIBLIOGRAPHY

AOU = American Ornithologist's Union.

All About Birds. "Arctic Tern." https://www.allaboutbirds.org/guide/Arctic_Tern/overview

American Bird Conservancy. "Hawaiian Common Gallinule ('Alae 'Ula)." https://abcbirds.org/bird/hawaiian-common-gallinule/

American Ornithologists' Union (AOU). *Check-list of North American Birds.* 7th ed. Washington, D.C.: American Ornithologists' Union, 1998. 829 pp.

AntWiki. "Leach, William Elford (1790-1836)." https://www.antwiki.org/wiki/Leach,_William_Elford_(1790-1836)

Bailey, A.M. *Birds of Midway and Laysan islands.* Denver Museum Pictorial No. 12: Museum of Natural History, 1956.

Banko, W.E. *History of endemic Hawaiian birds: specimens in museum collections.* CPSU/UH Avian History Report, Issue 2. Honolulu, Hawai'i: Cooperative National Park Resources Studies Unit, University of Hawaii at Manoa, Department of Botany, 1979.

Birds of the World. https://birdsoftheworld.org

Bloxam, A.J. "Diary of Andrew Bloxam naturalist of the 'Blonde.'" *Bernice P. Bishop Mus. Special Publ.* Volume 10, 1925.

Bryan, W. A. and A. Seale. "Notes on the birds of Kauai." *Occas. Pap. Bernice P. Bishop Museum,* Volume 1(3), 1901: 129-137.

Bryan, W. A. "Some birds of Molokai." *Occas. Pap. Bernice P. Bishop Mus.* 4 (2), 1908: 133-176.

Bryan, W. A. "Report of an expedition to Laysan Island in 1911: under the joint auspices of the United States Department of Agriculture and University of Iowa." *Bulletin / U.S. Department of Agriculture, Biological Survey;* no. 42 Washington, D.C.: U.S. Dept. of Agriculture, Biological Survey, 1912.

Cabanis, J. *Museum Heineanum*, Vol. 1. Halberstadt: R. Frantz, 1850. 233 pp.

Cassin, J. *United States Exploring Expedition. During the years 1838, 1839, 1840, 1841, 1842. Under the Command of Charles Wilkes, U. S. N. Mammalogy and ornithology.* Philadelphia: J. B. Lippincott & Co, 1858.

Caum, E.L. "The exotic birds of Hawaii." *Occas. Pap. B. P. Bishop Mus.* 10(9), 1933: 1-55. Honolulu, HI.

Cluett Pactol, Catherine. "Tagging Kioea: Learning about Molokai's Rare Shorebirds." https://themolokaidispatch.com/tagging-kioea-learning-about-molokais-rare-shorebirds/

Cook, J. and J. King. *A voyage to the Pacific Ocean... performed in His Majesty's Ships* Resolution and Discovery *in the years 1776, 1777, 1778, 1779, 1780.* 3 vols., London, 1784.

_____. *A voyage to the Pacific Ocean performed in His Majesty's Ships* Resolution and Discovery *in the years 1776, 1777, 1778, 1779, 1780.* Vol. 2. G. London: Nicol and T Cadell, 1784.

Dement'ev, G.P., and N.A. Gladkov. *Birds of the Soviet Union.* Vol. II. Gosudarstvennoe Izdatel'stvo "Sovetsdkaya Nauka," Moscow, 1951a. [English translation, Isreal Program for Scientific Translations, 1968; 704 pp.]

_____ and _____, eds. *Birds of the Soviet Union.* Vol. I. Gosudarstvennoe Izdatel'stvo "Sovetsdkaya Nauka," Moscow, 1951b. [English translation, Isreal Program for Scientific Translations, 1966; 553 pp.]

_____ and _____, eds. *Birds of the Soviet Union.* Vol. III. Gosudarstvennoe Izdatel'stvo "Sovetsdkaya Nauka," Moscow, 1951c. [English translation, Isreal Program for Scientific Translations, 1969; 756 pp.]

_____ and _____, eds. *Birds of the Soviet Union.* Vol. IV. Gosudarstvennoe Izdatel'stvo "Sovetsdkaya Nauka," Moscow, 1952. [English translation, Isreal Program for Scientific Translations, 1967; 683 pp.]

_____ and _____, eds. *Birds of the Soviet Union*. Vol. V. Gosudarstvennoe Izdatel'stvo "Sovetsdkaya Nauka," Moscow, 1954a. [English translation, Isreal Program for Scientific Translations, 1970; 957 pp.

_____ and _____, eds. *Birds of the Soviet Union*. Vol. VI. Gosudarstvennoe Izdatel'stvo "Sovetsdkaya Nauka," Moscow, 1954b. [English translation, Isreal Program for Scientific Translations, 1969; 546 pp.]

Denny, J. *The Birds of Kauai*. Honolulu: University of Hawaii Press, 1999. 120 pp.

Denny, J. *A Photographic Guide to the Birds of Hawaii: The main islands and offshore waters*. Honolulu: University of Hawaii Press, 2010. 210 pp. illus. ISBN: 978-0-8248-3383-1.

Dill, H. R. "Report on conditions on the Hawaiian Bird Reservation with list of the birds found on Laysan." *United States Dept. Agriculture, Biological Survey Bulletin* 42, 1912: 7-23.

Dole, S. B. "A synopsis of the birds hitherto described from the Hawaiian Islands. With notes by Sanford B. Dole, Esq., of Honolulu, Corresponding Member." *Proc. Boston Soc. Nat. Hist.* 12, 1869: 294-309.

Dole, Sanford. "List of birds of the Hawaiian Islands. Corrected for the Hawaiian Annual, with valuable additions." *Hawaiian Almanac and Annual for 1879*, 41-58. Honolulu, HI: Thomas G. Thrum, 1879.

E = *'Elepaio*. Journal of the Hawaiian Audubon Society.

eBird. https://ebird.org

Ellis, W. *An authentic narrative of a voyage performed by Captain Cook and Captain Clerke, in His Majesty's Ships* Resolution *and* Discovery *during the years 1776, 1777, 1778, 1779, 1780*. London: Robinson, Sewell and Debrett, 1782.

Evenhuis, N. J. *Barefoot on Lava: The journals and correspondence of naturalist R.C.L. Perkins in Hawai'i, 1892-1901*. Honolulu, HI: Bishop Museum Press, 2007. 412 pp.

Finch, O. "On the so-called "Sandwich Rail" in the Leiden Museum." *Notes of the Leiden Museum* 20, 1898: 77-80.

Fisher, W. K. "Notes on the birds peculiar to Laysan Island, Hawaiian group." *Auk* 20, 1903: 384-397.

Fisher, Harvey and Paul Baldwin. "War and the birds of Midway Atoll." *Condor* 48, 1946: 3-15.

Frohawk, F.W. "Description of a new species of rail from Laysan Island (North Pacific)." *Ann. Mag. Nat. Hist.* (6 Ser.) 9, 1892: 247-249.

Gering, E., M. Johnsson, P. Willis, T. Getty, and D. Wright. "Mixed ancestry and admixture in Kauai's feral chickens: invasion of domestic genes into ancient Red Junglefowl reservoirs." *Mol. Ecol.* May 2015; 24(9): 2112-24. doi: 10.1111/mec.13096. Epub 2015 Mar 6. PMID: 25655399.

Gill, R.E., T.L. Tibbitts, D.C. Douglas, C.M. Handel, D.M. Mulcahy, J.C. Gottschalck, N. Warnock, B.J. McCaffery, P.F. Battley, T. Piersma. "Extreme endurance flights by landbirds crossing the Pacific Ocean: ecological corridor rather than barrier?" *Proceedings of the Royal Society B*. 276 (1656), 2009: 447–457.

Gray, G.R. *Catalogue of the birds of the tropical islands of the Pacific Ocean in the collection of the British Museum*. London: Trustees of the British Museum, 1859. 72 pp.

Gregory, H.E. "Report of the director for 1930." *B.P. Bishop Mus. Bull.* 82, 1931: 1-36.

Hailer, Frank, Helen F. James, Storrs L. Olson, and Robert C. Fleischer. "Distinct and extinct: Genetic differentiation of the Hawaiian eagle." *Molecular Phylogenetics and Evolution*, 83, 2015: 40-43.

Hawaii Audubon Society. *Hawaii's birds*. Seventh Edition. Honolulu, HI: Hawaii Audubon Society, 2020. 160 pp.

Henshaw, H. W. *Birds of the Hawaiian Islands being a complete list of the birds of the Hawaiian possessions with notes on their habits*. Honolulu: Thos. G. Thrum, 1902.

Henshaw, H. W. "Description of a new shearwater from the Hawaiian Islands." *Auk* 17, 1900: 246-247.

Higgins, P.J., ed. *Handbook of Australian, New Zealand and Antarctic birds*. Vol. 4. Oxford, U.K.: Oxford University Press, 1999.

_____ and S.J.J.F. Davies. *Handbook of Australian, New Zealand, and Antarctic birds*. Vol 3. Oxford, U.K.: Oxford University Press, 1996.

Hume, Julian P. and Michael Walters. *Extinct Birds*. London: T&AD Poyser, an imprint of Bloomsbury Pub, 2012.

Islam, K. "Erckel's Francolin, Black Francolin, Gray Francolin." *Birds of N. Am.* 394-396, 1999: 1-24.

Iwaniuk, Andrew L., Storrs L. Olson, & Helen .F. James. "Extraordinary cranial specialization in a new genus of extinct ducks (Aves: Anseriformes) from Kaua'i, Hawaiian Islands." *Zootaxa* 2296, 2009: 47-67.

James, H.F. "A late Pleistocene avifauna from the island of Oahu, Hawaiian Islands." *Documents Labs. Geol. de Lyon* 99, 1987: 121-128.

James, Helen. F., and Storrs L. Olson. "Descriptions of thirty-two new species of birds from the Hawaiian Islands: Part II. Passeriformes." *Ornithological Monogr.* No 46, 1991.

_____. "A giant new species of Nukupuu (Fringillidae: Drepanidini: Hemignathus) from the island of Hawaii." *The Auk*, 120(4), 2003: 970-981.

_____. "The diversity and biogeography of koa-finches (Drepanidini: Rhodacanthis), with descriptions of two new species." *Zoological Journal of the Linnean Society* 144, 2005: 527-541.

_____. "A new species of Hawaiian finch (Drepanidini:Loxiodes) from Makauwahi Cave." *Auk*; Vol. 123 Issue 2, 2006. p335.

Jobling, James A. *The Helm Dictionary of Scientific Bird Names*. London: Christopher Helm, 2010. p. 148.

Kerr, Robert. *A General History and Collection of Voyages and Travels, arranged in systematic order: forming a complete history of the origin and progress of navigation, discovery, and commerce, by sea and land, from the earliest ages to the present time*. Vol. XVII. Edinburg: William Blackwood and London: T. Cadell, MDCCCXXIV, 1824. http://www.gutenberg.org/files/15425/15425-h/15425-h.htm

Latham, John. *A General Synopsis of Birds*. Vol. 1, Part 2. London: Benjamin White, 1782. https://archive.org/stream/generalsynopsi3111785lath/generalsynopsi3111785lath_djvu.txt

Lavretski; et al. "Genetic admixture supports an ancient hybrid origin of the endangered Hawaiian duck." Journal of Evolutionary Biology. 28 (5), 2015: 1005–1015. doi:10.1111/jeb.12637. PMID 25847706.

Lichtenstein, M. H. K. *Beitrag zur ornithologischen Fauna von Californien nebst Bemerkungen über die Artkennzeichender Pelicane und über einige Vögel von den Sandwich-Inseln*. Abh. Koniglichen Akad. Wissensch. Berlin, 1839: 417-451.

Mosher, Stephen M., Philip E. Taylor, and Matthew D. Burt. "Kalij Pheasants Established in the Wai`anae Mts. on O`ahu: Is Eradication Too Late?" https://manoa.hawaii.edu/hpicesu/DPW/HCC-2010/Mosher_et_al_2010_Kalij_Oahu_HCC%20Poster.pdf

Munro, G. C. *Birds of Hawaii*. 2nd Edition. Rutland, Vt. and Tokyo, Japan: Charles E. Tuttle Co., Inc., 1960

New Zealand Birds Online. https://www.nzbirdsonline.org.nz/

Newton, A. "On a new species of *Drepanis* discovered by Mr. R. C. L. Perkins." *Proc. of the Zoological Soc.* London, 1893, 690.

Oiseaux Birds. "Black Francolin." http://www.oiseaux-birds.com/card-black-francolin.html

Olson, Storrs L. and Helen F. James. "Prodromus of the fossil avifauna of the Hawaiian islands." *Smithsonian Contributions to Zoology*, 365, 1982 1–59.

_____. "Descriptions of thirty-two new species of birds from the Hawaiian Islands: Part 1. Non-Passeriformes." *Ornithological Monographs*, 45, 1991: 1-88.

Olson, Storrs L. "History and ornithological journals of the Tanager expedition of 1923 to the Northwestern Hawaiian Islands, Johnston and Wake Islands." *Atoll Research Bull.*, 1996, 433.

Pacific Rim Conservation. "Bird Translocations." https://pacificrimconservation.org/conservation/bird-translocations/

_____. "Project Coordination" https://pacificrimconservation.org/conservation/project-coordination/

Paxinos, Ellen E., Helen F. James, Storrs L. Olson, Michael D. Sorenson, Jennifer Jackson, and Robert C. Fleischer. "mtDNA from fossils reveals a radiation of Hawaiian geese recently derived from the Canada goose (*Brantacanadensis*)." *PNAS* 99, 2002: 1399-1404.

Peale, T. R. *United States Exploring Expedition. During the years 1838, 1839, 1840, 1841, 1842. Under the Command of Charles Wilkes, U. S. N. Vol. 8. Mammalia and Ornithology*. Philadelphia: C. Sherman, 1848.

Perkins, R. C. L. "Notes on some Hawaiian Birds." *Ibis* (7th ser.) 1, 1895: 117-129.

_____. "Vertebrata." Pp. 365-466 in D. Sharp, editor. *Fauna Hawaiiensis or the zoology of the Sandwich (Hawaiian) Isles*. Volume 1, Part IV, 1903. Cambridge, England: University Press.

Perkins, R. C. L. (Introduction). Pp. xv-ccxxvii in D. Sharp, editor. *Fauna Hawaiiensis or the zoology of the Sandwich (Hawaiian) Isles*. Volume 1, Part VI. Cambridge, England: University Press, 1913.

Perkins, R. C. L. "On a new genus and species of bird of the family Drepanididae from the Hawaiian Islands." *Annals and Mag. Nat. Hist.*, series 9, 3, 1919: 250-252.

Pratt, H. D., P.L. Bruner and D.G. Berrett. *A field guide to the birds of Hawaii and the tropical Pacific*. Princeton, N.J.: Princeton University Press, 1987.

Pratt, H. D. "The Hawaiian honeycreepers: Drepanidinae." *Bird Families of the World*. Oxford, England: Oxford University Press, 2005.

Pratt, H. D. "A consensus taxonomy for the Hawaiian honeycreepers." *Occasional Papers of the Museum of Natural Science*. Louisiana State University, No. 85, 2014. Available online at http://sites01.lsu.edu/wp/mnspapers/files/2014/10/85.pdf.

Pratt, Thane K., Cameron B. Kepler and Tonnie L. Casey. "Poouli (Melamprosops phaeosoma)." *The Birds of North America Online* (A. Poole, Ed.). Ithaca: Cornell Lab of Ornithology, 1997. Retrieved from the Birds of North America Online: http://bna.birds.cornell.edu/bna/species/272 doi:10.2173/bna.272 http://bna.birds.cornell.edu/bna/species/272/articles/measurements

Pyle, Peter, Daniel Webster, Robin W. Baird. "White-rumped Dark Storm-petrels in Hawaiian Island Waters." https://www.birdpop.org/docs/pubs/Pyle_et_al_2016_Leachs_vs_Band-rumped_Storm_Petrels.pdf

Pyle, Robert L. "The spring migration: Hawaiian Islands region." *American Birds* 37, 1983: 914-916.

_____. "The spring migration: Hawaiian Islands region." *American Birds* 37, 1987: 914-916.

_____. *American Birds*, Volume 43, Number 3, 1989.

Pyle, R.L., and P. Pyle. *The Birds of the Hawaiian Islands: Occurrence, History, Distribution, and Status.* Honolulu, HI: B.P. Bishop Museum, 2009. Version 1 (31 December 2009) http://hbs.bishopmuseum.org/birds/rlp-monograph

Richardson, Frank and John Bowles. "A survey of the birds of Kauai, Hawaii." *Bull. Bernice P. Bishop Mus.* No. 227, 1964.

Rothschild, W. "Types of three new Hawaiian birds." *Bull. Brit. Ornith. Club* 1, 1892: 16.

_____. On *Hemignathus lanaiensis. Bull. Brit. Ornith. Club* 1, 1893:24-25. [Reprinted Ibis 6 (5th Ser.): 256-257.

_____. *The avifauna of Laysan and the neighboring islands with a complete history to date of the birds of the Hawaiian possessions.* London: R. H. Porter, 1893-1900.

_____. Note on the *Loxops* of O'ahu. *Novit. Zool.* 2, 1895: 54.

Scott, J.M., S. Mountainspring, F.L. Ramsey, and C.B. Kepler. *Forest bird communities of the Hawaiian Islands: their dynamics, ecology, and conservation.* Studies Avian Biol. 9, 1986: 1-431.

Seattle Audubon Society. "Pomarine Jaeger." https://www.birdweb.org/birdweb/bird/pomarine_jaeger

Sharpe, R.B. "On *Pennula* and its allies." *Bull. Brit. Ornith. Club* 1, 1893a: 19-20. [Reprinted Ibis 6(5th Ser.): 252-253.

Sharpe, R.B. "On *Pennula sandwichensis.*" *Bull. Brit. Ornith. Club* 1, 1893b: 42-43. [Reprinted Ibis 6 (5th Ser.): 443-444.

Sibley, David. *Sibley Birds West: Field Guide to Birds of Western North America.* New York: Alfred A. Knopf, 2016.

Sorenson, Michael D., Alan Cooper, Ellen E. Paxinos, Thomas W. Quinn, Helen F. James, Storrs L. Olson, Robert C. Fleischer. "Relationships of the extinct moa-nalos, flightless Hawaiian waterfowl, based on ancient DNA." *Proc. R. Soc. Lond. B:* 1999 266 2187-2193; DOI: 10.1098/rspb.1999.0907. Published 7 November 1999.

Stejneger, L. "Birds of Kauai Island, Hawaiian Archipelago, collected by Mr. Valdemar Knudsen, with descriptions of new species." *Proceedings of the United States National Museum.* 10, 1887:75-102.

Schwartz, C.W. and E.R. Schwartz. "The game birds in Hawaii." Unpub. report. Honolulu, Hawaii: Hawaii Board of Agric. and Forestry, 1949.

Swedberg, G. "Hawaiian bird introductions." Unpub. report. Div. of Fish and Game, DLNR, Honolulu, HI. Copy on file, Honolulu: B.P. Bishop Museum, 1967.

Telfer, T. C. "Final Report: ecological study of the Erckel's Francolin on Kauai." Hawaii DLNR, Div. For. and Wildlife, 1986.

Tibbitts, T. Lee, Daniel R. Ruthrauff, Jared G. Underwood, Vijay P. Patil. "Factors promoting the recolonization of Oahu, Hawaii, by Bristle-thighed Curlews, Global Ecology and Conservation." Volume 21, 2020.

Townsend, J. K. *Narrative of a journey across the Rocky Mountains to the Columbia River and a visit to the Sandwich Islands, Chili, & c. with a scientific appendix.* Philadelphia: Henry Perkins, PA, 1839.

_____. *The Literary Record and Journal of the Linnaean Association of Pennsylvania College*, Volume 3. Gettysburg, Pennsylvania, 1846.

U.S. Fish and Wildlife Service. *Revised Recovery Plan for Hawaiian Forest Birds.* Portland, OR: Region 1, 2006.

VanderWerf, E. A., L. C. Young, and C. Blackburn. "First record of Tristram's Storm-petrel in the Southeastern Hawaiian Islands." *'Elepaio* 71 (7), 2011: 41-43.

VanderWerf, E. A. and Richard E. Downs. "Current distribution, abundance, and breeding biology of White Terns (*Gygis alba*) on Oahu, Hawaii." *The Wilson Journal of Ornithology* 130 (1): 297–304, 2018 https://pacificrimconservation.org/wp-content/uploads/2018/06/VanderWerf-and-Downs-2018-White-Terns-WJO.pdf

VanderWerf, E. A. and Rohrer J.L. "Discovery of an 'I'iwi population in the Ko'olau Mountains of O'ahu." *'Elepaio* 56, 1996: 25–28.

Von Kittlitz, F.H. "Nachricht von den Brüteplätzen einiger tropischen Seevögel im stillen Ocean." Mus. Senkenbergianum Abhandlungen aus dem Gebiete der beschreibenden Naturgeschite 1, 1834: 115-126.

Walther, Michael and Julian P. Hume. *Extinct Birds of Hawai'i.* Honolulu, HI: Mutual Publishing, 2016.

Wells, C. P., P. Lavretsky, M. D. Sorenson, J. L. Peters, J. M. DaCosta, S. Turnbull, K. J. Uyehara, C. P. Malachowski, B. D. Dugger, J. M. Eadie, and A. Engilis, Jr. "Persistence of an endangered native duck, feral mallards, and multiple hybrid swarms across the main Hawaiian Islands." *Molecular Ecology*, 28(24), 2019: 5203-5216.

Wikipedia. "Alexander Wilson (ornithologist)." https://en.wikipedia.org/wiki/Alexander_Wilson_(ornithologist)

_____. "Bonaparte's gull." https://en.wikipedia.org/wiki/Bonaparte%27s_gull

_____. "Chukar partridge." https://en.wikipedia.org/wiki/Chukar_partridge

_____. "Franklin's gull." https://en.wikipedia.org/wiki/Franklin%27s_gull

_____. "Henry Baker Tristram." https://en.wikipedia.org/wiki/Henry_Baker_Tristram

_____. "James Bulwer." https://en.wikipedia.org/wiki/James_Bulwer

_____. "Leonhard Stejneger." https://en.wikipedia.org/wiki/Leonhard_Stejneger

_____. "Sandwich tern." https://en.wikipedia.org/wiki/Sandwich_tern

_____. "Spencer Fullerton Baird." https://en.wikipedia.org/wiki/Spencer_Fullerton_Baird

_____. "Terek sandpiper." https://en.wikipedia.org/wiki/Terek_sandpiper#:~:text=The%20Terek%20sandpiper%20(Xenus%20cinereus,first%20observed%20around%20this%20area.

_____. "Walter Buller." https://en.wikipedia.org/wiki/Walter_Buller

Wilson, S.B. "Descriptions of some new species of Sandwich-Island birds." *Proc. Zool. Soc. of London* 6, 1889: 445-447.

Wilson, S. B. and A. H. Evans. *Aves Hawaiiensis: the birds of the Sandwich Islands.* London: R. H. Porter, 1890-99.

Wilson, S.B. "Descriptions of two new species of Sandwich-Island birds." *Annals and Magazine of Natural History* 6(7), 1891: 460.

Wu, Nina. "1st wild Bonin petrels fledged from their nests on Oahu's North Shore." *Star-Advertiser,* Aug. 3, 2021. https://www.staradvertiser.com/2021/08/03/breaking-news/1st-wild-bonin-petrels-fledged-from-their-nests-on-oahus-north-shore/

Young, Lindsay C., Eric A. VanderWerf, Matthew McKown, Paige Roberts, Jeff Schlueter, Adam Vorsino, and David Sischo. "Evidence of Newell's Shearwaters and Hawaiian Petrels on Oahu, Hawaii." https://pacificrimconservation.org/wp-content/uploads/2019/05/Young-et-al-2019-NESH-HAPE-Oahu.pdf

NON-PROFITS HELPING O'AHU'S BIRDS

American Bird Conservancy
www.abcbirds.org
(888) 247-3624

Bernice Pauahi Bishop Museum
www.bishopmuseum.org
(808) 847-3511

Hawai'i Audubon Society
www.hawaiiaudubon.org
(808) 528-1432

Pacific Rim Conservation
PO Box 61827
Honolulu, HI 96839
www.pacificrimconservation.org
(808) 377-7114

INDEX

ABOUT THE AUTHOR

Michael Walther was born in Cleveland, Ohio and raised in Margate, Florida and Southern California. He first visited Hawai'i in December 1972 for several months. In March 1980, he moved to Kaua'i and while living in Po'ipū Beach became interested in the native honeycreepers that survived in the remote Alaka'i Wilderness area. In January 1981, he returned to the mainland.

For the next fifteen years he lived and worked in California but the memory of the colorful and disappearing honeycreepers stayed with him. During his last year in college, the fate of Hawai'i's native birds became the focal point of his research. In 1994, he returned to Hawai'i which had become "the Endangered Species Capital of the World," to study its birds and do what he could to help them survive. For three months, he surveyed the native forest bird populations on Kaua'i to determine their status. His results were published in the journal of the Hawai'i Audubon Society: *'Elepaio.*

He returned to California to finish his degree in Anthropology with an emphasis in Environmental Studies from the University of California at Santa Barbara. After graduating with honors in March 1995, he moved to Maui and volunteered for The National Biological Survey. He participated in a project studying several of the rarest birds on Earth, including the Maui 'Ākepa, *Loxops coccineus ochraceous,* Maui Nukupu'u, *Hemignathus lucidus affinis,* Po'o-uli, *Melamprosops phaeosoma,* Kiwikiu, *Pseudonestor xanthophrys,* and 'Ākohekohe, *Palmeria dolei.* He worked on a research team that was surveying the wild, wet and windy slopes of the world's largest dormant volcano, Haleakalā.

Michael is the author of five books on native Hawaiian flora and fauna, including: *A Pocket Guide to Nature on O'ahu; Images of Natural Hawai'i: A Pictorial Guide of the Aloha State's Native Forest Birds and Plants; Pearls of Pearl Harbor and the Islands of Hawai'i, A Guide to Hawai'i's Coastal Plants,* and *Extinct Birds of Hawai'i,* as well as many articles in birding and nature publications.

In the fall of 1995, Michael, with the help of his brother Mark, started O'ahu Nature Tours. The company slogan is "Conservation through education."